INTERACTIVE MEDIA:
Working Methods and Practical Applications

ELLIS HORWOOD BOOKS IN COMPUTING SCIENCE
General Editors: Professor JOHN CAMPBELL, University College London, and BRIAN L. MEEK, King's College London (KQC), University of London

Series in Computers and their Applications
Series Editor: BRIAN L. MEEK, Computer Centre, King's College London (KQC), University of London

An up-to-date and readable list of texts on the theory and practice of computing, with the emphasis on computer applications and new or developing areas: a valuable nucleus for all computing science libraries and departments.

Series in Computer Communications and Networking
Series Editor: R. J. DEASINGTON, International Computers Limited (UK), Edinburgh

Books covering an area of growing current interest in data communications technology, local area networks (LANs) and wide area networks (WANs); aimed at both professional users of network and communication systems, as well as academics.

Series in Artificial Intelligence
Series Editor: Professor JOHN CAMPBELL, University College London

Books which reflect the latest and most important developments in the field of Artificial Intelligence, edited by a most prestigious and well respected authority of world renown.

Series in Cognitive Science
Series Editor: MASOUD YAZDANI, Department of Computer Science, University of Exeter

A series which reports on work being carried out in an emerging discipline, an area of artificial intelligence which is being recognised as an independent study in its own right.

ELLIS HORWOOD BOOKS IN INFORMATION TECHNOLOGY
General Editor: Dr JOHN M. M. PINKERTON, Principal, McLean Pinkerton Associates, Surrey (formerly General Manager of Strategic Requirements, ICL)

Books are planned in this area in knowledge engineering, expert systems, the human–computer interface, computational linguistics; and will cover the many applications of information technology.

If you would like more information on titles in any of these areas, please contact our distributors and ask them for a catalogue of our publications.

JOHN WILEY & SONS LTD
Baffins Lane
Chichester
West Sussex
England

Halsted Press: a division of
JOHN WILEY & SONS, INC
605 Third Avenue
New York, NY 10158
USA

INTERACTIVE MEDIA: Working Methods and Practical Applications

Editor:
DIANA LAURILLARD, B.Sc., Ph.D.
Lecturer and Head of Centre for Information Technology in Education
Institute of Educational Technology
The Open University

ELLIS HORWOOD LIMITED
Publishers · Chichester

Halsted Press: a division of
JOHN WILEY & SONS
New York · Chichester · Brisbane · Toronto

First published in 1987 by
ELLIS HORWOOD LIMITED
Market Cross House, Cooper Street,
Chichester, West Sussex, PO19 1EB, England
The publisher's colophon is reproduced from James Gillison's drawing of the ancient Market Cross, Chichester.

Distributors:
Australia and New Zealand:
JACARANDA WILEY LIMITED
GPO Box 859, Brisbane, Queensland 4001, Australia

Canada:
JOHN WILEY & SONS CANADA LIMITED
22 Worcester Road, Rexdale, Ontario, Canada

Europe and Africa:
JOHN WILEY & SONS LIMITED
Baffins Lane, Chichester, West Sussex, England

North and South America and the rest of the world:
Halsted Press: a division of
JOHN WILEY & SONS
605 Third Avenue, New York, NY 10158, USA

© 1987 D Laurillard/Ellis Horwood Limited

British Library Cataloguing in Publication Data
Interactive media: working methods and practical applications. —
(Ellis Horwood books in computing science: new technology in training).
1. Video tapes in education
I. Laurillard, Diana
371.3'35   LB1044.75

Library of Congress CIP available

ISBN 0–7458–0011–4 (Ellis Horwood Limited)
ISBN 0–470–20885–6 (Halsted Press)

Phototypeset in Times by Ellis Horwood Limited
Printed in Great Britain by R. J. Acford, Chichester

COPYRIGHT NOTICE
All Rights Reserved. No part of this publication may be reproduced, stored in a retrieval system, or transmitted, in any form or by any means, electronic, mechanical, photocopying, recording or otherwise, without the permission of Ellis Horwood Limited, Market Cross House, Cooper Street, Chichester, West Sussex, England.

Contents

List of contributors 9

Preface 10

Part 1 Instructional Design and Development for Interactive Media 11

1 Setting up an interactive videodisc project 15
Robert F. Fuller
   1.1 Introduction 15
   1.2 Should you use interactive video at all? 16
   1.3 Selection of content 16
   1.4 Starting an interactive videodisc project 18
   1.5 How much does it cost? 19
   1.6 Organising an interactive videodisc project 21
   1.7 Choosing hardware and software for the project 24
   1.8 Should you really do it? 25

2 Lessons from computer-based learning 28
Alfred Bork
   2.1 Models of interaction 29
   2.2 An example of a computer dialogue 31
   2.3 Consequences of interaction 32
   2.4 Degree of interaction 34
   2.5 Quality of interaction 35
   2.6 Designing interactive material 37
   2.7 Implementing interactive material 39
   2.8 Evaluation of interactive materials 40
   2.9 The role of video in interaction 41
   2.10 Conclusions 42

3 Computer-assisted learning and interactive video 44
Philip G. Butcher
   3.1 Introduction 44
   3.2 IV, CAL and educational paradigms 45
   3.3 Educational interactions with IV 50
   3.4 Interactions in computer-controlled video 55
   3.5 Summary 58

4 Twenty-first century books: an assessment of the role of videodisc in the next 25 years   60
David R. Clark
- 4.1 Introduction   60
- 4.2 The capacity of the videodisc   61
- 4.3 Pedagogical exploitation of the capacity of the videodisc   68
- 4.4 Conclusion   72

5 Pedagogical design for interactive video   74
Diana Laurillard
- 5.1 IV as a form of educational technology   74
- 5.2 Evaluation of interactive video   75
- 5.3 An evaluation case study   77
- 5.4 Pedagogical design aspects   85
- 5.5 Summary of instructional design points   88

6 Why do instructional designers need conversation theory?   91
Gary Boyd and Gordon Pask
- 6.1 Introduction   91
- 6.2 The theoretical contribution of CT   91
- 6.3 Contributions from research on instructional TV   93
- 6.4 Using CT   94
- 6.5 Concluding points   95

7 Conversation theory as a basis for instructional design   97
Gordon Pask and Gary Boyd
- 7.1 Introduction   97
- 7.2 Conversation theory   97
- 7.3 Ambiguous interpretation   101
- 7.4 Logic of Lp   103
- 7.5 Videodisc and other technologies in Lp   108
- 7.6 Lp and other representations   108
- 7.7 Authoring and learning   109
- 7.8 Implementation and operation   110
- 7.9 Transportable systems   112

8 From trigger video to videodisc: a case study in interpersonal skills   116
Nick Rushby
- 8.1 Introduction   116
- 8.2 Trigger video   117
- 8.3 The role of the trainer   117
- 8.4 Towards interactive video   119
- 8.5 'Who do you think you're talking to?'   119
- 8.6 Design   119
- 8.7 Structure   121
- 8.8 Prototyping and developmental testing   124
- 8.9 Technical aspects   125
- 8.10 Screen presentation   127
- 8.11 Costing   127

	8.12 Future developments	128
	8.13 Interpersonal skills and technology based training	128
9	**The creation of an integrated IVD curriculum**	**132**
	Richard C. Smith	
	9.1 Introduction	132
	9.2 Planning	133
	9.3 Special IVD choices for the prescriber/provider	135
	9.4 Integrated course creation	136
	9.5 Composition of staff	137
	9.6 Selection of media mix	140
	9.7 The relationship between provider and prescriber	140
	9.8 Project scheduling	141
	9.9 Production database	141
	9.10 Conclusion	142

Part 2   Exploiting the Technology

10	**A question of delivery — an outline classification of interactive video delivery systems**	**145**
	Rupert Dowling and Bert Camstra	
	10.1 Introduction	145
	10.2 Interactive video applications	146
	10.3 Levels of interactivity	148
	10.4 Video equipment	150
	10.5 Interactive video systems	153
	10.6 Current developments	157
11	**Interactive video — a producer's medium**	**160**
	Martin Wright and David Nelson	
	11.1 Introduction	160
	11.2 Conventional video to videodisc	160
	11.3 The new tools	161
	11.4 Using the new tools	166
	11.5 Conclusion	169
12	**The political economy of interactive video in British higher education**	**171**
	Andrew Hart	
	12.1 Introduction	171
	12.2 The potential of interactive video	172
	12.3 Communication and interaction	173
	12.4 Costs and benefits in training	174
	12.5 The higher education context	175
	12.6 A development case-study	176
	12.7 Technology and innovation in teaching	178
	12.8 A survey of existing European material	180
	12.9 The evaluation vacuum	181
	12.10 Alternative applications of interactive video	183

	12.11 Interactive video and continuing education	185
	12.12 Conclusion	186
13	**Interactive video as a school resource: Rolls-Royce or Model T Ford?**	190
	Colin Mably	
	13.1 Introduction	190
	13.2 A primary school case study	190
	13.3 Interactive video and school education	193
	13.4 Potential school uses	195
	13.5 Hardware issues	197
	13.6 Software — a modular approach?	200
	13.7 Affordability	204
14	**Producing resource discs — the Domesday project experience**	205
	Peter Armstrong	
	14.1 Introduction	205
	14.2 Building the data base	207
	14.3 The copyright nightmare	208
	14.4 Checking and double checking	209
	14.5 Conclusions	210
15	**Videodisc and videotex: love-match or passing acquaintance?**	211
	Colin Jackson	
	15.1 Introduction	211
	15.2 The project	211
	15.3 Interface design	212
	15.4 Hardware	214
	15.5 Content and organisation of the disc	215
	15.6 System problems	217
	15.7 The lessons learned	218
	15.8 Project phase two — a different approach	219
	15.9 Summary	220
Postscript		222
Bibliography		224
About the contributors		233
Index		239

List of Contributors

Peter Armstrong
    Head of Television South & East, BBC Elstree Centre, Clarendon Road, Boreham Wood, Herts WD6 1JF.

Professor Alfred Bork
    Educational Technology Centre, Information and Computer Science, University of California, Irvine, Ca 92717, USA.

Professor Gary Boyd
    AudioVisual Department, Concordia University, 1455 De Maisonneuve Blvd. W, Montreal, Quebec H3G 1M8, Canada.

Philip Butcher
    Academic Computing Service, Open University, Milton Keynes MK7 6AA.

Dr Bert Camstra
    Courseware Europe bv, Nieuwstraat 59, 1441 CL Purmerend, Netherlands.

Dr David Clark
    University of London Audio Visual Centre, North Wing Studios, Senate House, Malet Street, London WC1E 7JZ.

Dr Rupert Dowling
    Courseware Ireland Ltd, 14 Upper Fitzwilliam Street, Dublin 2, Ireland.

Professor Robert Fuller
    Physics Department, University of Nebraska, Lincoln, Nebraska 68588, USA.

Dr Andrew Hart
    Department of Teaching Media, University of Southampton, Highfield, Southampton SO9 5NH.

Colin Jackson
    Department of Computing and Cybernetics, Brighton Polytechnic, Lewes Road, Brighton BN2 4GJ.

Dr Colin Mably
    School of Independent Study, North East London Polytechnic, Holbrook Road, London E15 3EA.

David Nelson
    BBC/OUP, Walton Hall, Milton Keynes MK7 6AA.

Professor Gordon Pask
    57, Queenswood Court, King's Avenue, London SW4.

Nick Rushby
    Centre for Staff Development in Higher Education, 2 Taviton Street, London, WC1H 0BT.

Richard Smith
    Physics Department, University of West Florida, Pensacola, Florida 32514, USA.

Martin Wright
    BBC/OUP, Walton Hall, Milton Keynes, MK7 6AA.

Preface

All the authors contributing to this book have had experience of the design, development or use of interactive media materials for education or training. The aim of the book is to capture that experience, from both sides of the Atlantic, and articulate it for other practitioners in the field, in the hope that this will enhance its progress. Because the chapters are written from experience, rather than to an overall plan, the book should be seen as a collection of differing perspectives: not as a handbook, but as a basis for a conceptual understanding of what interactive media contribute to the educational world. The varying styles of the chapters reflect the authors' differing responses to their experience, from the practical to the philosophical.

The term 'interactive media' in the title is a catch-all phrase that embraces all forms of computer-controlled media (video and audio, disc and tape), as well as the stand-alone forms of these media, insofar as they are designed to be user-controlled. The one discussed most in the book is computer-controlled videodisc, normally referred to as 'interactive video', but many of the experiences are relevant to all forms of interactive media, focusing as they do on the fundamental aspects of interaction, presentation, control and logistics.

The expected audience for the book is educators and trainers who are using or planning to use the new technology in their teaching. Most of the examples discussed here are drawn from education rather than training. It has not been possible to achieve the desirable balance between the two, because the training world has a commercial bias that makes it protective of its knowledge. While the financial and logistic contexts are very different in the two worlds, however, there is little difference in their requirements of the technical and pedagogical aspects of the new technology, and in these respects the book will speak equally to both kinds of practitioners.

February 1987 Diana Laurillard

Note: Throughout this book, I use 'they', 'their', 'them', for the third person singular, as it seems to me the only reasonable solution to the absence of a non-sexist third person singular pronoun. The practice is given grudging approval by the *Shorter Oxford Dictionary*: 'used instead of "his or her" when the gender is inclusive or uncertain. (Regarded as ungrammatical.)', supported by quotes from such eminent persons as Thakeray, 'A person can't help their birth', and Shaw, 'It's enough to drive anyone out of their senses'.

Part 1

Instructional Design and Development for Interactive Media

The advent of interactive media as a new kind of instructional technology presents a considerable challenge to the educational world. This is partly because they offer a radically different way of designing educational material, and partly because they require a radically different way of developing that material.

Teachers usually approach teaching in a subject-oriented way, assembling and ordering a curriculum, revising it according to state-of-the-art knowledge and presenting it in a logical, rationalised and coherent way. Interactive media turn this around and require the teacher to think in a learner-oriented way. The point of these new instructional forms is to make the learner active, rather than allow them to be a passive recipient of knowledge, and it follows that the activities they undertake must be 'mathemagenic' — they must 'give birth to learning'. However, precisely what kinds of activities are mathemagenic for a particular curriculum topic is a challenging question. Assembling educational material for an interactive video lesson is therefore radically different from assembling material for a lecture: it is not sufficient to expose the student to the topic; the teacher has to decide how they will interact with it, what mathemagenic activities the lesson should encourage.

The new interactive media also present a challenge to the teacher's authority over the development of educational material. The classic face-to-face lecture or tutorial gives the teacher total control over the material presented. Any instructional medium interferes with that control in the sense that the teacher is dependent on technical help in developing the material. Interactive media make the teacher highly dependent on technical assistance from both producers and programmers, and inevitably their authority over what is presented and how is compromised as a result.

These issues force educators to consider carefully how far interactive media bring welcome assistance to the teacher, and how far they bring unwelcome problems. It is important, therefore, to clarify both the nature of instructional design and the development process within which it occurs, if we are to understand how to achieve a favourable balance between the advantages and disadvantages of interactive media.

The development process for any instructional material should in theory begin with an analysis of educational needs. In practice, however, interactive media have typically developed from a desire to explore or exploit a new medium. This may be inevitable in the early days of a new method, but it has to be recognised that this focuses the design on the medium rather than on the instruction, and for this reason, early developments have often been disappointing from a pedagogical point of view. The authors in this book are all writing from the perspective of practitioners who have already gone through the early stages of exploration, and are now able to articulate that experience and express a preferred mode of development, based on that experience. There are four crucial issues that recur throughout Part 1 of the book, but there is not always a consensus about what should be done.

First, the selection of the topic for interactive media has to take account of its unique features and be capable of exploiting them to the full. Interactive video (IV) in particular is sufficiently expensive to develop that it has to be used in areas where there is already a recognised teaching (education or training) problem, where it is conceivable that a new approach could make a significant difference to the quality and/or the quantity of teaching done. Suppose, for example, that IV is used to replace a successful instruction manual. Undoubtedly it could use its unique features to make a better job of the presentational style, and being interactive is probably more fun and therefore more motivating to use. But if the manual is already successful, in the sense that it meets the training need in terms of both quantity and quality of results, then it is impossible to fully exploit the additional features of IV — the added sophistication cannot be matched by significantly improved results. There is only any point in using this complex medium if its unique features can be fully exploited. This point is elaborated by Bob Fuller and Al Bork, who both consider the features of IV that differentiate it from all other media, emphasising the importance of this consideration in planning an IV project.

Secondly, interactive video in particular, requires team-work to an extent that is unmatched by any other educational medium dreamed up so far. The minimum skills necessary are subject expert, systems analyst, video producer, instructional designer, as well as the technical assistance all these experts need (programmers, graphic designers, camera operators, actors, researchers, etc.). One principal difficulty experienced by many projects to date has been the ticklish question of who is in charge. Views differ, even among those who have been through the process, and depend on the expertise of the person concerned. Some will argue that the subject expert should be in charge because they know what should be taught and have experience of teaching the topic. Others make a case for the video producer to take control because when the video material is shot, they have control over what finally appears on the screen, and they know what viewers need. The case to be made for the systems analyst is that the programmer has ultimate control over what appears to the learner because they can always program the lesson to edit the video material as they wish. My own view, as an instructional designer, is that the instructional designer should have overall control, because they have researched this particular medium, they know how learners learn, and therefore they know how learners react to this unique collection of pedagogic features. Opinions vary, according to perspective. Bob Fuller, Al Bork, Phil Butcher and David Clark represent the perspectives of the subject expert, the instructional designer, the systems designer and the video producer respectively, and their chapters reflect the different kinds of skills and ways of thinking that each brings to the subject, underlining the importance of team work in such a complex medium. On the other hand, Dick Smith describes how a typical IV project team works in practice, and concludes that there should be one single person identified as the designer in overall control of the entire project. But who should that be? Perhaps interactive media will eventually create the equivalent of the film director — the mastermind who can author the material by marshalling all the component technical and creative resources the medium needs.

The third issue concerns authoring systems. Many educators have looked to authoring systems to provide a solution to the problem of the teacher's loss of control over the development process. The idea of an authoring system is that it takes the technical expertise out of development, leaving the teacher with just the pedagogical decisions. Unfortunately, in practice it takes away the pedagogical expertise as well, and provides a very poor substitute. The most common way to make teaching programs easy for teachers to produce is to offer multiple choice questions (mcq's) as the principal form of student–computer interaction, which any self-respecting teacher would reject as being pedagogically unsound. If the teacher is being at all imaginative about the use of interactive media, then necessarily there will be no provision for it in an existing authoring system — it will have to be programmed in. The reader will discover a variety of arguments against the use of both authoring systems and mcq's in all the Part 1 chapters. Good team collaboration between teacher and programmer is the only way to produce good material, accepting the problems of negotiating overall control that this implies.

Finally, it is generally recognised that instructional design is the core problem of the use of interactive media for teaching — what does the medium offer that will contribute so much to the improvement of teaching and learning, and how do we make use of it? There are several fundamental issues that interactive media prompt us to address:

(1) *The nature of knowledge* Knowledge has traditionally been articulated, transmitted and stored through language and text, which impose particular kinds of structure; digitised data and pictures offer new kinds of structure in which to capture what we know.
(2) *Access to knowledge* The forms of access to knowledge have used the text-based techniques of indexes and contents lists; interactive media bring new kinds of access techniques, such as iconic maps, conceptual maps, networks, user-constructed queries.
(3) *Forms of interaction with knowledge* These have been very restricted, with the emphasis on transmission of knowledge rather than interaction

with it, tutorials and laboratory practicals, at their best, coming closest to allowing a student to explore and test the world they are trying to learn about; interactive media by their nature afford radically new ways of enabling a student to interact with knowledge, and thereby offer a major challenge to educational thinking.

(4) *Control over interaction with knowledge* Control is a double-edged sword for interactive media because while they can support a high degree of user control, it is equally possible for the program to take complete control of what the user does; teachers have always tried to maximise their control over the teaching–learning process, but computers give them the opportunity to exercise even more control over what the student does, and when, and in what order, an opportunity that is all too frequently seized upon.

All these issues are addressed throughout the book. In particular, in Part 1, David Clark argues that because words and pictures are distinct logical types, and because videodiscs now make pictures as accessible as words, knowledge will be encoded and accessed differently in future. The theoretical challenge of interactive media is confronted by Gordon Pask and Gary Boyd who explain how Conversation Theory can provide a disciplined way of thinking about and exploring these issues: how concepts can be represented and manipulated, and how the form of representation chosen, the entailment mesh, allows us to develop a theoretical framework for instructional design that forces designers to make explicit their decisions about who has control over the knowledge represented in the system, how it is accessed and how it is manipulated. At a more detailed level, the forms of interaction facilitated by interactive media are documented and categorised in different ways in the chapters by Phil Butcher, Al Bork, Nick Rushby and myself. There is, as yet, no single agreed way of defining these forms. Practitioners and researchers are in the process of discovering what is possible, and articulating what students experience in confronting this new way of learning, and this process will continue, no doubt, for some time before a consensus is established.

The same is true of all the issues thrown up by interactive media. The contributions here should be seen as mapping the terrain to be explored rather than as defining the navigable routes: as a starting point on which we hope other practitioners will be able to build.

1

Setting up an interactive videodisc project

Robert G. Fuller

1.1 INTRODUCTION

This chapter contains hints and recommendations about interactive videodisc projects based on my experiences with six different interactive videodisc projects from 1979 to the present. All of these projects produced videodisc-based physics lessons intended for university students. The video images on these discs include such varied scenes as archival film of a bridge collapse, a television trial about blind teddy bears, fixed camera pictures of performing gymnasts, and vibrating string experiments in a physics laboratory setting. The interactivity levels of the various lessons include Level 1 (designed for stand-alone use of a videodisc player using chapters), Level 2 (lesson branch points are coded into the videodisc and read into the memory of a Level 2 player), and Level 3 (computer graphics are overlaid onto the videodisc images and the control of the lesson is managed by computer software).

I am a physicist whose professional career, since the early 1970s, has increasingly overlapped into areas of science education and instructional technology. Before I started my first videodisc project in 1979, I had produced single concept films for physics instruction, taught large lecture-recitation sections of introductory college physics classes, used self-paced, mastery-based instruction for three different levels of college physics courses, and developed a Piagetian-based physics course for non-science, first-year college students. As a part of my work with these areas of physics instruction I led a number of faculty development workshops to teach other faculty members about these different teaching strategies.

Each of the interactive videodisc projects with which I have been involved has been developed by a production team. Sometimes the team was a specific group with each person having well defined tasks. Other times the production team featured a variety of changing personnel and tasks were assigned, or made-up as the project went along.

All of the projects viewed the videodisc lessons as a means to not only enhance the science knowledge base of the learners but also as a way to encourage them to improve their use of scientific reasoning. These lessons were influenced by my own belief in a constructivist view of learning as espoused by Jean Piaget, William Perry and others. While we have generally followed the precepts of the reinforcement theory of learning we have not been deceived by thinking that training a person to carry out repetitive tasks is sufficient for improved problem solving. As a result the learner may come to the end of some of our interactive videodisc lessons with a haunting sense of a lack of closure. For example, if you work completely through *The Puzzle of the Tacoma Narrows Bridge Collapse* videodisc (Fuller *et al.*, 1982), some three hours after you have started, you will find yourself confronted with the task of constructing for yourself, from the various experiences you have had with the disc, your own explanation of why the bridge collapsed. Hopefully, these interactive science learning experiences will encourage people to *wonder* about nature. A sense of wonder is the beginning of wisdom.

1.2 SHOULD YOU USE INTERACTIVE VIDEO AT ALL?

Not every educational task merits the use of interactive video. Just because the videodisc will allow you to put a high quality video image with stereo sound on the screen of a television monitor in an educational setting does not mean that it is appropriate in all instructional settings. I personally favour the videodisc for many of the educational tasks now done with 35 mm slides and 16 mm films, but I happen to see the functions of those media as *interactive* modes of group instruction if they are to be effective in enhancing learning. Typical show-and-tell presentations do not need the features of a videodisc and are very adequately done using a videotape/video projector, or 35 mm slides/projector system. Before you begin an interactive video project you need to evaluate your reasons for wanting to do such a project.

There are two essential questions, I think, that you need to consider before you begin an interactive video project — how can *interaction* with a video image enhance the learning environment of this lesson? and how can this interaction increase the students' *active learning*? If you are unable to give compelling answers to these two questions, then interactive video is likely to not be the appropriate medium for your lesson. Notice that both of these questions focus your attention on the activity of the learner rather than on the content of the lesson. I think it is important to begin by focusing your attention on how the learner will interact with the totality of the video lesson rather than on what video images you will provide.

1.3 SELECTION OF CONTENT

The structure of the discipline you wish to teach from your lessons will help you to select the visual content of your videodisc lessons.

In physics we have a good list of possible criteria for selection based upon the 1970 Millikan Lecture given by Professor Franklin Miller, Jr. In Professor Miller's lecture, 'A Long Look at the Short Film' (1970), he suggests several reasons for using single concept films to teach physics:

- the phenomenon is too small to be easily seen by a group, e.g. the magnetic domain microstructure of a crystal.
- the phenomenon is too large to be shown in a classroom setting, e.g. a sphere dropped from the mast of a moving ship.
- the phenomenon is too fast to be easily seen, e.g. the recoil of a rifle upon firing a bullet.
- the phenomenon is too slow to be conveniently used in a typical instructional setting, e.g. radioactive decay of long lifetime can be shown using time-lapse photography.
- the phenomenon is too hazardous to be used with a group, e.g. a high pressure critical temperature experiment.
- the phenomenon is a rare event, e.g. the launch of the lunar lander from the moon.
- the phenomenon is too uncertain to be easily used with a group, e.g. many electrostatic phenomena depend upon a dry atmosphere to be observed.
- the equipment needed to show the phenomenon is not readily available, e.g. the behaviour of liquid helium at 3°K.
- the presentation of the phenomenon can be aided by graphics overlay, e.g. a sine wave on top of an oscillating mass.
- the students can quantitatively analyse the phenomenon by taking data directly from the video image on a monitor, e.g. plot the centre of mass of a diver during a high dive into a swimming pool.

Professor Miller's reasons for using single concept films in physics teaching provide us with clues as to the type of images that may make good videodisc lessons.

Similar criteria can be developed for your discipline and can be useful in suggesting to you ideas for the content, or visual images, that you want to put in your interactive videodisc lesson:

- You may have an instructional task that you have not been able to do satisfactorily using traditional media, e.g. film a gymnast for use in a physics class where it can be shown in slow motion for quantitative analysis.
- You have some excellent visual material that you would like to convert into an interactive lesson, e.g. the archival film footage of the collapse of the Tacoma Narrows Bridge.
- You may have a linear sequence of video material that, because of its non-interactive nature, did not seem to be as effective as you wished, e.g. the 'Eye for an Eye' television programme for the materials science course of The Open University.
- You may want to provide real world visual images to motivate students to study the subject, e.g. motion sequences of aircraft for air-force cadets to analyse using Newton's laws of motion.

Begin your work on the content of your videodisc lessons with some brainstorming sessions to make lists of all the possible visual images that might be useful to help students become involved in your lessons.

1.4 STARTING AN INTERACTIVE VIDEODISC PROJECT

There is *no* substitute for hands-on experience with interactive video. If you are serious about creating an interactive videodisc lesson you must go somewhere and play with someone else's interactive videodisc system and work at least part way through someone else's lesson. Again, I repeat, there is no substitute for concrete experience with this technology! Everyone has their own personal preferences about how interactive lessons should work. You need to develop your own style. If you have not spent a few hours just playing with some interactive videodisc material, please set this book aside and do that! Turn on the frame display number of the videodisc player so you can see where you are on the videodisc as you go through the lesson and become aware of the structure of the information on the disc. A part of every videodisc lesson design is the decision about what video material to put where on the disc. You need to see how some other people have done it. You need to have some concrete experience with videodisc lessons before you continue planning.

You also need to read some of the how-to-do-it materials in other books about interactive video. The *Handbook of Interactive Video* (Floyd and Floyd, 1982) includes a chapter by Patric McEntree that goes through the steps of producing interactive video programs. In a similar way, *The Videodisc Book, A Guide and Directory* (Daynes and Butler, 1984) has several chapters on videodisc design and production. A good resource on the technical information about interactive technologies is the book *Interactive Video* (Parsloe, 1983). The more information you have before you start, based on the experiences of others, the fewer common mistakes you will repeat.

Find someone who has already worked on a complete interactive video project to be part of your working group. There is no substitute for real experience in this business. Try to find a person who has done part of a project and participated actively in the whole project from beginning to end, from the start of the idea through the post-production stretch to the instructional use finish line. This technology has its own jargon and concepts, e.g. field dominance, 3–2 pull down, white flags, frame jitter, etc., that will be important in the quality of your final product. It is better to work with someone who already knows about these kinds of issues. I discovered a case of mind-boggling stupidity that illustrates the importance of doing adequate preparation before you begin an interactive video-project and of having the courage to ask experienced persons for help and advice. The following classic case of self-satisfied ignorance illustrates this point. A group of academics, in a country and institution that shall remain nameless, were invited to bring their institution into the interactive video generation.

After some study of the field, they decided that interactive videodiscs were too expensive (a false economy of decision-making, to which I will turn later) so they proceeded to produce an interactive videotape lesson. They also ordered a videotape player to use in their classrooms. Since it was obtained by a bidding process, they obtained the best of the mono soundtrack videotape players. This group of academics had overlooked the fact that to do interactive video with tape you must put the frame location data on the second sound-track, so when you ask the controlling computer to look for a particular frame or motion sequence it can use audio information on the second sound-track. Many hours of academic thinking time later this group has an interactive lesson on videotape that can be silent with flexible access to the images or that can have sound with a very slow searching system. Such obvious mistakes are easily avoided if you seek the help of someone who has experience with interactive video already. Warning: beware of those in this field who *talk* much about it but really have not done much. The unexpected booby traps in this business seem to hunt down the inexperienced. Seek and get advice from experienced others!

1.5 HOW MUCH DOES IT COST?

You need to arrange for enough financial support to be able to complete the project, at least through to the production of some discs. After you have completed the production of the videodisc you can arrange to work on the interactive software a little bit at a time. Until you get your disc produced there is no great need for you to finish your software lessons. How much money do you need? I have been involved in projects that have cost from a few thousand US dollars to about two hundred thousand dollars. I have recently heard rumours about costs of six hundred thousand dollars per lesson. What the total cost will be depends upon the services you have to hire. You will need to pay a manufacturer a videodisc set-up charge, that is about $2000, and then about $10 per copy of the disc. I recommend that you make at least 100 copies of your disc. Even if you do not plan to sell them you will be surprised at the number of educators who will want a copy of your disc in the next few years. Some of the projects in the early years only made about ten copies of their discs. So few copies makes it extremely difficult for other developers to see your disc and learn from it. Anyway, 100 copies means a minimum cost of about US $3000, only $30 per disc. There are some companies that are beginning to specialise in interactive videodiscs for education and that are willing to share some of the production costs in return for the right to sell the discs to educational institutions. For our least expensive project we used nearly all pre-existing film that was available from government or public service companies. The new video scenes were made using a university videotape team. The pre-mastering, converting everything to 1 inch videotape master, was done in a university media centre at no cost. The narrator was a student. The complete master tape, ready to be sent off to a videodisc mastering company, had cost less than $300 assuming that the professional time of the authors is not counted. This brings me back to the comment that I made in the previous section. Many groups that get into the interactive video business are used to the usual academic way of developing new courses and curricula. Those development tasks are assigned to various faculty members and the development of the course or curriculum is an assumed part of their professional work. There is never any financial accounting made of the cost in professional time that is committed to the new course or curriculum. Academic groups tend to approach interactive video lessons in the same way and stumble over the minimum cost of about $3000 to master any reasonable number of discs. So they may turn to what they see as a less expensive medium, video-tape. Do not be deceived. *The professional development time/cost is much, much greater than any of the costs associated with the production and mastering of the video material!* At The Open University the academic cost of a video lesson is about seven times the television production cost. For the interactive video lessons on which I have worked the professional design and development time has had a financial value about *ten times* the costs of the production, pre-mastering, and mastering of the discs and lessons. The point is that if you really want to do effective interactive video and expect to spend a reasonable amount of time trying to do the best lessons that you can, then *do not* be pound foolish and pence wise and opt for the least expensive production and distribution technology. The professional development costs will be so much greater than the production costs that you *should* provide your lessons with the highest quality distribution technology that you can. Of course, much of that professional cost can come out of your professional flesh. You can do videodisc lessons instead of your other professional work and the time you use on these lessons can be stolen from other tasks that you have to do. That is even more reason to make sure that you take care of all the work you have done and give your interactive lessons the best chance for success. Today, the best is interactive videodiscs. Use it. You need to make sure that you have enough financial backing to pay for the real costs that you will incur. You will need from US $3000 on up. Then you will have at least one hundred copies of your own videodisc and a chance to develop the interactive lessons for it. We estimate that it takes us about 1000 person-hours to conceive, script, and produce the interactive lessons that use one side of a videodisc, about three hours of learner time.

To summarise this section let me cite my own experience. My first disc project was supported by the National Science Foundation for a total of US $60,000 which included the purchase of three equivalent sets of videodisc hardware (and that was back when the players cost $2500 each!). I worked on this project with two other physics educators quite experienced in the production and use of single concept 8 mm films for physics teaching. All of the original video material and the post-production work was done with the Nebraska Videodisc Design/Production group which had already produced nine videodiscs by the time they began to work with us. Even so we have made our share of blunders in our proof disc, e.g. flicker stills when the two scan down fields of the same video image are different, wrong audio when the narration does not match the image, and dead-end loops where the 'go to' instructions in the video image send the viewer to a non-existent disc location. We managed to correct or compensate for all of those errors in the final published version of the disc. We ended up with a level two videodisc of which we are proud, the first commercially available interactive videodisc specifically designed for classroom use, *The Puzzle of the Tacoma Narrows Bridge Collapse* (Fuller *et al.*, 1982).

1.6 ORGANISING AN INTERACTIVE VIDEODISC PROJECT?

You must organise the interactive videodisc project so that it will operate effectively in the institutional environment in which you find yourself. The structure of your project *team* needs to fit your institution and enable you to accomplish the tasks required to complete the project.

You will notice that I use the word team. I have never done a complete interactive videodisc project completely by myself. I consider such an approach unwise. Interactive video is not a single person technology. The poorest quality videodisc project with which I have been involved was the one in which we had the least help from other persons. Plan to organise a project team to accomplish the specific tasks discussed below. If you favour the 'single creative teacher dispels the ignorance of the learner' model of instruction, do something else rather than interactive video. Both you and the world will be better served.

Your project team needs to be able to accomplish a variety of tasks, so you need to make sure that you have the expertise on your team to get them all done correctly (and punctually, if you are working against a production deadline). Your interactive video lesson will need *content, instructional design and evaluation, interactive software,* and *video images*. You need to make sure that these four aspects of the project can be carried out by your team.

Content Some people on the team need to be very familiar with the content to be taught by the interactive video lessons. If the content specialists have taught the lesson content in typical educational settings, then you can use their experience to design more effective interactive learning activities. We had all had classroom and laboratory experience teaching the physics of standing waves on vibrating ropes before we started the Tacoma Narrows Bridge videodisc. It was on the basis of that experience that we chose the ropes, weights, and lengths to show on the disc. I am now helping script a *Science of Flight* videodisc. Five physicists who are experienced pilot instructors are serving as content consultants. I find no adequate substitute for the experience of having taught the concepts with live students as a basis for the design of a videodisc lesson.

Instructional design and evaluation Your interactive lessons will be best if they follow some overall instructional plan. Evaluation of your lessons can help you make better lessons in the future. The evaluation of the Tacoma Narrows Bridge lessons showed that the seven minute opening documentary film of the collapse was an excellent motivator for the students and most of them worked through the remaining two to three hours of material on the disc to try to solve the puzzle of the bridge collapse. On the other hand, we designed the *Studies In Motion* disc (Zollman and Fuller, 1983) to begin with a ballet which had impossible, 'trick' motions done by the dancer. When the disc was finally done there were three trick notions in about four minutes of ballet. The evaluation of the disc by students showed that the opening ballet failed to puzzle them enough to interest them in the later parts of the lesson. Fortunately, the subsequent motions of divers and gymnasts proved to be high in intrinsic interest and the students readily studied those portions of the disc. As a result, a disc, presently under development, on the physics of sports goes straight to the sports action scenes.

If some of the people on your team are experienced in instructional and video screen design they can help keep the various parts of the lessons working towards common instructional goals and help with the evaluation of your project. One important aspect of interactive video is the design of the individual frames. At which location on the monitor screen is the main action shown? Where and what size letters can you overlay onto that action?

Interactive software Some members of your team need to be familiar with the capability of the computers and languages that you will be using for delivering and authoring your interactive lessons. If they have had previous experience with interactive lessons they can be a valuable resource for the team. Good computer ideas can overcome weaknesses in your video materials. On the *Teddy Bear* disc (Williams *et al.*, 1984) the student applies increasing tension on a steel rod in the tensile testing machine using the >arrow key on the computer. When the rod exceeds its elastic limit, the software puts the videodisc into the play mode and the rod snaps with a loud noise. The visual images on this section of the disc are not very exciting, a steel rod between two clamps and a line on a piece of graph paper, but the dynamic interaction between the input of the student and the final breaking of the rod, with its accompanying loud sound, draws students into the lesson content. From one point of view interactive video is computer-based education illustrated with video images.

Video images Some people should have experience with both educational television and videodisc production. They will have the important task of making sure that the video content you want on the disc can be done effectively and in ways appropriate to a videodisc. Your interactive lesson can feature stills, computer overlays, and television special effects. Good television advice is essential. Outstanding visual images can motivate students to study even the most pedantic subjects. The parabolic motion of an object projected into the air near the surface of the earth seems to be much more interesting when it is the body of a gymnast, or a diver, and can be shown both forward and backward in time. From this point of view your video lesson is outstanding television images enhanced by interactive computer software.

How many people you will need on your team and who they are will be determined by the interests and abilities of the people you have available.

On several of our projects the academic content specialists served as the instructional designers, evaluators, and software developers. The only additional expertise we used was from television specialists. In retrospect those projects suffered from the lack of video input from the beginning and some of the video sequences failed to achieve our instructional goals.

I believe that the best interactive video projects on which I have worked have been those that were carried out by a course team modelled after the Open University structure. In those cases the different functions that need to be done for an interactive video project are represented by different people. All of them were involved, more or less, from the beginning of the projects and all of them were able to make suggestions about the structure, content, flow, production, and evaluation of the interactive lesson as the project developed. While this did mean that the content specialists lost some of their control of the final product the interactive lesson that resulted was probably better than it might have otherwise been. Also, in those particular projects all of the members of the project had had previous experience with interactive lessons or interactive video. On such a project team there is a great deal of expertise and an exceptionally good project is most likely to occur.

Most universities are organised into quite separate departments. There is not very much co-operation among members of the various parts of the university. In these circumstances putting together an interdisciplinary project team may be quite difficult and using content specialists and video consultants might be your best choice. If you intend to get into the interactive video production business on a continuing basis then I strongly recommend that you try to construct an interdisciplinary team of professionals that can work together for several years on a number of different projects.

Finally, the issue of control will have to be faced. Who decides exactly what view and images are in each video scene? Who decides what the computer messages say? Who decides what content is included and what is omitted from the lesson? Interactive video raises to a higher level the importance of each individual frame of video and computer material. This new importance for each frame makes every decision more important, i.e. do you fade or dissolve from one scene to the next? do you use a narrator or let the computer text carry the storyline? can you use trick video images to provoke inquiry on the part of the learner or will interactive computer dialogue work best? etc. For many of these decisions there may be no correct answers. What is decided will be worked out in the give and take of the control of the project team. How your project finally turns out may be more influenced by who had the control of the project rather than by what makes the best lesson. Be prepared to be involved in a professional power struggle. Work for what you think will make the best project but recognise that in the end you may not have the power to make it happen the way you want. If you do not work well in situations where professionals disagree with one another about what should be done then you had better not work in interactive video.

1.7 CHOOSING HARDWARE AND SOFTWARE FOR THE PROJECT

Your materials should be authored on the most powerful and most flexible system that you can afford. The best projects of mine have had the software developed on mainframe computers and delivered on micros using a standard high-level language like Pascal. On several of my projects the computers that we were going to use to deliver the lessons to the students were also the machines that we used for authoring. This tends to limit the size of the interactive lesson that you can write. Today the greatest changes are occurring more rapidly in microcomputers than in the videodisc players. All of the main videodisc players are nearly the same. So the choice of what computer to use is more difficult to make. It seems to me that high resolution computer graphics that can overlay onto the video are a minimum requirement. A two screen system with multi-tasking for the computer would seem to offer you the best of both worlds. The computer screen can show the student any message you wish, such as the table of contents and the actual location of the student in the overall structure of the lesson, while at the same time delivering interactive materials on a combined videodisc/computer graphics screen. I have had experience with two different projects that made excellent use of the two screens. The first was a physics lesson in which the students were using the computer cursor on the video images to obtain the time, x-location, and y-location of a gymnast during her vault. The computer screen was used to display a spreadsheet page on which the numerical data were shown each time a cursor location was entered. The students had the ability to decide what data to collect by looking at their spreadsheet numerical results or at the dots on the video screen. This use of two screens seemed superior to our earlier use of a single screen where the students toggled back and forth between the video image and a spreadsheet. A second case is the interactive instructor workstation that we are developing at the US Air Force Academy. In addition to the computer overlay/video colour monitor that can be viewed by the students, the instructor will have access to a monochrome screen that will show the lesson outline and prompts for the instructor. I am convinced that the wise use of a two-screen system will prove to be the best. Of course, if you desire to only use the computer overlay/video screen you can turn off the computer screen with the software, but at least you will have the option of using the second screen if you wish. I think that the growing use of multi-tasking, desk-top computer software accessories is going to increase the use of two-screen interactive videodisc systems.

Try to match the components of your system intelligently and try not to be overly swayed by your budget limitations. One project had a $2500 videodisc player controlled by a $400 computer. The final product was ludicrous, black and white block graphics and square lettering appeared in conjunction with fine quality colour video. Likewise, it would be silly to use a $10,000 computer to control a $600 videodisc player. There is a concept called impedance matching in physics and it seems to have an analogous concept in the interactive video business that roughly works out to be *cost matching*. Try to get the costs and capabilities of all the aspects of your systems to be about the same. And remember that professional thinking time and costs will far outweigh your production costs and the costs of your delivery hardware. Do not cheat your lessons by trying to deliver cutting edge interactive lessons on the hardware of the previous electronic generation. On the other hand, I tend not to favour being the first person in the world to use a particular interactive video hardware system for the authoring and/or delivery of my lessons. I like to take a system that someone else has already got to work satisfactorily and then push it to its limits to see what is the best lesson I can create using a system that I know will work.

So far, I have not been impressed by authoring languages for interactive lessons. I realise that every company that sells interactive lessons to users prides itself on its own special authoring system. I have never used them. All of the projects that I have done have used a standard computer language such as Pascal and clever programmers to make the interactive lessons do what I wanted them to do. The idea of having an authoring language so that I could sit down at a computer terminal and write my own lesson directly into computer code does not appeal to me. In fact, I think that such a system would always tend to impose some software constraints on the way I would develop my lessons and incline me to make my lessons easier to program and, perhaps, not as interesting or effective as if someone else has to make the computer do what I want the lesson to do.

1.8 SHOULD YOU REALLY DO IT?

Perhaps by now you are put off about interactive video because of all the advice offered in this chapter. While an interactive video project does have several components that have to be brought together to make it all come out right, it is really not so bad. To help you organise your thinking about your interactive video project I have included Fig 1.1 that presents the suggestions of this chapter in outline form.

Producing an interactive videodisc lesson from start to finish is one of the most interesting and enjoyable tasks a professional educator can undertake. It is a combination of writing a movie script, a textbook, and a computer game, all rolled into one. Each of the videodisc projects in which I have been involved has taken on a distinct personality of its own as the project evolved. Finally, it seems, with the disc about two-thirds of the way finished, the disc personality takes over the creative process and drives the project team to the conclusion of the lesson. I have the most vivid memories of this occurring for both the Tacoma Narrows and the Bicycle videodiscs. With a few thousand frames left to script for each disc, the project team ground to a halt and had to reassess the total content of the disc and decide how to bring it all to a conclusion. From the previous work on the disc and a rethinking of the physics involved, each project personality seemed to indicate the direction to go to conclude the disc. Thus the threefold ending on the Tacoma Narrows concludes with the Ella Fitzgerald Memorex ad. The Bicycle disc

INTERACTIVE VIDEODISC (IV) CHECK-LIST

Problems to solve	Hints towards solutions
Deciding to do IV	Consider interactivity and active learning
Choosing IV content	Examine discipline-based structure and criteria (try brainstorming for visual images)
Raising money — how much?	Do your budget analysis (total costs can vary from US $3000 to $600,000 for 100 discs)
Organising your project team	Get the help you need Content specialists Instructional design/evaluation Interactive computer software Video images
Obtaining hardware and software	Match videodisc player and computer hardware costs. (Try for the best, latest computer you can afford.) Use a standard high level computer language Provide computer overlay onto videodisc images
Getting started	Put your hands on IV equipment Do background reading Talk to an experienced IV author/producer
Doing it	Try it You'll Like It

Fig. 1.1 — Setting up an interactive videodisc project.

(Fuller and Zollman, 1984) ends with the puzzle of the output energy of the bicycle being much greater than the energy input as calculated from the disc by the students, how can that be? Neither ending was what we had in mind when we started the two discs.

Not only do interactive video lessons promise enhanced learning opportunities for students, they also offer academics a new avenue for creative expression. So take up your pen, your video camera, and your computer keyboard and start creating! I think you'll like it!

REFERENCES

Daynes, R. and Butler, B. (eds) (1984) *The Videodisc Book, A Guide and Directory*, John Wiley, New York.

Floyd, S. and Floyd, B. (eds) (1982) *Handbook of Interactive Video*, Knowledge Industry Publications.

Fuller, R. G. and Zollman, D. (1984) *Energy Transformations Featuring the Bicycle*, Great Plains Media Center, University of Nebraska–Lincoln, Lincoln, NE.

Fuller, R. G., Zollman, D. and Campbell, T. C. (1982) *The Puzzle of the Tacoma Narrows Bridge Collapse*, John Wiley, New York.

Miller, F. (1970) *Amer. J. Phys.,* **39**(1), 5–8.

Parsloe, E. (ed.) (1983) *Interactive Video*, Sigma Technical Press.

Williams, K., Wright, M. *et al.* (1984) *Introduction to Materials Science*, The Open University/BBC, Milton Keynes, UK.

Zollman, D. and Fuller, R. G. (1983) *Studies in Motion*, Great Plains Media Center, University of Nebraska–Lincoln, Lincoln, NE.

2

Interaction: lessons from computer-based learning

Alfred Bork

Interaction, involving detailed communication, is a critical human activity. The major advantage of interactive video over older forms of video lies in the concept of interaction, and in its consequences. But examination of existing material described as interactive video shows that it is precisely this interaction that the new material is most wanting. Indeed, much of what has been produced so far might be best described as *slightly* interactive video. Few projects currently available use the full capability of the medium.

For designers who have worked much of their lives in non-interactive modes, the linear producers, *any* interaction seems marvellous. So the person with considerable passive video experience is unfortunately often more than satisfied with primitive levels of interaction, compared with what is possible with the computer. So it is not too surprising that interactive video often shows weak interaction.

I am concerned in this chapter with material to promote learning, in the broad sense of the term that includes schools, industrial training and home learning. The idea of learning *interactively,* with the learner an active participant in the process, is not new. But as we have been faced, for thousands of years, with the difficult problem of educating more and more students, we have used less interactive forms of learning, such as the lecture and the book.

The learner, today, is primarily a spectator in our formal learning institutions. In a room with twenty-five, or thirty, students, only an exceptional teacher can offer fully individualised attention. So we do not react to individual differences in most cases. I do not mean to blame the teacher for this situation, but only point out the impossibility of full individualisation in lecture-based classes. Good teachers do manage to provide some individualisation, through questioning students and in other ways, but this is limited. Most current use of video is also passive. A central problem of education and training today is to create active learning systems that pay attention to each person.

It is the purpose of this chapter to focus on the term 'interactive' and thus to lead toward a reasonable standard for interactive video. I do not think we will use interactive video effectively until we begin to use the full interactive facilities of the modern computer as well as the best current video practices. We have much to learn in this process.

2.1. MODELS OF INTERACTION

One object can interact with another object in a variety of ways. They can bump into each other, or one can exert a gravitational pull on the other. But interaction, as it applies to my concerns in the chapter, is particularly a property of higher life, in that it assumes entities that can *communicate* with each other. Such communication need not be verbal — body movements, pictures, and other non-verbal components may be involved. We will be primarily concerned with interactive verbal and visual communication.

2.1.1 Human interaction

Two humans can engage in an interactive conversation, each saying things that depend on what has already been said. Such a conversation is not truly interactive unless each person is *listening* to the other. Listening is just as important in dialogue as talking. Each reply considers what the other person has said. In such an interactive conversation, each person talks frequently; speeches of several minutes in length make the conversation less interactive, more of a one-way street. Humans may also use such media as the blackboard, or paper, in the interactive process.

Not all interactive conversations concern learning, so we are interested in a subset of interactive conversations. The typical learning dialogue might be one that takes place in a teacher's office, with one to three students. Such a conversation is a useful one to keep in mind in considering interactive learning via modern technology. Although some teachers would deliver a non-interactive lecture to several students in the office, most of us would try to profit from the small group size. Designers of interactive units can use this office situation as a model.

How does a teacher engage in a learning dialogue in the office? We have all seen such conversations. The typical mode might be with the teacher asking questions, and then responding to student replies with other questions. Small amounts of 'information' might also be supplied by the instructor. The student may also ask questions; for example, if the student has tried to work a problem in a science or mathematics course, he or she might ask for suggestions about how to proceed at a given point.

The learning dialogue with the teacher as questioner was made famous by Socrates, in fifth century BC Athens. We do not know what Socrates actually did, but we have the many dialogues of Plato that illustrate this approach to learning. The several students who were with Socrates were engaging in a highly interactive learning experience, it would seem.

This type of learning activity, with one highly skilled teacher working interactively in a conversational mode with only a few students, has been much admired throughout human history. The tutorial system in Oxford and Cambridge is a more recent example. But the pressure of numbers to be educated has made such a system impractical economically. We have in the world too many students, and too few good teachers, to depend on such dialogues between teachers and students as the major delivery system in education. For the past one hundred years the average class size in the public school system in the United States has been nineteen students. The 'typical' class is larger, because the average includes small rural schools, special education classes and other small classes.

Hence education has been dominated for the last two thousand years by modes of learning that are *not* interactive. Such education is far from perfect in offering assistance to each student unique to that student's needs. But, given the economics of interactive education based on excellent teachers, we as a world people have not been able to do better.

The consequences of passive learning are enormous losses in realising the full potential of human beings. Students who do not do well in the current system, perhaps two-thirds of the students, quickly develop an 'I cannot learn' attitude. In some areas, such as ethics, education of all types has been a complete failure; we still have wars. My aim, using interactive technology, is to move to an interactive learning environment for *all* students, in all parts of the world.

2.1.2 Human–computer interaction

Until recently, the only type of learning dialogue involved two humans. But the development of the modern computer has led to another form of interaction. The learning conversations can all be planned in advance, by a group of skilled teachers, and the computer can be programmed to 'deliver' the learning conversation to individual students. I will refer to such an interactive programs as a 'dialogue'.

So far computer and video dialogues are conducted differently from the common way of conducting human dialogues. Typically the student side of the dialogue is conducted through typing, or through pointing mechanisms. The computer can talk, but this is still rare in practice. Analysis of student speech is still to come. Video can supply sound, either through the built-in sound track inherent in the video format, or through compressed audio stored on the disc.

Text and visual information are displayed on the screen. In a system with only a computer, the information is all generated by the computer; with videodisc or compact disc storage, part of this content may be coming from the disc, including speech, graphics, and textual information.

It would be foolish to claim that we *now* can conduct a computer–student dialogue with the same skill that a highly skilled teacher can conduct a teacher–student dialogue. Indeed, we may never be able to do this, notwithstanding some of the claims one sees for intelligent tutoring systems.

But we must remember that in learning environments today, worldwide, *very little* of learning is delivered through dialogues with an excellent teacher. The technology-based dialogue need not compete with the teacher--student dialogue; it must compete well with the typical learning modes economically practical for large-scale education now and in the reasonable future. In this area we can compete very well. We are already skilled enough to develop student–computer dialogues far superior to the passive learning seen in most learning environments today.

We cannot reasonably expect to have enough good teachers to conduct all education interactively with teachers. But we can, with computers, amplify the effect of the few teachers with great skills in this direction by persuading them to develop technology-based learning material, assuming we can provide them with a reasonable development environment. In direct conversation these teachers can reach few students, but through the surrogate of the computer they can, potentially, reach vast worldwide audiences. Further, they can reach these audiences interactively, rather than in the passive learning mode provided by traditional linear video.

At this point, ideally, the reader should stop looking at this chapter, and look at several hours of excellent examples of highly interactive technology-based learning material. It is difficult to describe, verbally, the notion of student–computer interaction. The actual experience is needed. As a substitute, in the next section I describe an example. But I highly recommend the real thing!

2.2 AN EXAMPLE OF A COMPUTER DIALOGUE

The example I will use is from the introductory section of a computer dialogue called Heat and Temperature. This dialogue is part of a series of programs called the Scientific Reasoning Series. No video is involved. The overall aim of these learning modules is to help students begin to approach problems as a scientist would. Thus they are concerned with problem solving and critical thinking, in science. Each of these dialogues is a coherent learning experience, not needing other learning media. The typical program in the series is about two hours long, for the average student.

The Scientific Reasoning Series is commerically available from IBM. The programs were developed at the Educational Technology Center, in the Department of Information and Computer Science, University of California, Irvine. Initial support was from the National Science Foundation and the Fund for the Development of Postsecondary Education.

This particular learning dialogue, Heat and Temperature, is concerned with developing a new concept, heat, as it might be developed in a scientific investigation. Thus it avoids the approach often seen in classes, an arbitrary definition of a term presented by a teacher or book. In a scientific investigation, the definition often slowly emerges from a series of empirical investigations. In this dialogue, the evidence is simple everyday phenomena that can be viewed in any kitchen. The emphasis is on conveying the spirit of scientific investigation, as with the other dialogues in the Scientific Reasoning Series.

After the title page to the first module is displayed, the screen is erased, and the student is told, in one sentence, that he or she is probably familar with measuring temperature. Then a question appears on the screen: How do you measure your own body temperature? The machine waits for an answer. The question is in English, and the student is expected to type an English answer. (A French version is also available, developed at the University of Geneva). Only a few seconds have elapsed before the student is replying to a question, the hallmark of an interactive conversation. Only two sentences have appeared on the screen, the second a question. Most of the screen is blank. It is important to emphasise how quickly interaction begins.

Almost everyone at this point types something like 'use a thermometer'. Many spelling errors will be overlooked. The computer agrees with this answer, drawing a thermometer on the screen. The next question, presented immediately after this, asks if the thermometer, below body temperature, will read correctly if it is left in the mouth for only a few seconds. Most users say 'no'. Then we immediately ask about what should be done to get a better reading.

The question just presented to the student allows a variety of forms of input, as different people will answer it differently. The program will respond favourably to such student-constructed replies as these:

— Keep it in my mouth longer.
— Wait three minutes before taking out.
— Keep it in several minutes.

In almost all instances, the computer's reply to student input is responsive. Again I emphasise how little in the way of text and visuals occurs between each student input. The flavour is highly conversational.

The next investigation involves two thermometers, one in a pan of hot water sitting on the table, and one attached to the wall of the room. We continue to ask questions to the student about what will happen in this situation. Slowly the student actively arrives at the new concept.

Thus the program provides an interactive learning conversation between the student, and the group teachers involved in developing the program. The full heat dialogue requires about ninety minutes for the average student, but this time can vary considerably from one student to another.

Again I suggest that the reader access programs such as this, to gain experience with interactive modules. The Scientific Reasoning Series, ten discs, is available from IBM.

2.3 CONSEQUENCES OF INTERACTION

So far I have discussed interactive learning, contrasting it with older passive learning modes. The primary idea is a learning conversation between the student and the computer, possibly with video also involved. Interaction also has important educational consequences. This section is concerned with two of these consequences, both important in learning, individualisation and motivation.

2.3.1 Individualisation of learning

We have long known that each person is unique. For learning this implies that students have different backgrounds, different learning styles, different rates of learning, different interests. So different approaches to learning are essential in an effective learning system.

> "The more we learn, the more we recognise the unique complexity of any one individual intellect and the stronger the conclusion becomes that the individuality inherent in our brain networks makes that of fingerprints or facial features gross and simple by comparison. The need for educational tests and policy measures to identify, accommodate, and serve the differentially specialised forms of individual intellectual potential becomes increasingly evident (Sperry, 1982)."
>
> Roger Sperry, Nobel Prize Speech December 8, 1981
> Science September 23, 1982, page 1223

But our present dominant learning systems react to each individual student in only crude ways; these systems tend to treat every student almost identically. A good example is the lecture, where everyone in the class, regardless of background or learning style, hears the same lecture. Another example is the usual linear video learning sequence, again the same for all students.

Current classroom environments do provide some individual attention, such as office hours or similar arrangements. But a brief glance at the time available, and the numbers of students involved, demonstrates that little time can be devoted to each student. Mass production in education, non-individualised learning, is not a modern invention. Plato complains about learning from lectures and written material.

Modern technology offers us, through interactive learning, the opportunity to treat students as unique individuals. Because the program is interacting frequently with the student, the program can gather rich knowledge about the student. Background weaknesses can be easily spotted, because good teachers designing interactive material know what weaknesses are likely to occur. Similarly, frequent student errors and misconceptions, perhaps based on naive world views held by students, can be individually addressed.

A sophisticated program can build up a model of how the student learns; currently we are weak in this regard, but we can expect progress with additional experimentation. In the tradition of Benjamin Bloom's concept of mastery learning, students can be kept at a task until they can perform perfectly on the task. Alternate learning sequences can be offered to students who did not learn with the initial approach. We *can* achieve the very desirable goals of treating everyone as an individual, and of assuring that everyone learns.

2.3.2 Motivation for learning

An important aspect of learning is motivation. Students learn more if they spend more quality time on a task. Interesting material increases time spent on the task.

Motivation should not be confused with entertainment. Learning is often difficult. The notion that all learning can occur through play is simplistic. Unfortunately, computer games with little or no learning value have already become common in classes all over the world. Games can be valuable learning experience, but this is a rare rather than a common experience. In a similar fashion, the notion that all learning can take place through video or computer-generated cartoons is also highly questionable.

Our experiences in the Educational Technology Center at the University of California, Irvine, show that highly interactive material is *intrinscally* motivating. For many years we have tested computer-based learning material in the public library. The programs are available, but no one is present to offer help to the students; evaluators are located elsewhere, with monitors to watch what the students are doing. The environment can be desicribed as 'free'; students are under no pressure to continue to work at a program, neither pressure due to the presence of a teacher, nor pressure due to a future examination that will cover the material. Under these circumstances we can empirically identify motivationally weak sections of the dialogues by gathering the data on where students leave the program. These sections can be improved, and tested again in a free environment.

Our experience indicates strongly that the major places where many students leave are those with poor interaction, as discussed in the next two sections. So an important consequence of good interaction is increased motivation. But I would not claim that this is the only aspect of motivation.

2.4 DEGREE OF INTERACTION

So far I have frequently used the word interaction. I also have implied that not all interactions are equally important. In this section and the next one I consider the difficult topic of good and bad interaction, beginning the process of setting up a standard for interaction. First I consider the amount or frequency of interaction, and in the next section the quality of individual interactions. Both factors are important.

Two numerical factors affect degree of interaction. A critical factor is the average time between interactions, for all the users of the computer dialogue. The figure that we strive for at the Educational Technology Centre at Irvine is an average interaction time of 15 to 20 seconds. This time is measured as follows: the clock starts when the student presses return or enter, after having answered a question, and the clock stops when the student begins to think about how to respond to the next query. Designers may choose longer or shorter times, depending on the pedagogical intent. And the average time may differ considerably from student to student. Individual inputs may vary from this average.

A second factor is the time for the student response. Long times correspond to a non-interactive situation. Some computer dialogues 'watch the clock' and attempt to stimulate student response when nothing has happened for some time. Short times are often not desirable in a learning environment, because we want to encourage thinking as part of the learning process. When a student replies to a question, we want the student to think about the question, not just to react. In some places the developers may even want to discourage a quick response, because too little thought-time has gone into the process. In other situations, such as building student intuition, a rapid response is desirable.

2.5 QUALITY OF INTERACTION

Another important interaction issue is the quality of each individual student–computer interaction. Each time the dialogue proceeds, with something from the computer, followed by something from the student, quality is an important consideration, just as it is in human–human interaction.

It is convenient to distinguish three quality issues concerning interaction, the nature of the student input, the analysis made on student input, and the resulting internal actions.

2.5.1 Type of student input

Student input can take a variety of forms. It might be, for example, that all the student does is press return or some other key, such as the space bar. But meaningful input involves more than this.

The best type of input is the student's everyday language, as in the *heat* example presented earlier. It is not difficult, with a reasonable design process and with simple computer techniques, to build programs that do a remarkably good job of responding to typical student inputs in everyday language. The key to being responsive to students is that the designers must be good teachers who are sensitive to student problems and to student vocabulary. The designers specify, in the design sessions, the likely student responses to the questions. Simple string matching, with some logic, is usually sufficient. We have found it better to match on beginning fragments of words, rather than whole words, to overcome some typing and spelling problems. When the material is used with students, in the formative evaluation process, new possibilities that the designers overlooked will come to light, and the material can be improved and tested again.

Such an analysis using only simple matching of strings plus logic (for example, does the input contain one of these strings, plus one of those strings) will not be 100 per cent perfect. But even when a human speaks with another human we do not have 100 per cent comprehension.

A particularly poor form of input is multiple choice. Multiple guess decisions, as they are described by students, seldom correspond to the real world. In most important decisions there are far more than four or five possibilities, so multiple choice questions seldom test for the situations that the students will encounter in life. They encourage a student to guess at the answer. The literature on how to take exams, primarily directed to multiple choice exams, is particularly revealing in this regard.

Such exams are often demeaning to the student, in that they are 'user unfriendly'. One only needs to look at the student lore about multiple choice exams to see this. Cartoons often depect multiple choice in an unfavourable light. I recall seeing a Peanuts cartoon in which Lucy complains about an example, saying that she prefers a multiple choice exam in which she does not need to think!

Multiple choice is a sign of weak interaction, wherever it occurs in learning material. Furthermore it is almost never needed with a computer, except possibly as a variant on style once in a great while. Its widespread use in current interactive video reflects the poor quality of much of this material. There is no excuse for multiple choice, either with the computer or with interactive video. The use of multiple choice is the single worst feature in many existing materials.

Pointer input is often simply an alternate form of multiple choice, not a sophisticated input form. Because of touch screens in many video systems, multiple choice is, unfortunately, often used. However, it is only appropriate where there is only a finite number of possible answers.

2.5.2 Analysis of student input

Another factor altering the quality of interaction is the analysis of student input. It is difficult to classify this analysis, as it is often highly dependent on the pedagogical needs at the particular point. Some situations may not need any analysis at all. Perhaps the purpose of the interaction was simply to get the student to spend time thinking about the issues involved, and nothing further is required.

In other cases detailed and complex analyses of the student input may be useful. In the future these analyses may even include some use of natural language recognition, although, as mentioned already, most student input can be recognised without such tactics, using only, as suggested, matching of strings combined with simple logic decisions. A group of good teachers in the design group can do an excellent job of anticipating possible student input.

2.5.3 Action taken on the basis of student input

An important factor in the quality of interaction is the consequence of what the student typed. As we have stated, the hallmark of a human conversation is that people *listen* to each other; the conversation depends fully on what has already been said. A simple mechanical toy can always reply in the same way, regardless of what has already happened. But we hope to do much better with technology-based learning material. Each time a student types something, or inputs in other ways, decisions must be made by the designers as to how to proceed. These decisions can be complex, based on all the replies of the student over a long period of time.

In our context the fundamental issues are learning issues. We can ask a variety of questions:

(1) What does the student already know? A major piece of advice from modern psychology is that good learning starts with the current knowledge of the student. We can determine this current knowledge directly in the interactive situation, through a series of carefully chosen questions. We may also be able to learn something of the misconceptions held by the students, ideas that may interfere with the learning process.
(2) Given what the student does not know, what learning aids can be provided to assist in learning this material? Generally more than one such aid is needed, because not all students learn in the same way. If a student has not learned the material with one approach, repeating that learning sequence is not the best possibility. A different approach is usually desirable. At present we do not know enough about learning to select the best approach for each student, so we can only offer alternative approaches.
(3) Can we be sure that students have learned what we hope they have learned? The critical issue is *mastery learning*. We want all students to master the concepts, not just a few. We can interact with students, making certain that each student has fully learned the material. If they have not achieved mastery, we should provide an alternate learning strategy. Learning time may vary from student to student.

Although the designers can strive toward effective mastery learning, empirical studies with students will be needed to determine the quality of interaction in this important regard. But many pieces of interactive learning material do not even make the attempt, so they will not realise the goals of mastery.

Although I have discussed the issues of both amount and quality of interaction for computer-based learning material, such standards should probably hold equally for interactive video material. Most of the issues are issues of interaction, not issues of the particular technology involved. But additional research here might show some differences for different media. Perhaps, for example, video sequences can be somewhat longer than fifteen seconds.

2.6 DESIGNING INTERACTIVE MATERIAL

The model I have suggested for technology-based interactive learning material is that of a teacher or professor with several students working with the professor directly in the office. But we must design not just one such learning conversation, but, in a sense, all possible teacher–student conversations. The computer program must be able to react differently to different students, just as a skilled teacher does. This task structures the design process.

The word design has come to have in everyday speech, a variety of meanings. My concern is with pedagogical design, the decisions that must be made to determine how the material works with students. Several issues are involved.

2.6.1 Who are the designers?

Our experience at Irvine indicates that design of interactive modules is best done in groups of about four or five. Fewer people in the group leads to less interactive material, because parts of the 'conversation' for some students are ignored. Too many people lead to quarrels that cannot be resolved.

Three types of people may be involved in the design group; the best possible teachers for the subject matter and target audience, those who have done research in how people learn in those areas, and media consultants, perhaps one for each of the media involved. There may be no useful research.

2.6.2 Training the designers

The main aim of the training sequence, usually in our groups a morning at the beginning of a design session of a week or two, is to acquaint the designers with the characteristics of interactive learning, as already discussed. Many have used interactive techniques only partially in their own class activities. Many of the design group will have been successful in non-interactive learning media — lecturing, writing textbooks, making films, etc. Hence they will tend to use tactics that have worked successfully in those media. They must be brought to realise the full power of interacton, so the interactive role must be fully stressed in these introductory workshops.

2.6.3 Design format

The design group also needs a format to record their pedagogical decisions. A variety of structures are possible. We have developed one such format at Irvine over many years, a design specification document that we refer to as a *script*. It provides an easy way for teachers to specify the full details of what is to appear on the screen, and the details of the interaction. The designers need not be familiar with this or other mechanisms of recording the group decisions; this can be quickly learned by the group.

The script must specify everything that is to happen when students run the program — messages that appear on the screen, computer-generated graphics, video sequences to be shown, slides to be shown, audio output, analysis of student input and actions taken on the basis of student input. For examples of scripts developed for computer-based modules at the Educational Technology Center, see *Personal Computers for Education* (1985) and *Designing Computer Based Learning Material* (1987).

2.6.4 How do the designers know if the material is interactive?

From the script it should be possible to determine when the design has too much text, or too much in the way of pictures. The script will have some mechanism of showing the various logic decisions to be made, based on student input. Typically this may be with lines running round the page. The density of these lines reflects the interaction of the computer material. Large blocks of non-interactive text material are obvious in the script.

2.7 IMPLEMENTING INTERACTIVE MATERIAL

The section considers the computer aspects of implementing interactive material, the process of starting with the script and producing the running programs.

2.7.1 The programs are complex

Any full scale highly interactive modules involve programs that are long and complex. Beginners in this area are often misled, seeing trivial 'sample' programs and assuming that the programming task is a minor one. If one seeks examples of good interactive material it is clear that this material is complex, and that the programs are non-trivial, typically thousands of lines of code. The Scientific Reasoning Series, for example, has about 300,000 lines of Pascal code. The methodology for developing these programs must be based on the fact that the programs will be long.

2.7.2 Learning programs change frequently

Further, it is important to recognise that frequent revisions will be necessary. Modifications are based on testing during development, later corrections and additions, movements to new computers, addition of new capabilities as they become available, and other factors. A program will be altered hundreds of times before a final product is attained.

2.7.3 Software engineering

A discipline within computer science is concerned with programming. It considers exactly the situation just outlined, large programs needing frequent revision. This discipline is software engineering. We should reasonably insist that careful implementation of the computer components of interactive video would be based on modern software engineering practices. Unfortunately most developers in this area have never heard of software engineering, and are not acquainted with these practices. Hence material is often poorly developed, not following good modern standards.

If code is to be modifiable, it must be readable. This implies also that the code must be highly modular, that all quantities must be carefully defined, that it be well commented, that the identifiers have clear meaning. It implies too, that code must be designed, and that coding projects must be managed on modern standards. The literature of software engineering provides further details.

2.7.4 Avoid authoring systems and languages

A common, but useless, direction in developing interactive material is to 'pick' an authoring language or system for coding the material. Indeed, beginners often believe that this is the only direction to follow. Vendors are eager to sell such systems. Yet little effective highly interactive material has ever been written in these systems. They tend to restrict the possibilities, allowing only simplistic units to be prepared. They are particularly weak with regard to the major theme of this chapter, producing interactive material, because they tend to focus developers' attention away from interaction.

Furthermore authoring systems tend to violate everything that is known about software engineering. Often the language design is such as to make it very difficult to modify the program. Authoring systems are, almost always, a waste of time and money.

Video developers are no exception. They may believe that they need an authoring system to control the videodisc or compact disc. The tasks are trivial, and can be handled by a competent programmer rapidly. For example, the following tasks might be required: (1) Go to a place on the disc; (2) Play x frames on the disc, forward or backward, starting from y, with sound off or on, at speed z; (3) Show a slide at x; (4) Play compressed audio message at a; (5) Place the video output in a window on the screen at a specified location; (6) Place the slide at x in a buffer; Show the slide in the buffer in a window on the screen. An authoring system is not needed for such a small number of commands.

Developers in the area are strongly urged to avoid all authoring systems and languages. They should be developing in the powerful general purpose languages that satisfy the criteria of moden structured programming, such as Pascal, Modula II or Ada. Software may be useful in aiding the programmers, and should be provided for the common tasks. But authors should not code, just as authors of books should not learn to run the printing press!

2.8 EVALUATION OF INTERACTIVE MATERIALS

An important component of educational development is the review and evaluation of the product. This can occur at a variety of stages, starting with initial design. The purpose of each of these evaluative stages, from the standpoint of the developer, is to improve the material. Hence each review or evaluation stage should be followed by a revision stage.

Unfortunately the most common strategy has much to be desired. Often much of the internal review is peer review by the developers or others brought in for this purpose. While peer review is important in the earlier stages of the process the emphasis should shift, during the development cycle, toward evaluation involving *students* from the target population. The critical thing is not how the material works with experienced individuals, or their opinion of the material, but how it works with those who have the need to learn. Several cycles of evaluation-improvements, formative evaluation, with larger and larger numbers of students, are suggested.

Evaluation is a critical component in assuring interaction. The designers make assumptions about how the students will react in certain places, based on their own experiences with students. But the real test is what happens when typical students use the material. New student responses for example, may be discovered. Almost always the initial views of the designers can be improved, leading to more interactive materials.

Evaluation is often minimal, because of the expense in budgeting for a quality development effort. But excellent material cannot be developed without serious evaluation. At Irvine, about one-third of the budget of many of our computer projects goes for evaluation and improvement.

2.9 THE ROLE OF VIDEO IN INTERACTION

So far, in the vein of the title of this chapter, I have been concerned primarily with the computer, as the computer provides the interactive dialogue. It will be recalled that my aim was to move interactive video toward quality interaction, away from the very slightly interactive material that has mostly been developed by linear producers to this point. The computer allows the interaction, and so that has led to emphasis on the computer.

Some lessons are to be learned for the video itself. If the material is to be interactive, to satisfy the standards suggested above for the amount of interaction, *short* video sequences should be used. Long video sequences, more than 20 to 30 seconds, probably will create a spectator sport once more, and so promote passive learning. If they have to be long, the video sequences must be of high quality, providing strong student motivation.

Because of the need for primarily short video sequences, it is unlikely that existing film and video material will be highly useful for good interactive video products, although there are exceptions to this. Generally the video segments in existing interactive video material are far too long. Interactive video is a *new* learning medium! This may be dependent on the nature of the project. In some cases, access to a vast film library may provide adequate video.

In a similar vein I would claim that the 'generic' videodisc is unlikely to lead to highly interactive material. The entire conception, I believe, came out of failure. Initially no one talked about generic videodisc. But when people expended all their energy and funds on developing the video portion, so nothing was left over for interactive computer material, they proclaimed a new type of disc. Someone else later was to prepare the computer material. In a few areas this may indeed be a possibility. But generally generic discs are not likely to lead to high quality interaction.

The key is that both the computer interaction, and the associated video material, need in most instances to be *planned together!* The design groups mentioned above should consider this as a single problem, and not a pair of problems. The design group fully specifies both the computer components and the video components, following the ideas suggested in this chapter. Then separate production teams are involved in preparing computer and video units. Product integration must occur, bringing the two together.

The emphasis on short video sequences, and the use of other media such as compressed sound and slides, indicates that the future highly interactive material may perhaps best be done with the newer CD-I (compact disc interactive) technology. Here not too much space is available, in present formats, for large numbers of video sequences. So the discipline of working with this medium may push designers into being more cautious about what video is needed, and the material may therefore become more interactive.

In many cases traditional video is effectively used only for sound, with the visuals playing an almost trivial role. If so, the video is certainly not needed. My test of this is to face away from a video sequence, listening only to the sound, and to see how much of the message can be picked up. Or better, have students do this. An alternative test is turn down the volume of the sound to zero, but to continue to watch the picture to see how much of the content can be picked up. Many well known television programmes in education have almost zero content in the visuals, as measured by these tests. I stress that I am not trying to play off visuals versus sound, but simply to get people to understand what is needed in a particular situation, sound or video.

2.10 CONCLUSIONS

In this section I stress, by listing them, a few important points.

1. Most of the existing interactive video material could be best described as 'very slight interactive'. That is, the interaction is weak.
2. Interaction comes primarily from the computer component. Media specialists for both the video and interactive computer material are needed in design.
3. Good teachers, who listen to students, are the key to designing good interactive material. Detailed experience with the student populations desired is essential.
4. Interactive material is best developed in groups of about four or five.
5. Students should have a meaningful input to the program about once every fifteen seconds.
6. The quality of each input must be carefully considered.
7. Multiple choice should be avoided.
8. The role of visuals and sound must be carefully considered, separately, in designing good learning material.
9. Authoring languages and systems are the work of the devil. But programming tools are useful.
10. In implementing the computer component of interactive material, principles of good modern software engineering should be dominant.
11. Evaluation with student populations, and improvement based on this evaluation, is essential for high quality material.

REFERENCES

Bork, A. (1980) *Computer Assisted Learning in Physics Education,* Pergamon Press, Oxford.
Bork, A. (1981) *Learning with Computers,* Digital Press, Bedford, Massachusetts.

Bork, A. (1985) *Personal Computers for Education,* Harper & Row, New York.
Bork, A. (1987) *Learning with Personal Computers,* Harper & Row, New York.
Bork, A. and Weinstock, H. (eds) (1987) *Designing Computer-based Learning material,* Springer, in press.
Bork, A. (1984) Producing computer based learning material at the educational Technology center, *Journal of Computer-based Instruction,* **11,** 3, Summer.
Bork, A. (1984) Production systems for computer-based learning. In Decker F. Walker and Robert D. Hess, (eds), *Instructional Software: Principles and Perspectives for Design and Use.* Wadsworth Publishing Company, Belmont, California.
Bork, A. (1985) Why has the interactive videodisc had so little impact on education? *The Videodisc Monitor,* **111,** 8, September.
Bork, A. (1981) Aspects of marketing intelligent videodisc learning material, *Proceedings of Conference on Interactive Video Learning Systems,* Society for Applied Learning Technology, August 1981.
Bork, A. (1980) Development of the intelligent disc, *Videodisc News,* **1,** 5, June.
Sperry, R. (1982) Nobel Prize Speech, 8 December 1981, *Science,* September, 1223.

3
Computer-assisted learning and interactive video

Philip G. Butcher

3.1 INTRODUCTION

The design team for an instructional interactive videodisc typically comprises a subject-matter expert, a video producer and a Computer-Assisted Learning (CAL) author. The subject-matter expert is the teacher or trainer who has the original teaching problem to overcome and believes that IV holds the answer. They are responsible for specifying the aims, objectives and contents of the IV materials. The video producer is the team member responsible for the production of the videodisc. They coordinate actors, cameramen, graphic artists, videotape, etc. in putting together the master videotape, and consequently the disc. The CAL author handles the interaction with the student; presenting text, graphics and video, accepting input from the student by keyboard, touch screen or mouse, building a profile of the student's understanding and comparing this with some teaching strategy before selecting the next computer/video sequence. While each member of this team has a distinct role, each in turn cannot carry out this role without full knowledge of the capabilities and intentions of the others. As an example, the video producer is responsible for laying down sequences of images on the videodisc, but in doing so must be cognisant of the fact that it is the CAL author who is to select these images for display to the student and it is the CAL author who must state whether there is a computing requirement that the images be laid down in a certain, CAL related, order on the videodisc. Equally, it is the CAL author's task to ascertain the competence of the student on the topic under study, but it is the subject-matter expert who specifies what the topic is and what is to be done with the student who is failing to demonstrate understanding of a key principle. This chapter will consider interactive video from the viewpoint of the CAL author.

Interactive video combines the attractions of pictures and sound, which form a compelling, yet from the student's view passive educational medium, with the much less attractive but highly responsive computing environment. While there are areas in which the two media overlap, e.g. both can present text and 'stylised' graphics, it is in the areas where the media complement each other that the attractions and uniqueness of IV lie. Over the past few years technologists have gradually been bringing computers and video together. Initially the connection was purely one of the computer controlling the videodisc player (Fig. 3.1A). It soon became possible to place the two images, (one from the computer, the other from the videodisc player) on the same screen, but not at the same time (Fig. 3.1B). Direct overlay of computer-generated text and graphics came about through two technologies. Philips, using teletext technology enabled computer-generated teletext text and graphics to be superimposed on the video image when displayed on a teletext TV (Fig. 3.1C) while several individual video houses competed to provide video-mixing boards such that full screen computer images could be directly overlaid on the video image (Fig. 3.1D).

In the mid-seventies, interactive CAL was primarily delivered through teletypes, which were akin to typewriters, being able to print text, often only upper case. With the advent of the microcomputer the CAL author had to consider screen design first for text, then black and white graphics and subsequently colour graphics. Now in the mid-eighties the CAL author finds they are able to draw on the full complement of CAL techniques and combine these quite readily with a full video capability all on the one screen. The latest video-mixing boards provide what is probably a glimpse of things to come in the facilities that they provide for manipulating the computer and video images (e.g. fade up, fade down) at run time under computer control. If they are to use all these techniques to the full, the CAL author is going to be a very busy and very skilled person. More likely they will call on the skills of others, e.g. screen designers, graphic designers, and will rely on a software toolbox which provides, for instance, graphics editors, author languages, programming languages and videodisc controllers all within the one development environment. The IVIS system of Digital Equipment Co. is an example of such a development environment. Using a VAX computer as host, the IV programming team has access to a full range of mainframe computer facilities for developing the IV courseware prior to downlining the software to a microcomputer for subsequent delivery to students.

We can see that, through technological developments, the CAL/IV author finds himself with an increasing choice of presentational styles, and therefore must be aware of how technological changes influence the teaching and learning environment provided up to now by the computer alone. In seeking to describe these presentational styles and their educational impact it is useful to consider an existing analysis of educational paradigms supported by CAL and reflect on how they may be influenced by IV. The major UK evaluation of CAL in education is provided by MacDonald *et al.* (1977) and their analysis forms the basis for the next two sections of this chapter.

3.2 IV, CAL AND EDUCATIONAL PARADIGMS

At the end of the UK National Development Programme in Computer Assisted Learning the team of educational evaluators, MacDonald *et al.*, writing in the Final Report of the director provided three major educational

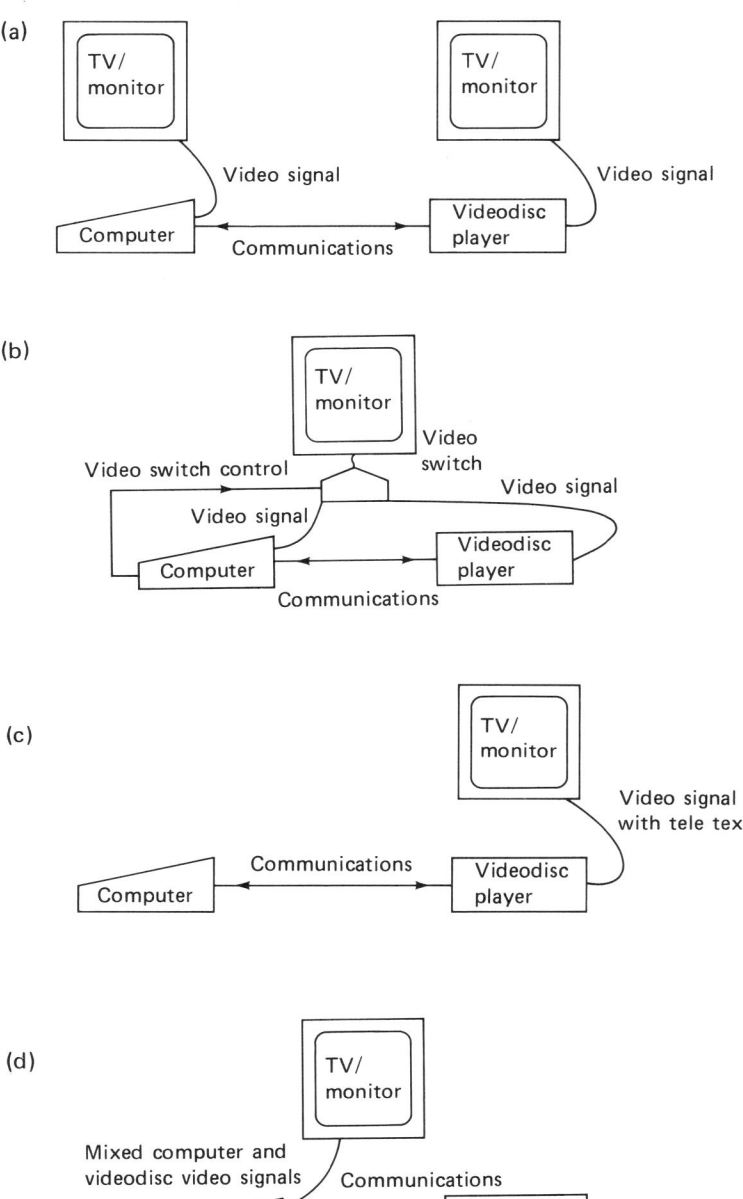

Fig. 3.1 — Interactive video hardware configurations.

paradigms for CAL and a typology of five student–CAL interactions (Kemmis, 1976) to describe student learning. How are the three educational paradigms and five student–CAL interactions affected by the interactive videodisc and in what ways can the videodisc enhance the learning process?

The three main educational paradigms identified by MacDonald *et al.* were:

— the instructional paradigm
— the revolutionary pardigm, and
— the conjectural paradigm

As its name implies the instructional paradigm is concerned with the transfer of knowledge through the transmission of information by the computer and its reception by the student. It covers at one extreme, drill requiring responses which are simply acts of recall or recognition (often aided by the correct answer being hidden in a multiple choice list), and at the other extreme, complex problem-solving skills where the computer is on hand to evaluate and advise on the student's solution or partial solution to the problem. The latter approach, often described as tutorial or adaptive-tutorial, requires the student to apply knowledge rather than simply recall it and is most often characterised by questions which require the student to synthesise their answer rather than select it from a multiple-choice list. The well programmed adaptive-CAL tutorial is able to evaluate the student's approach and proceed accordingly. Of the National Development Programme's projects, the CALCHEM project (Ayscough, 1977) was a major use of the adaptive-tutorial style. To give a flavour of the kind of interaction that can be supported in this style, Fig. 3.2 contains an excerpt from a program on the interpretation of nuclear magnetic spectra. The reader should not attempt to follow the science involved in this example but should concentrate on the interaction between student and computer. The student has been presented with a recorded spectrum of an organic compound and the dialogue shows his attempts to interpret the spectrum in the presence of the computer. Note that the computer not only accepts correct answers, but is able to advise students why incorrect answers are incorrect.

The facilities needed to support this style of student–CAL interaction are described in more detail later in this chapter.

MacDonald *et al.* attributed three roles to the computer in the instructional paradigm; 'presentation of content, task prescription (and), student motivation through fast feedback'. In each of these three roles, presentation, task prescription and student motivation, video can improve on computer-based techniques. As a presentation medium and for providing motivation video is a far more impressive than is a computer. Video can show real situations, can add human interest, can contain a story line and can entertain. Who has seen a computer make a subtle joke? At the same time 'task prescription' need not be purely verbal nor limited to stylised graphics but may make full use of pictures and sound.

The second of the educational paradigms is the revolutionary paradigm.

The data you have typed in is as follows:

Identity	Mean Peak position (in delta)	Multiplicity	Relative number of protons
1	14.1	1	2
2	1.23	1	6
3	2.63	1	2

What group (or type) of protons is responsible for the signal at 14.1 delta?
    2 COOH

Correct. COOH would explain the low field proton(s).

This leaves: 4*C   8*H   to be accounted for.

What group (or type) of protons is responsible for the signal at 1.23 delta?
    CH3

You are on the right lines, however this arrangement would not account for 6 protons.
Please reconsider your answer and try again.

    C2H5

CH3.CH2 would probably give rise to a signal at about 1.23 delta.
It would give rise to a signal with a multiplicity of 3
** not 1 which is observed **

Please try again.

    2 CH3

Note: The 'full' answer would be
'2 magnetically equivalent' CH3. groups

This would explain the 6 equivalent protons.

What atom(s) or group(s) would have to be adjacent to each CH3 group to give rise to a signal at 1.23 delta?
    C=C

CH3.C=C. would not give rise to a signal at 1.23 delta but at about 1.95 delta.

The CH3. group(s) which resonate at 1.23 delta must be attached to something less electronegative than the group(s) you have suggested.
Please try again.

Fig. 3.2 — An extract from a student dialogue with a CALCHEM program concerning the interpretation of Nuclear Magnetic Resonance spectra (Morris and Archer, 1977).

It is typified by two different categories of program, simulation and information handling. With simulation programs the student is allowed to manipulate variables and from observations of the effects of these manipulations the student 'is expected to develop an intuitive understanding' of the underlying theoretical model. There may be no correct answer to the problem, the student is allowed simply to observe the result of his actions. For simulations of physical phenomena, i.e. simulations that can be precisely defined by equations, where the student is interested in the exact numerical answers that his change to the input parameters causes, it is difficult to see how a videodisc with its prespecified pictures can be readily attached. A simulation to demonstrate the Gas Laws would be one such physical simulation. However, there are a growing number of simulations of non-physical phenomena being explored as learning environments through computer-based techniques. If these simulations have a finite number of possible pathways then it is feasible to provide video reinforcement. For instance, a business game may set a student the task of improving his (imaginary) company's performance in a market regulated by the computer. If during the game the company's managing director appears on screen asking for either improvements or resignation, the motivating effect can be imagined. A major factor of IV simulations is the videodisc's ability to display real environments so that the student may learn from interacting with these environments and while not experiencing real situations, can come as close to them as technology will allow.

Information handling programs can also be influenced by interactive video. A disc of still frames and a computer program to handle the 'picture-base' allows IV to extend the revelatory paradigm. The combination of a data and pictorial mass storage device (plus appropriate retrieval software) as a learning device is superbly illustrated by the concepts in the BBC's Domesday discs described elsewhere in this book.

The third educational paradigm described by MacDonald *et al.* is the conjectural paradigm which is concerned with providing an environment for the 'articulation and manipulation of ideas and hypothesis-testing'. For this paradigm the computer's role is to provide a fast computational service allowing students to construct and test models; by creating their computer model the students learn more about the underlying theories of the system under study; by running the model on the computer the students can test the assumptions of their model. For example engineering students may be given the task of modelling the behaviour of structures under load. To achieve this the students would have to construct a model consisting of equations describing the forces within, and displacements of, the various structural members when the structure was subjected to loading. When run on a computer the model could be tested with a variety of loads and the performance of the model could be evaluated against real data.

While IV cannot influence the reactive computing environment, which is the central feature of applications described by the conjectural paradigm, it can enrich the educational impact of the environment by providing supporting pictorial information. In our example, IV sequences showing structures undergoing loading could provide the real data that the student was being asked to model. Students could observe the effects of loading, take measurements of displacements and even freeze the experiment at critical moments by halting the video. With the current example the ultimate goal would be for the student to superimpose a graphical representation of his model on the video of the real structure and to try to match the behaviour of the modelled and filmed structures.

In summary, while the impact of IV on educational materials described by the conjectural paradigm will be peripheral, we should expect to see IV making a substantial impact when applied to educational materials developed in the instructional and revolutionary paradigms described for CAL which in turn will be reflected in the student–IV interactions.

3.3 EDUCATIONAL INTERACTIONS WITH IV

The five interactions for students with CAL programs described by MacDonald *et al.* are:

— recognition
— recall
— reconstructive understanding or comprehension
— global reconstructive or intuitive understanding
— constructive understanding

These 'five 'types' refer to the interactions between the student and the immediate CAL context. What distinguishes the types is the kinds of opportunity they offer for learning . . . .' (MacDonald *et al.* 1977).

The simplest interaction is described as recognition where 'the student is merely required to indicate whether or not the information provided by the machine . . . has been presented previously'. The question form most often involved with recognition interactions is of the multiple choice or binary choice (True/false, Yes/No) type. IV offers a much richer medium for this type of interaction than does straight CAL. With CAL the student can only be presented with verbal or simple graphical information and consequently the recognition interaction can only test in a rather tedious way with few demands being made on the able student. IV on the other hand can also test recognition of visual and aural sequences and by combining the various messages the student can be involved in a more dynamic and realistic test of their abilities.

The videodisc player, with its capability to display the video images at a variety of speeds in both forwards and backwards directions offers fine control over the presentation of pictures, while the newer videomixing boards mentioned earlier offer more sophisticated computer control of the video image. Thus sequences can be played and the student asked to indicate that he has 'recognised' a particular instance by, for example, pressing a key or touching the screen. Most modern videodisc players offer status information to the computer such that on recognising the student's response the computer is able to ascertain the frame number on display at the moment and can compare this with the pre-stored correct answer.

If the student fails the test, then the sequence may be highlighted in a variety of ways:

— the sequence may be played again at a much slower speed or halted on the target frame
— text captions can be provided
— peepholes can be created by a computer-generated overlay thereby allowing just part of the video image to show through.
— twin audio tracks can contain different commentaries at different levels of explanation

An example from the Open University's 'Teddy Bear' disc on the structure of materials (Open University, 1984; Laurillard, 1985; Butcher, 1986) shows a metal specimen undergoing a tensile test to determine its yield point and ultimate tensile strength. The test, recorded in the laboratory, is first shown to the student with a descriptive audio commentary. The student is allowed to control several such experiments recorded on the disc (without commentary) before he is asked to show that he now understands, in practical terms, what is meant by yield point and ultimate tensile strength. For this, the tensile test is shown again but without sound; the student is asked to press a key when the critical points are reached. The computer awaits the student's response and compares the currently showing frame number with the programmed values for the correct answers. After two attempts, if the student is unable to correctly identify the critical frames, the video is played again with sound and also with highlighting boxes of text which pinpoint the moments when the metal specimen fails.

In this example, the same video sequence is used in four different ways. Initially the sequence is shown as instruction. This is followed by allowing the student to control the loading and observe the effects on the test specimen; the sequence is used as a simulation. Having completed the tests to his own satisfaction the video is used as a vehicle for testing the student's recognition of the critical phases shown in the tests and finally for the weak students the video is presented as reinforcement with text and graphics added to the still frames of the failure points.

Next in the typology is recall, which 'requires the student to do more than recognise information presented, but it does not call for understanding'. Here the student may be required to construct, by recall, his own answer and enter it into the computer. This in turn demands that the computer can recognise the student's response, i.e. the computer should possess some answer matching capabilities.

As our example from the CALCHEM NMR program (Fig. 3.2) shows, once we have questioned the student and received his response we need facilities for analysing that response. These facilities should not simply be of the numeric or multiple choice variety, but should include powerful response matching routines enabling the author to exercise the student by requiring him to provide his own answer. It is in the possession of such response handling facilities that 'author' languages are most readily differentiated from 'normal' computer languages. Inexperienced authors are often sceptical about the capabilities of a machine to ask an open-ended question and to analyse the student's response accurately. How can a machine do this? Of course it cannot, and any attempt to explore the boundaries of machine 'intelligence' take us away from CAL and towards Artificial Intelligence. What can readily be achieved, however, using powerful authoring facilities is the capability of asking a question that is apparently open-ended, but in reality is not. Thus the author needs response handling facilities which can cater for the phraseology within which the student may set their answer. To facilitate this he must set the question in such a way that correct, partially correct and incorrect student responses can be readily anticipated. Such a technique is clearly not applicable to all teaching situations but there are wide areas in maths, science and technology where open-ended questioning techniques can be readily applied with the consequent improvement of the interaction as a learning aid.

To illustrate this further, consider the following question which has well defined correct answers:

'What are the two vitamins in cod liver oil?'

A complete answer to this question must contain vitamin A (retinol) and vitamin D (cholecalciferol). Answer matching algorithms are designed to make it easier for the author to match the variety of ways in which the student may express his answer. We can demonstrate some of the functions of these languages by analysing some possible replies. Of the following nine replies, the first seven are correct while the last two are partially correct.

vitamin A and vitamin D
vitamin D and vitamin A
retinol and cholecalciferol
cholecalciferol and retinol
retinol and vitamin D
D and A
Cod liver oil contains both vitamin A and vitamin D
retinol
vitamin D

What facilities does the author require to deal readily with all the above (and more) variants?

Two obvious obstacles to easy response matching in the above examples are the extra, uniformative, words and the other of the words. Consequently, we should like firstly, a facility for ignoring extra words and secondly, a facility for ignoring the order of words.

Next we must recognise that not all students are good typists and for long words such as cholecalciferol we should be willing to permit a degree of misspelling. In some languages this is implemented by allowing subsets of the whole word to be matched e.g. colcalfrol for cholecalciferol, while other approaches to this problem included the use of wildcards and algorithms based on SOUNDEX (i.e. sounds like) systems.

Finally for this example we must be able to deal easily with synonyms, thus 'VITAMIN A' and 'RETINOL' can be considered equivalent.

An author with the above facilities could then write his answer matching in the following form

> If the student's answer contains in any order
>> (the sequence RETNOL in any one word) OR
>> (exactly A as a word)
>
>> AND
>
>> (the sequence COLCALFROL in any one word) OR
>> (exactly D as a word)
>
> THEN the answer is complete and correct.
>
> ELSE IF the student's answer contains
>> (the sequence RETNOL in any one word) OR
>> (exactly A as a word)
>
> THEN prompt for the missing vitamin, vitamin D.
>
> ELSE IF the student's answer contains
>> (the sequence COLCALFROL in any one word) OR
>> (exactly D as a word)
>
> THEN prompt for the missing vitamin, vitamin A.
>
> ELSE the student's response is wrong.

Most modern author languages allow rather more control of the answer matching than that shown above, and in a somewhat more concise representation! For a fuller description of languages suitable for CAL, some of which possess IV commands, the reader is referred to Dean and Whitlock (1983) and Barker (1983–85).

Although the above answer matching example may appear to cater for all possibilities of correct and partially correct responses, this must be confirmed in practice by analysing the ways in which students do respond to the question. The ability to collect such student responses under a variety of author controlled constraints is a further response related feature found in all good author languages.

The third category in the typology — reconstructive understanding or comprehension — calls for the student to understand a principle under discussion by for example solving a problem using rules which the teacher hopes that he has conveyed to the student. If, for instance a student of chemistry is taught the following rules:

- electrons in an atom are contained in shells described by the principal quantum number 'n'
- each shell contains 'n' sub-shells with secondary quantum number 'l' varying from 0 to $n-1$
- sub-shells are labelled s for $l=0$, p for $l=1$ and d for $l=2$
- each sub-shell contains $2l+1$ orbitals
- an orbital can hold 2 electrons
- the order of filling of shells is 1, 2, 3 . . .
- the order of filling of sub-shells is s, p, d . . .

then to answer the question

'What is the electronic structure of the chlorine atom which has 17 electrons?'

the student would have to understand and apply the above eight rules to construct the correct answer of

'$1s2$ $2s2$ $2p6$ $3s2$ $3p5$'

(This question is taken from an Open University CAL program used on the university's Science Foundation Course (Butcher and Harding, 1978).)

Using the answer matching facilities referred to above, the CAL author's task is not only to match the correct answer, but also to comment on anticipated incorrect answers. In this case, the student's conceptions of the rules can be inferred from errors made in the number of electrons assigned to a sub-shell, or the wrong order of filling the sub-shells etc.

At the single question level this implies that there are a variety of further questions or hints which are selected as appropriate based on the student's response. Adaptive CAL programs should be able to build a profile of a student's ability over a range of such questions enabling them to employ a teaching strategy which bases its selections on this profile to govern the sequencing of subsequent materials.

Comprehension is not limited to verbal expression; a car mechanic will diagnose a fault by sound and sight; a doctor will take the vital signs of his patient. Although the student can only respond constructively through the keyword, IV can be used for vastly expanding the range of subjects over which comprehension can be tested. More real life experiences can be shown by IV than by any other educational media and the student's understanding of what they have seen can be tested, through the interactive program.

The fourth type of interaction will similarly benefit from the ability of IV to show stills or sequences of real life images. The interaction is described as global reconstructive or intuitive understanding which involves "getting a feel" for an idea, developing sophisticated pattern-recognition skills, or a sense of strategy' and is closely linked with the use of simulations. The potential impact of IV in interactions within this category is clearly shown by the current wave of video games where, to survive, the player has to build a conceptual model of the enviroment within which the game is played.

The final interaction type is constructive understanding in which the student enagages in open enquiry. While the student may not manipulate the contents of his pictorial database through computer programs, there is no doubt that the combination of pictorial information with superimposed data will provide a very attractive environment for engaging students in open enquiry. The BBC Domesday disc is pioneering a 'hybrid' technology (pictures and data on the same videodisc), as it shows ordnance survey maps of the UK from the video and overlays these maps with numerous forms of statistical data taken from UK census information. On the disc the audio track is used as a digital data store in a manner analogous to the technology for storing very large amounts of data on compact discs.

3.4 INTERACTIONS IN COMPUTER-CONTROLLED VIDEO

This chapter ends by considering the major computing constructs necessary to control an interactive videodisc and thereby support the student–IV interactions described above. These constructs can be seen as extensions to author languages (for the recall, recognition and comprehension interactions), to ordinary programming languages (for simulations) and to database packages (for data manipulation programs). The constructs can be grouped by function into three categories:

> those which control the display of the videodisc (VIDEO, AUDIO, STILL and PLAY);
> those which control the positioning of the videodisc (SEARCH and STEP);
> and those which provide information on the current operating settings of the videodisc player (FRAME and STATUS).

IV design considerations are included with the description of each of the functions that follow and an example showing how commands can be combined to provide a more sophisticated interaction is described. While it is accepted that videodisc players vary between manufacturers, all the following videodisc player functions are usually available under computer control.

VIDEO on/off The video picture may be turned on and off. With the video picture turned off, a black video background is provided on which computer images may be superimposed. As both audio tracks can be played without the video picture it is possible to combine audio with computer-generated text and graphics. Work at the Open University has shown that students appreciate hearing their tutors talk them through difficult subjects — the talks are recorded on and distributed through audiocassette — and the technique can be equally well used with IV, for instance to describe a computer graphic where the student needs to concentrate on the graphic while hearing the description.

AUDIO 1/2 on/off   The two audio channels can be turned on and off independently. The twin audio tracks have several possible uses, for example different commentaries at different levels of explanation can cover the same video sequence, or different languages can be used, or audio which has no matching video can be hidden under an unrelated video sequence.

STILL   This command displays a single still frame. With active play laservision videodiscs, a still frame may be held for long periods of time with no degradation of the video image enabling computer-generated text and graphic overlays to be used to instruct and test the student on the contents of the image.

SEARCH frame-number   The videodisc player searches for the specified frame and responds when it finds it. During the process the current video picture is lost and the video screen becomes black. The delay in searching is related to the distance that the videodisc player has to travel over the disc. Longest case times from end to end of the disc are gradually reducing, but to reduce black screen times even further the CAL author and video producer must have a clear idea of each other's needs before the disc is laid down.

STEP forwards/backwards   The STEP function is similar in concept to SEARCH. The difference is that the movement of the disc-player is relative to the current position rather than being an absolute position on the disc. STEP moves the disc-player head to the next frame, forwards or backwards. In achieving this movement there is no loss of video image (in contrast to SEARCH); the image simply changes with no intervening black. By defining the STEP function to accept a parameter it is possible to step forwards and backwards over groups of images, e.g. STEP 4 would step 4 frames forwards while STEP -2 would step 2 frames backwards.

With current technology, stepping over images but not resting on them is not a successful way of moving across the disc if the intervening images are different. The eye is sensitive to change and even though the intervening images are only fleetingly seen they are registered by the eye and can confuse the student. It is expected that this problem will disappear in the next generation of disc-players which will have the capability of providing instant jumps to local frames, within a range of say fifty frames either side of the current frame, without loss of the video signal and with no display of the intervening frames.

FRAME number   The computer interrogates the disc player to obtain the frame number of the currently diplayed video image. This function is the basis for the concurrent computer, video and audio presentations which are the hallmark of IV applications. For example, computer overlays can be provided at preset frame numbers, or the sound-tracks may be switched off over a preset sequence of frames. The function is equally valuable in testing students' powers of observation, for example students may be set the task of interrupting a video sequence when a key event occurs. By reading the frame number at the instant the student hits a computer key, the computer can decide, from preprogrammed ranges of frames, just how observant the student is.

STATUS Most modern players with computer connections can provide the controlling computer with current player status information. Thus the computer can be informed when a video sequence has ended or when a prescribed frame has been reached.

The order of actions and the sequencing of the computer–videodisc player interactions in all the above is quite straightforward. The computer issues the instruction and the player carries it out. Apart from the SEARCH facility all instructions are carried out almost instantaneously.

PLAY Plays video sequence — at a variety of speeds, in either direction, with or without a specified terminating frame.

This final video command uses the features of the videodisc player to the full, yet at the same time, unless programmed carefully, can impose artificial constraints on the student–IV interaction. Complications can arise because of the possibility of concurrency, that is, the computer or the student may wish to perform some action while a video sequence is playing.

As an example, consider an implementation of the PLAY command which operates in a manner analogous to the SEARCH command, where the computer issues the PLAY command and waits for a signal that a prespecified frame is reached. The videodisc player on receiving the command plays the video at the instructed speed until the specified frame is reached, when it sends the appropriate message back to the computer which on receiving the message carries on with its next instruction.

Within this sequence, first the computer is in control, then the disc player is in control and finally the computer is in control again. At no point is the student in control. Even though they have a medium that can theoretically be halted on any frame, this ability has been taken out of the student's hands by the simple command sequence that we have defined. The inadequacy of the above command sequence first came to the author's attention while watching students interacting with a laboratory experiment recorded on videodisc. Too often, the students reached out for the SLOW, STILL and BACK buttons as the video showed significant parts of the experiment, but the video carried on regardless. The students wished to exercise their own control over the speed and number of times that they observed the experiment being performed — a perfectly respectable point of view considering the capabilities of the videodisc player. Clearly what was needed, and was soon developed, was a sharing of control between computer and student, with the computer specifying the sequence of video to be shown (the disc was of the instructional paradigm classification) but at the same time providing the student with full control over the speed and direction of the video sequence. This was achieved by creating a software cycle that checked first the current position on the videodisc (with FRAME) followed by checking the keyboard for a student command. The cycle was simply repeated until either the end of sequence was detected or a student command was received. Upon receipt of a student command the command was obeyed and the software checking cycle restarted.

The description of the above constructs is included to give the reader some insight into the basic functionality provided by a computer-controlled videodisc. The last example, on concurrent operations, is important as it shows not only how simple constructs can be combined to support more sophisticated interactions but also illustrates the role of students in determining the form of the finished product. IV authors, like CAL authors, should be mindful of the need to evaluate their interactive materials and to change them according to student reaction.

3.5 SUMMARY

The previous three sections have covered styles of IV uses, types of IV interactions and the computing constructs required for supporting the full range of videodisc applications. The chapter was written with a view to giving the CAL author some evidence of the impact that IV will have on their medium and to create an awareness for video producers of some previous analyses of CAL as an educational tool.

IV offers the widest range of features of all educational technologies but to exploit these features fully it is essential that the experienced exponents of the television arts become familiar with the capabilities of computer-based media and similarly that CAL authors realise the dramatic potential that video can bring. Only through mutual understanding of the strengths of the two media can they be totally integrated to produce a true IV interaction — which should be contrasted to some early 'IV' materials where the two media were crudely bolted together.

Starting from this knowledge of the strengths of the independent media we should not be surprised to see creative design teams produce new uses and interactions specific to IV such that in a few years time a critique of IV applications can be written along the lines of the report by MacDonald *et al.* on CAL in the 1970s.

REFERENCES

Ayscough, P. B. (1977) CALCHEM: Final Review Report, Department of Physical Chemistry, The University of Leeds.

Barker, P. G. (1983–85) A practical introduction to authoring for computer assisted instruction: Parts 1–5, *British Journal of Educational Technology*, **14** 26, 174; **15**, 82; **16** 115, 218.

Butcher, P. G. and Harding, C. J. (1978) *Electronic Configurations*, Academic Computing Service, The Open University, Milton Keynes.

Butcher, P. G. (1986) Computing aspects of interactive video, *Computers and Education*, **10**, 1.

Dean, C. and Whitlock, Q. (1983) *A Handbook of Computer Based Training*, Kogan-Page.

Kemmis, S. (1976) *The Educational Potential of Computer Assisted Learning: Qualitative Evidence about Student Learning*, University of East Anglia, Centre for Applied Research in Education.

Laurillard, D. (1985) The teddy bear's disc, *Media in Education and Development*, March.

MacDonald, B., Atkin, R., Jenkins, D. & Kemmis, S. (1977) Computer assisted learning: its educational potential, in *National Development Programme in Computer Assisted Learning*. Final Report of the Director, R. Hooper, CET.

Morris, H. and Archer, D. (1977) *The Interpretation of NMR Spectra*, CALCHEM, Department of Physical Chemistry, The University, Leeds.

Open University (1984) *An Eye for an Eye (The Teddy Bear disc)*, Open University Educational Enterprises, Milton Keynes.

4

Twenty-first Century Books: An assessment of the role of Videodisc in the next 25 years

David R. Clark

4.1 INTRODUCTION

For some 450 years we have used just two data-types as the permanent mediators of ideas: *words* and *pictures*. They have served us well in the task of fixing in time and space the evanescence of speech and thought. As our whole civilisation is based on the printed word and the whole of its culture inextricably entwined with pictures, the vehicle that carries these wonderful items, which we call the book, is the focal point of all of human existence that is not merely animal. Any new device that seeks a comparable place in the world of the future must be at least a match for what a colleague of mine once called the **B**asic **O**rganised **O**ptical **K**nowledge system. But the book is under attack. A new data-type that, since its invention at the start of this century, and its mechanisation in the last forty years, threatens to dominate the mediation of ideas for the foreseeable future. This 'new' form is *digital data*.

The ubiquity of digital data needs little emphasis. It has proved possible to encode both words and pictures in this form and, as such, to render them amenable to analysis and manipulation by mechanical devices programmed to execute algorithms which express a wide range of logical intentions. What is required in the modern world, therefore, is a device that is at home just as much with this 'new' data type as with the more conventional material to be found in books. But the simple expedient of holding all the world's wisdom as digital data is not the answer. Words and pictures are distinct logical types and their requirements for comprehension, reproduction and manipulation are different (Clark, 1983).

Whilst it is undoubtedly true that words represent a higher level of abstraction than images, this very fact militates against their comprehension, since the abstraction has taken place according to a set of rules which, if they are not shared by all users of the words, render the words incomprehensible to those who do not understand the code.

Pictures may be less codified than words; that is to say, their meanings are less open to arbitrary assignment than words. The mechanism for picture analysis (seeing!) is intrinsic; it is hard-wired into our brains in the sense that we decompose the visual stimulus into 'objects' without any undue effort or prompting. The relationships that we create amongst these 'objects', that is to say the syntax of visual perception, are less clearly related to 'meaning' than the corresponding relationships in linguistic structures. This implies that pictures are less restrictive of meaning than words. Indeed, it is not clear that a picture can have meaning in the way that a word can; a picture is more of a peg on which may hang any number of word-formed ideas. The capacity of a picture to act as a resonator or mode-mixer for disparate ideas is what underpins the use of pictures as vital tools for explanation and clarification of unassimilated ideas.

To a large degree the appearance and the meaning of *words* are separable. The 8-bit ASCII code is sufficient for the representation of the meanings contained in all the world's written languages, including those that are based on ideograms. This fact has ensured the success of digital computation when applied to texts. The same is not true for 'pictures', where there is no 'alphabet' and the notion of meaning is less clearly defined, inextricably bound up with appearance, and where ambiguity is a virtue rather than a vice. Speaking loosely, pictures are for the eye and brain together, whereas words are for the brain alone. This ridiculously crude division contains one important truth: pictures are designed to be *seen*; the physical properties and capabilities of the eye are a matter of significance for pictures. It follows from this that any device that trades in pictures will gain an advance if it is tailored to the performance of the eye. Video is just such a medium.

4.2 THE CAPACITY OF THE VIDEODISC

The precise properties of the video signal have been defined with respect to the performance of the human eye and take into account many of the complex interactions between eye and brain that we loosely call seeing. For example, the human eye–brain gains the vast majority of its information from 'brightness' detail, and the video signal is designed to exploit this fact. There are 575 picture lines in the (PAL) video raster; when the resolving power of the eye is taken into account, at a distance of more than about six picture-heights from the screen the video line-structure is invisible.

The intrinsic resolving power imposed by the horizontal line structure itself imposes an equivalent vertical resolution: 'square pixels' are obtained by having $(4/3)*575=768$ elements in each horizontal line. Since the total of 625 lines must occur every 1/25 of a second, each full line takes $64\mu s$ to draw. As there must be time allowed for re-positioning the beam between each line, the time allowed for each 'active line-time' is 52 μs so that the corresponding horizontal frequency of pixels is 14.77 Mpixels/sec. Since the highest frequency at which any change can be conveyed is half this pixel rate (it takes two pixels to make a difference!), the highest horizontal frequency is about 7MHz. Historically, because of the poor performance of the first

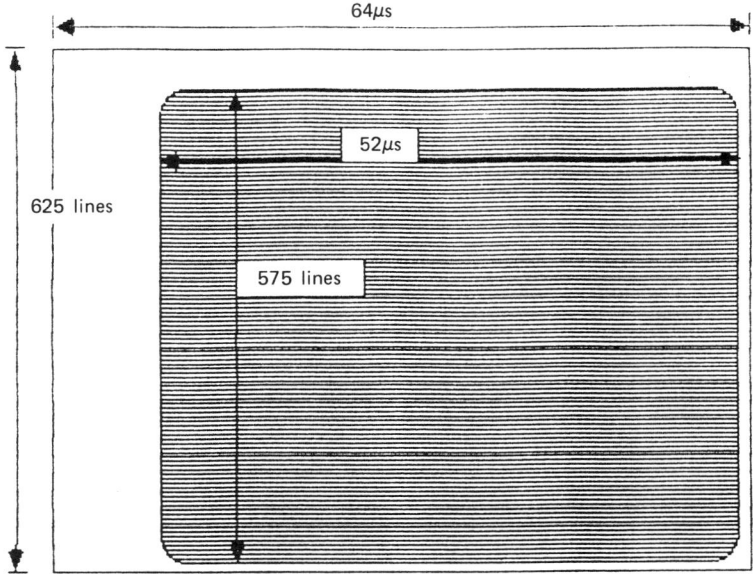

Fig. 4.1 — The 'active picture area' in the video frame. The frame consists of two interleaved fields each containing 312.5 lines.

cameras, which scanned more than one line at a time, the current limit of high frequencies in the video signal is about 5.5 MHz. This corresponds to an effective vertical resolution of 430 lines. As the video signal is a serial flow of information which represents a two-dimensional picture, the upshot of all this calculation is that the effective bandwidth of the video signal is 5.5 MHz.

The eye–brain treats 'brightness' and colour differently. Colour spatial resolution is at least an order of magnitude less acute than monochrome definition and the coding system used in video to hold the colour and brightness information of a picture trades on this difference between luminance and chrominance resolution to reduce the bandwidth required to hold an acceptable image. Although a camera decomposes the light from a scene into red, green and blue components, these are not the basic elements of a video signal. Since it is the 'brightness', which is a mixture of all of these colours, which is important, the video signal consists of three different components, called Y, U and V, which allow for the different sensitivities to colour and brightness. U and V, the chrominance components, are held in the video signal at a far lower fidelity than that for Y, the luminance component (Clark, 1980). Historically, this was the way that the three signals required for colour reproduction were compressed into the space occupied originally by just a monochrome transmission.

It is fortunate that the eye's brightness resolution is one part in 2^8 or worse. This degree of discrimination between adjacent distinct levels of brightness corresponds to a signal-to-noise ratio of about 50 dB and, as such, is within the range of performance easily obtainable by conventional analogue electronic circuits.

These facts taken together ensure that the analogue video signal is a most effective way of first encoding, then presenting pictorial information to humans. The global acceptance of television is no mean confirmation of this state of affairs.

These technical matters have been dwelt on to emphasise the intrinsic differences in the forms of presentation that have been developed for the data-types that we use to mediate our ideas. The requirements of appearance of a printed (text) page are different from those of a picture. The intention here is to demonstrate the viability of the videodisc as the preferred carrier of all the mediated messages that we as humans may need to convey. It is worth studying the video signal in some detail since, in one form or another it will be with us for a long time to come. For those who doubt the viability of analogue video, it is worth remembering that over half the degradation in the picture-quality that occurs in the whole chain from camera to receiver occurs in the domestic TV set. This is purely a price-sensitive technological constraint that can be relaxed at the manufacturers' discretion; the electronic signal that represents the television picture is more data-dense and carries more information than today's, or even tomorrow's TV set can display. Furthermore, the requirement that the video signal be broadcastable, that is to say put on a carrierwave sent from a transmitter, has added additional constraints to the fidelity of 'TV'. In the videodisc, these factors are not so severe and the new generation of videodisc players provide R, G and B signals at a fidelity comparable with reasonable video cameras.

As it was specifically designed for the job, it is tautological to say that the videodisc is good for holding pictures. A more important question in the present context is to ask how good is the videodisc at holding digital data. This has been an active field for research since the invention of the laser disc. The information held on the surface of a videodisc is *not* digital data. The meaning of the pits and islands in the reflective surface is quite different from that on the other laser-read device, the Compact Disc. This fact has been the source of much confusion so it is worth spelling out the difference between the two systems, especially as there are now several variants of the CD system appearing that purport to offer some aspects of a general-purpose information handler.

The important difference between the LaserVision and the CD formats is that the former is an analogue signal whereas the latter is a digital signal. The LaserVision system stays very close to the usual system for transmitting and recording video signals, namely the frequency modulation of a carrier wave. The purpose of this system is to avoid the problems that arise with the need to transmit 'no change'. Since all transmission channels are noisy, there is always the problem of deciding whether a small variation is signal or noise; in particular, if the something to be transmitted is 'nothing' — black in the case of pictures — it is a very bad idea to send nothing because then the noise is bigger than the intended signal! The classical solution is to let a particular frequency of a carrier wave represent 'nothing' and deviations from this frequency to represent the deviation of the signal from this reference. The video signal is a cunning mixture of information representing brightness, colour and sound and the instantaneous combination of all these factors is used to 'modulate' a carrier wave; the continuously varying frequencies that result from this modulation are stored on the videodisc as a train of pits and islands that alter their relative lengths according to the modulation.

The pits and islands on the compact disc, on the other hand, represent pure digital data (Anon, 1982). In the original format designed for sound reproduction, each channel was sampled some 44 000 times per second to an accuracy of one part in 2^{16}, giving 4 bytes per stereo sample. These 32 bits were augmented by extra bits to give a high degree of error protection and these new, lengthened, words shuffled to ensure that in any adjacent group of bits there would be no more than 1 bit from any of the original sample bytes. This is the Reed–Solomon error-correcting system and it has been implemented in silicon. There is one further refinement. On the disc, it is the *change* from a pit to an island, or an island to a pit, that represents a '1'; this means that in the shuffled data there must be no adjacent 1's. This requires another level of coding, referred to as EFM, again done in hardware, that contributes to the very high resistance to error that the CD disc displays. In the latest releases of the *videodisc* players, this system has been incorporated into the modulated carrier system to give the perfect combination of picture- and data-carrying capacity.

This matter of the difference between the digital and analogue methods of holding data really comes to a head over the question of pictures. The information on each side of a videodisc is held in a spiral track of pits and islands some 31 Km long making a total of 55 000 turns. Each turn of the spiral is, on a Constant Angular Velocity disc, sufficient, even at the inner radius, to hold the analogue representation of an almost-broadcast-standard video image. The equivalent digital data density is about threequarters of a megabyte per picture. This means that a videodisc holds, in analogue form, the equivalent of about 42 gigabytes (42 000 megabytes) of digital data. This is about seventy times the digital capacity of a Compact Disc. Since the track-length on an LV disc is seven times longer (due to the larger size of the videodisc) than a CD track, the equivalent digital data density of an LV disc is ten times that of a CD disc. Or to put it the other way round, a compact disc can hold, in digital form, about 800 pictures at videodisc quality; this is 1.4% of the capacity of a videodisc or 10% of the capacity of a videodisc of the same size as a CD disc. As the analogue representation is tailored to human requirements, the videodisc is undoubtedly the way to hold large numbers of pictures designed for eyes to look at. Furthermore, it is specifically designed to provide *moving pictures,* a thing that compact discs, using digital data find almost impossible.

But this is not all that the videodisc can do. It can also be made to hold digital data in the analogue video format and it can also be made to hold both digital data and analogue pictures simultaneously on the same track!

Taking the digital-as-analogue case first. The video signal is a rather unusual signal in that the two essential components of a signalling system, namely synchronising information and message information, are kept separate and distinct. As about 23% of the signal space is given over to synchronising information (most of the remaining space in Fig. 4.1), the video signal is very robust. From a digital point of view it is also very noise-free. By making the arbitrary assignment: black=0, white=1, each TV line in a frame can easily hold forty 8-bit bytes of digital data. This is a very conservative number that can be increased by at least two factors of 2 with current technology; even so, the data capacity of one side of a videodisc using this value is a staggering 1200 Megabytes. This is 'raw bit' capacity that has to be used in conjunction with an error-correction scheme to compensate for the errors that inevitably occur in all mechanical systems; nevertheless, when the appropriate schemes are applied, one side of a videodisc can hold and return a full gigabyte (10^9 bytes) of error-corrected data.

Such a large number needs to be put into a more everyday context (Clark, 1984). In a medium that can hold 55 000 analogue video pictures or 1 Gigabyte of digital data, or any combination in between, the possibilities for information handling are hard to grasp. Take, for example the 24 volumes of the *Encyclopaedia Britannica*; they contain between them some 43 million words and 23 000 pictures. Assigning one video track to each picture leaves 32 500 tracks for digital data. As an English word contains on average, six characters, including the inter-character space, and each character requires 1 byte, if ASCII coded, the 43 million words require just over a quarter of a gigabyte to hold them. This amount of data occupies 14 320 picture tracks, so that the whole of EB, words and pictures, when stored this way occupies just over *two-thirds of one side of one videodisc*. This leaves us with the great problem of the twenty-first century: what do we do with the other third? The 17 000 remaining tracks represent over a quarter of a gigabyte of digital data. The most extravagant program to search this database might occupy 10 megabytes, and this is less than 3% of the available free space!

As a comparison, the CD system could hold all the words of the EB and then have room only for about 500 of the 23 000 pictures (2%) at video quality. For all its fashionableness, CD is a very poor second to LV and only transient commercial factors are giving it its spurious dawn for anything other than music.

The videodisc as originally designed did not just hold pictures; it held two music-quality sound channels as well. There have been a number of LaserVision variants that have differed in a way that reflects the differences between the European (PAL) and the American (NTSC) video systems. In both cases the sound channels, which require a smaller bandwidth than the vision channel, have been held in the low-frequency region of the power spectrum (Fig. 4.2). High quality digital audio is produced by sampling the analogue audio signal at about 44 KHz. This allows frequencies up to about 20 KHz to be recovered accurately and frequencies in this region are outside the normal hearing range (the 4th harmonic of C_8, the highest 'C' on the piano, is about 19.6 KHz and the six harmonics required to give an almost perfect audition of a note are available up to A_7). The samples need to be at least 12 bits deep to avoid noticeable 'quantising error' on reconstruction

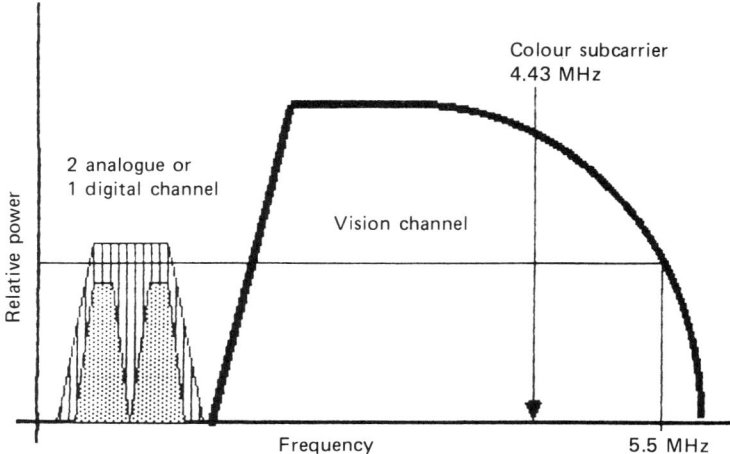

Fig. 4.2 — The distribution of signals in the frequency space.

and it is now conventional to use 2 bytes for each channel, giving a digital bit rate, after the EFM process, of about 2 Mbit s^{-1}. Such a data rate requires about 2 MHz of bandwidth and this can be accommodated below the video on a modulated carrier. The advantage of this system, which is employed in the new Philips player (VP415) for the Domesday project, is that it allows the videodisc to carry analogue video pictures and digital data 'simultaneously'.

This simultaneous availability of analogue pictures and digital data confers a significant advantage on the LV system in comparison to any other for holding information. The ability to associate text, which is most economically held as digital data, with a picture, which is most economically held as an analogue image, confers on the videodisc the joint mastery of the two basic data types: words and pictures. That the digital data may also be statistical information, map overlays or even computer programs, gives the videodisc that added flexibility that will take it, as the preferred medium, into the twenty-first century.

In fact, there are problems. No mechanical system is error-free. In a record/replay device there are two types of error: 'hard' and 'soft'. Hard errors occur during recording or in damage to the medium and are permanent; soft errors occur on replay and are transient. They are indistinguishable if only one replay act is allowed and many different schemes for recovering data from an erroneous reading have been developed. The commonest error is a misreading, called a 'drop-out' where for a short time the readout from the disc is interrupted. Because of the particular form of the error-correcting system used to proof the digital data against 'drop-out' of the signal recovered from the disc, the digital data representing logically adjacent pieces of information are no longer physically adjacent; they are dispersed over a small region of the disc which is large in comparison with the size of the disturbance producing the drop-out. This means that, unlike the video signal from the disc, in which there is an instantaneous correspondence between the signal from the disc and the video raster, the recovered digital data are delayed with respect to the instantaneous position of the reading head. This means that there can be no instantaneous correspondence between data and pictures; synchronisation has to be achieved by some intermediate digital storage and this introduces complications into the design of the player and the disc mastering process. Nevertheless, such a system has been designed to provide digital stereo sound with movies.

The great benefit is to be gained when the digital data is not audio, but arbitrary digital information. The sampling rate of 44 KHz corresponds to about 7 Kbytes in each 1/25th of a second. The conservative figure of 6K of error-corrected data per video frame has been accepted as a working standard for the next generation of players, so this gives a digital capacity of 0.33 Gby *in addition* to the 55 500 video frames. This 6K of data is distributed over three or four adjacent video tracks. The major drawbacks to this system are that it is not easy to prepare the digital data in the correct form for mastering onto the disc and that the precise form of the record structure has been defined by the manufacturer of the electronics. With the digital-as-analogue method for holding the data, the whole process is independent of the videosdisc player since the recorded signal is standard video which has been generated privately in a way convenient to the task in hand.

The capacity of a videodisc is best represented as an area spanned by the two axes of analogue picture tracks and digital data (Fig. 4.3). The digital data can be on either the picture tracks, instead of the picture, or in the 'sound space', in which case it can be present along with the picture tracks. There are many ways in which information can be distributed between data and pictures. The 6K bytes that can go with each image can be thought of both as bibliographic material and more general indexing or graphical data. It represents about 1000 words or 1 bit for every nine TV pixels. This bit-map representation may be the most useful in that it can represent useful abstractions of pictures: the pipe-routes on a map or the outlines of relevant objects in a photograph, or some special codification of the image to make it word-free computer searchable.

Some possible combinations of pictures and data are indicated. They are:

(1) 600 pictures, each with 10 seconds of digital hi-fi stereo sound
(2) 1000 spacecraft images in both analogue and digital form
(3) 10 000 pictures each with 20 seconds of 'telephone quality' speech
(4) 15 000 pictures each with 20K of digital data (1 bit/TV pixel)
(5) 50/50 disc: half pictures, half digital data
(6) Surrogate Travel programme.

These options are in addition to either analogue sound or any digital data in the 'sound space', and range from cases where most of the disc is taken up

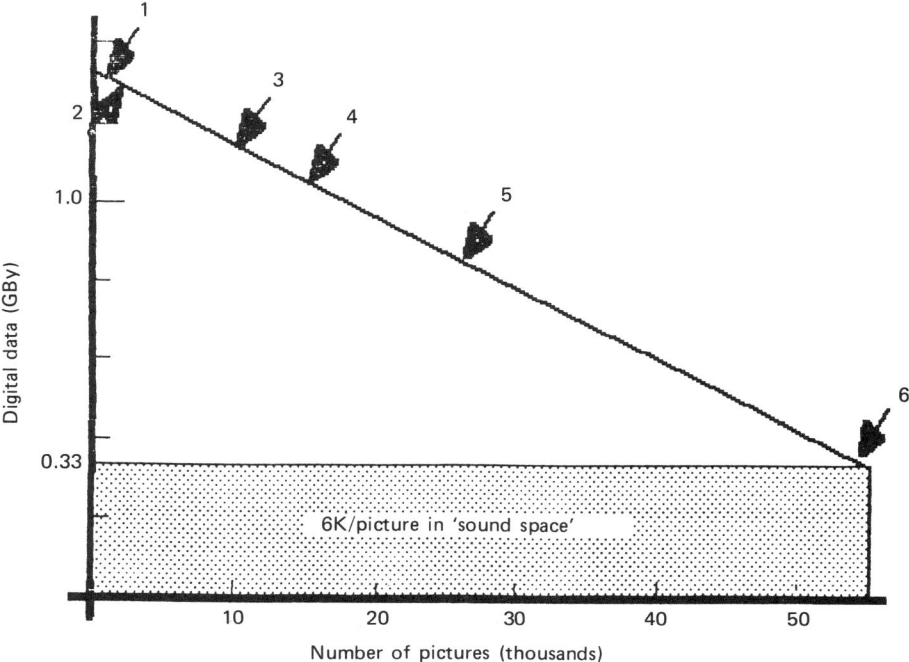

Fig. 4.3 — The capacity of a videodisc in terms of combinations of analogue pictures and digital data. (*Adapted from a diagram by David Backinsell, VDS*).

with data in the video space to an example where a database and some control programs, occupying of the order of a megabyte, serve to manage the passage through a large number of pictures in a Surrogate Travel programme.

It is interesting to note that the words part of the *Encyclopaedia Britannica* will fit into the 'simultaneous data' part of the disc, leaving the whole of the video portion free for pictures.

There are many developments in the laser disc field to come in the near future and we can look forward to machines that can offer a range of facilities and each application can be developed on the one that suits it best; the playback machinery will be able to cope with all the possibilities.

4.3 PEDAGOGICAL EXPLOITATION OF THE CAPACITY OF THE VIDEODISC

So much for the details of the capacity of the Videodisc. Why is it so significant that this device is so capacious? It all has to do with the fundamental processes by which we gain understanding about the world.

Consider the following proposition: *the American space missions need not have happened*. Their purpose was to collect data and, over the years, they have done so, in abundance. But, for all practical purposes, this information does not exist. It sits on magnetic tape in warehouses across America whence it is far too difficult for all but the most diligent researcher to obtain. Much of the data are pictures and this means that they are impossible to codify for content-searching by machine. They must be 'browsed', that is to say examined by eye with the expectation of being rejected. The form in which they are currently held precludes browsing and therefore 90% of the research is carried out on 10% of the data. A videodisc will hold 1000 browsable pictures *and* the digital data for those pictures on the same side of a disc. Issuing the digital data alone on CD, as the Jet Propulsion Lab. are doing, is completely to miss the point.

That anecdote illustrates the role of videodisc in marshalling resources; there is also the role of videodisc in education and training.

Learning is unquestionably an active, rather than a passive process. This is why learning strategies that involve a high degree of participation are so effective, all other things being equal. There is another aspect of the learning process that is often overlooked: learning is an individual, private process. It takes place in a frame of mind in which time, in particular, takes on a special significance. Objective time, marked by the passage of the clock, is of little relevance; the learner moves in a Subjective Time that dilates and contracts in ways related to the rate of acquisition of understanding. This flow of time is part and parcel of the conceptualisation process and must not be disrupted if concentration is to be maintained; any mechanical device that is designed to support the learner in the quest for understanding must not impose an arbitrary measure on the flow of this Subjective Time.

There are several interesting facets of Subjective Time in relation to learning. One concerns the inherent effectiveness of film and video as media for the development of understanding. In the act of watching a film, the viewer enters into a contract with the film-maker. This contract entails the viewer surrendering all rights to the control of time; the corresponding obligation that this contract imposes on the film-maker is that the film present a believable temporal universe. From this contract flow the rules both of editing and of narrative structure. These structural devices have served the audience well, but by so surrendering control over time, each viewer is deprived of the power of rational thought. This must be the case because the essence of analytical thought is that it takes place in a private, personal, Subjective Time which cannot co-exist with that temporal scheme imposed by the film-maker. The temporal universe of the film can only be accepted by a passive viewer, and this passive mode is antithetical to the kinds of thought that occur on the way from confusion to understanding; thinking, we agree, is an active process. As Goebbels knew, and succeeding generations of propagandists and advertisers know only too well, films act on the emotions far more than on reason. They effect changes in mood, not understanding. Modern methods and devices which seek to facilitate learning must favour Subjective Time at least as well as the book has done. In the new world of Interactive Videodisc, which is one aspect of the twenty-first century book, the management of time comes naturally: the system does nothing until it is prodded; it must then react speedily to return an appropriate response. Not only the pace of the interaction, but also its trajectory, is determined *entirely* by the learner. In this way, the maximum scope for individual imagination is provided in a way that is responsive to the particular train and pace of thought.

Another interesting facet in the maintenance of Subjective Time, is the effect of the devices used to mediate the interaction on the user's level of concentration. This is the true arena in which the battle of the mouse-and-icon must be fought. Unfortunately for all those proponents of the touch screen, or even the keyboard, the battle has already been won and the mouse is the victor on physiological and psychological grounds. As the researchers at Xerox PARC discovered (Card, English and Burr, 1977), human hand–eye co-ordination with the mouse-and-icon is both very efficient and is managed at a mental level distinct from that deployed in the kinds of thought involved in understanding. This hand–eye co-ordination, involving small movements of the arm in an unstressed position, is the least disruptive of thought of any of the possible input mediations. But that is only true for a real mouse — the one with just ONE button! Just as soon as the user has to decide which button to press, the whole advantage of the device is thrown away: the user has to take time out from the 'real' thinking to manage the mouse and this 'mode switch' is distracting and disruptive. The steady mouse-inflation, first to two buttons with Little Blue, then to three for later arrivals like the AMX, reveals a lack of understanding of the basic principles on which mouse-and-icon interaction should be based.

The valuable aspect of *activity* in the process of acquiring understanding is not just the participation; there is always in the process of learning a private moment when the learner does not 'know', for certain, the next step. The only way forward is by an act of imagination: the synthesis of all that the learner understands appears as an 'educated guess'. If that guess turns out to be correct, then the imagination becomes knowledge; if not, the imagination must be refined and improved. The only way forward is by making that imagination real, that is to say, by making an action. It is at this point that all the properties of interactive videodisc converge to produce the best medium yet devised for the imparting of understanding. This is because it alone so far, apart from the (unmediated) 'real world', provides the arena in which these acts of imagination can be first engendered, then realised. And it is in this realisation that the capacity of a videodisc, on which so much stress has been laid, becomes crucial. The action is always a choice between many alternatives; each of these alternatives has consequences and those consequences are the data that must be used to tune the imagination. This is just a grandiose way of saying that the way to learn is from your own mistakes. The value of the videodisc is that it has the capacity to hold a sufficient range of alternatives and their consequences, and allows you to make your mistakes in private without damage.

With no empirical justification as yet, it seems to me that a ratio of 10:1 in favour of erroneous options might provide a universe of sufficient versatility that within it genuine choices could be made. A videodisc, then, becomes a large collection of errors waiting to be made, and a videotape can be defined as the least interesting path through an interactive videodisc — it is the enforced sequence of all the 'true' choices.

This aspect of videodisc philosophy invites comparison with methods of imparting understanding that rely on *simulation*. In these methods there is an underlying model which is repeatedly invoked with new input conditions chosen by the user who then sees the computed consequences that the model predicts on the basis of these choices. The currently fashionable examples are to be found in medical teaching. The supposed virtue of these simulations is their 'reality'; they mimic the real situation because of the accuracy of the model and the 'real-time' nature of the event. Recent work by David Hon has confirmed the notion that all that is required of such an interactive program is that the participant *feels as though* the system is 'real'. The quest for real-time simulation is often misbegotten if there is no new information to be obtained, that is to say, if the simulation is for teaching, not for research.

Choice between a small number of predetermined alternatives is all that is required to give a convincing sensation for realism: there is no need for the global precision of a mathematical model. The challenge of interactive videodisc design is, in part, the selection of this minimum set of alternatives. A metaphor for this kind of interaction is the attempt to escape from the maze at Hampton Court; to escape takes the full concentration of the escapee, who is interacting continuously with the maze and receives all sorts of more or less useful indications on how to proceed; the maze itself is as unchanged as it was when Queen Bess played hide-and-seek in it as a child in 1540.

It is in the selection and creation of the universe of choice that the role of the teacher becomes paramount. By definition, a teacher is someone who ought to know what the areas of difficulty are that students most frequently encounter. A good teacher not only anticipates these common pitfalls but should also know what to do to help the student understand their nature. These two pieces of information, what the problems are and what to do about them, determine the selection of material to be included on a disc and the uses to which they are put. As education or instruction is at least in part the process of mastering and applying the (word) codes that define the subject under study, any device that stands at least partly across that code boundary must be a help in mastering novel abstractions. Visual images, because of their flexibility of meaning, are valuable and effective mediators of ideas. The usage *'let's look at this another way'* is more than a metaphor; there is some reason to suppose that the way we 'see', which is, of course, a mental rather than an ocular process, is intimately connected with the way we think. This close relationship between seeing, thinking and understanding argues for the need to bring images into the ambit of interactive learning in as detailed and effective manner as possible.

In a paper (Clark and Sandford, 1986) dealing with the attribution of meaning to pictures in such a way that they can be searched without the use of words, Neil Sandford and I discuss a technique that has liberated the designers of interactive videodisc teaching from the tyranny of the multiple choice question in all its hateful variants. In essence, we detail a way that allows an image to be presented straight, so to speak, with no qualificatory information; the aim is to pose a question in precisely the proper domain, with no other extraneous clues as to the appropriate response. If this can be achieved, then the student is exposed to the most genuine and, therefore most effective learning situation short of the 'real thing'. For example, (Lloyd, 1986), in a programme based on our 'Resource disc' on the Knee, students are asked to identify the anterior cruciate ligament. They can do this by pointing to the region of their choice and mouse-clicking: their only guide is a good picture of the dissected flexed knee and a prompt to point and click. The question and answer are in the same domain — the picture.

4.4 CONCLUSION

These considerations convince me that the videodisc is the medium *par excellence* for the next generation of implements designed to help people to think and to gain understanding. There is, however, a structural factor that militates against their immediate acceptance: their sheer power. By any measure, the videodisc offers at least a thousand-fold improvement over the current ways of managing information; such a step up is very hard to cope with. An advance usually offers a factor of two or so on current capabilities; the increase in the capacity of disc-drives or the increase in gate-density on silicon chips are familiar examples of such rates of improvement. To be confronted with a device that can hold the words and pictures of thousands of ordinary books in a form that is ideal for machine interaction is to be confronted with a terrifying monster. This in part explains the current vogue for the compact disc; its capabilities are rather more comfortably manageable by the less imaginative of today's system designers. In the rush to make CD work as a database medium, they have attempted to use it for encyclopaedias; every demonstration I have seen gives examples that end up, trumphantly, with a picture. In so doing, they demonstrate at once the primacy of pictures and the fundamental unsuitability of the digital disc to cope with them.

At the University of London Audio-Visual Centre we have, with the aid of a large grant from the DoTI and support from Thorn-EMI, explored the use of videodisc for education and training across a wide spectrum. We divide the videodisc universe into 'Resource discs', in which each image is present in its own right, and 'Concept discs', in which the images are contingent on the particular task for which the disc is designed. As a prime example of Resource discs we have instituted the University of London Videodisc Library of Anatomy. Two subjects have been covered so far under the guidance of Dr John Pegington (UCL), the Knee and the Inguinal Region. These discs have been developed in conjunction with a programming environment based on the Soft Option extensions to Microtext and currently are being given to program developers working in a uniform 'mouse-and-icon' style. The plan is to release the discs together with a suite of programs to illustrate the versatility of the system.

The Concept disc mode was used for a videogame presentation of one aspect of the English legal system. To help law students and solicitors in training get a good feel for the practicalities of Civil Procedure, Dr Martin Dockray (KCL) devised a highly-branched program in the style of an elaborate role-play 'simulation' in which the player takes the part of a solicitor who acquires a client and then conducts a case for him.

Perhaps the most innovative part of the whole videodisc project has been a Videodisc Guide to your Dog. This disc, which bridges the Resource and Concept categories, was designed to work with the simplest possible player and with no larger-scale computer support. To achieve this goal we have developed, with the assistance of David Rumball of RAG, a 'one-touch' handset that is set to revitalise the use of videodisc in the home. Without a viable consumer market for LaserVision, there is no chance of its survival in education; for purely self-interested reasons, therefore, we intend to stimulate just such a market.

All in all, the future is bright. Just at the time when we need the tools to enable people to re-educate themselves for changing needs in ways that are consistent with earning a living at the same time, just as the need for continuing professional education is being accepted and just at the time when we must give serious thought to the schoolteaching of modern science and technology, along comes the very device we need; one that has both the capacity and the capability to contain, manage and present the ideas in the heads of the people who understand their subjects. The work now going on in videodiscs will help to set the tone and style for education in the twenty-first century; by that time someone will have produced the videodisc equivalent of the novel and the book as we know it will have become the papyrus of a bygone age.

REFERENCES

Anon. (1982) Compact Disc Digital Audio, *Philips Technical Review,* **40** 6.

Card, S. K., English, W. K. and Burr, B. (1977) Evaluation of mouse, rate-controlled isometric joystick, step keys and text keys for text selection on a CRT, Xerox Palo Alto Research Centre, SSL-77-1, April.

Clark, D. R. (1983) Interactive video discs, *Professional Video,* 24–5, Feb.

Clark, D. R. (ed.) (1980) *Computers for Imagemaking,* Pergamon Press, Oxford.

Clark, D. R. (1984) Interactive videodisc in Education and training, *Media in Education and Development,* 190–4, Dec.

Clark, D. R. and Sandford, N. (1986) Semantic descriptors and maps of meaning for videodisc images, *Programmed Learning and Educational Technology (PLET),* **23,** 84–90, Feb.

Lloyd, P. (1986) Exploring the thinkies, *AudioVisual,* 46–7, Sept.

5

Pedagogical design for interactive video

Diana Laurillard

5.1 IV AS A FORM OF EDUCATIONAL TECHNOLOGY

This chapter attempts to situate interactive video within the field of educational technology, as one of a range of teaching media, each one of which is appropriate for only some teaching tasks. It may be helpful to begin by describing what educational technology does, in order to make clear what role it has as a framework for interactive video. It is not, after all, universally acknowledged that IV *should* be seen as a part of educational technology, and many developments have taken place outside this framework, in the context of systems software design, or video production, for example. It is my aim in this chapter to argue that IV for educational applications should always be carried out within such a framework.

Educational technology is an enterprise that uses research and development techniques in close combination to build knowledge and understanding of how students learn through different kinds of teaching media and methods, and how these should best be used in order to facilitate efficient and desired learning. Included in teaching media and methods are the whole gamut of techniques available to the teacher, from the traditional lecture or tutorial, through group methods, books, workbooks, AV, to computer programs and the computer-controlled media we are principally concerned with in this book. In every case the problem is to understand how the technique operates, what makes it work, or not, and why. Research and development are closely linked because each needs the other: research can only be carried out on students learning from the method concerned, and the method can only be developed satisfactorily in the light of information from research studies about how it operates.

As knowledge and understanding develop, it becomes possible for educational technologists to articulate the methodology to be used in instructional development, and the descriptions of, for example, forms of learning, student models, media typologies, etc. This kind of approach to education is important because it is the only way the teaching profession can know what it knows about teaching. Teachers know about and are trained in the content of their subject, but they have very little access to an understanding of the process of teaching it. Lawyers have time-honoured traditions to tell them how to handle the written law; doctors are given constantly updated research-based practices; teachers have little more than native wit to tell them how to teach people to understand their subject. It is the goal of educational technology to supplement this with good quality information about what they and their students are doing.

Educational technology describes a rational and systematic procedure for developing instructional materials. The framework it provides takes the general form of a cycle of analysis, development and evaluation:

Instructional needs analysis → learning objectives →
→ learning activities → choice of media →
→ instructional design → development →
→ evaluation → instructional design

but being rational, it is, of course, an idealistic framework. In practice it is usually the case that 'choice of media' is the first decision, followed by a fleeting design stage, an extensive development stage, and no evaluation at all. This is particularly important when it comes to considering the pedagogical design of interactive media, because unless interactive video, for example, is chosen after careful analysis of the needs, objectives and suitable learning activities for its potential audience, there is a considerable risk that the resulting material will fail to exploit the medium and fail to provide effective teaching. For many of the current implementations of interactive video, the teaching could have been done more effectively and much more cheaply by other means. That is why educational technologists must continue to argue for a rational design and development procedure, rather than accepting uncritically the way the world prefers to work.

Because the logical place for evaluation is at the end of the development cycle, it tends to assume a lesser importance than it deserves, and may even be left out altogether for want of time or resources. In this chapter, I want to emphasise its importance by putting it at the start, in order to demonstrate that it can both inform the development of a particular disc, and contribute to the general understanding of how interactive media are best used in teaching. With the results of one particular case study, we can then go on to develop some more general points about the principles of design for such media.

5.2 EVALUATION OF INTERACTIVE VIDEO

The kind of evaluation study necessary for interactive video is similar to that for any other computer-based medium. The aims of the study will be both 'formative', i.e. to find out what improvements should be made to the courseware, and 'summative', i.e. to generalise the formative findings and to describe the nature of this kind of learning experience.

The aims are not usually comparative. It only makes sense to carry out a comparative study of interactive video against some other teaching method if it is intended to exactly replace that method. In that case it is reasonable that the standards of judgement should be the same for the two media. In most applications, however, the interactive video is being used precisely because it makes some unique contribution that other media cannot make — indeed one might argue that if it does not, then IV should not be used because it is generally more expensive than other media. Therefore either it is essentially different from other media implementations, and is therefore non-comparable, or it is comparable but inefficient and therefore should not be used at all.

The formative and summative aims are descriptive rather than comparative. The aim is to find out, in particular, (a) what kind of thinking the medium promotes in the user, and (b) what aspects of the design help to promote learning. This information will then help teachers and trainers to decide where interactive video is needed for pedagogical reasons, and will help instructional designers to use the medium effectively.

A suitable methodology for such an evaluation study is outlined below:

Specify objectives — these are usually implicit in the nature of the disc, rather than explicitly defined during the design process. They must be explicitly defined for the evaluation, however, as it is this that determines the type of learning outcomes looked for, and how they will be tested.

Specify prerequisite knowledge — there is typically an implicit assumption by the designer that users will know certain things before they start. The evaluation should test this, however, partly because it may be an unwarranted assumption, and may make the disc more difficult to use; also because it often turns out that the prerequisite knowledge is poorly understood, but the material greatly improves the user's understanding of it. This then counts as a learning outcome.

Design pre- and post-tests — these are used to test both the pre-knowledge and the learning outcomes. The two tests are identical, the first half being questions the users are expected to be able to answer (the pre-knowledge), and the second half being questions the users can only be expected to answer well after using the material (the learning objectives). The difference in performance on the two tests can then be used to help to identify what has been learned with the help of the disc.

Observation — probably the best quality data in the evaluation study comes from the observation of two typical users working through the disc. This is when any major user problems come to light, but it can also tell the evaluator a lot about the kind of learning experience the material provides. The observation should record at least the users' inputs (which may also be done by a computer-monitoring program), the time at which these occur, and the conversation between the two users as they work together and any other actions they take (such as reading notes, drawing diagrams, etc.). The record of user inputs will provide information about the strategy used; the times will provide an estimate of how long the various forms of interaction take and what proportion of user time is spent on what kind of activity; the conversation will provide an externalisation of the kind of thinking the disc promotes in the user, which in turn aids an assessment of the kind of learning that might have taken place.

Interviews — interviews with users soon after the learning session will enable the evaluator to 'triangulate' the other evidence, i.e. to collect data about the same events in a different form. The interview can ask the user, for example, to explain concepts or procedures to check on learning gains, and to describe their experience of it and why they did what they did, to assist in the assessment of how the material might be improved.

Questionnaires — once the above forms of data collection have been carried out with a few users, the principal parameters of the evaluation will be known, and it will be possible to devise a more automated form of data collection using standard questionnaires, or even a computerised questionnaire. This will allow the evaluator to assess, for example, the importance to the typical user of particular design aspects, or the range of learning gains for the user population.

Evaluation studies are rare, even when the medium is as new and untried as interactive video. Once the disc is completed, the idea of evaluation is an unwanted intrusion in the atmosphere of self-congratulation and relief that inevitably engulfs the over-worked design team. However, the staffing required to carry out the above methods is very low — about 20 person-days — in comparison with the staffing required for the production of the disc, and in comparison with the value of the resulting data, both for the disc concerned and for the future of the medium. As an illustration, the following section describes a particular evaluation study of the Open University 'Teddy Bear's Disc'.

5.3 AN EVALUATION CASE STUDY

5.3.1 Description of the disc

The 'Teddy Bear's Disc' was developed for a second level course in technology, on the structure of materials. The course covers a wide variety of concepts in metallurgy and materials technology, and the aim of the disc was to provide a synthesis of all these by bringing them to bear on a real life problem. The video was used to present the problem, its context, and the visual aspects of the concepts involved; the computer interaction was used to allow the student to perform surrogate experiments, and to test their knowledge and understanding of the content.

The structure of the disc was based on an existing television programme from the course, which put the problem in the form of a court case assessing the responsibility for blindness in teddy bears: was it the fault of the manufacturers of the teddy bears' eyes, or did the fault lie with the people who made the washers that held the eyes in place? The court had to hear the arguments from both sides, and decide the issue on the basis of evidence about the properties of the materials involved.

The structure of this programme gives a framework to the material presented on the disc, and provides a rationale for the integrated computer-based exercises. The barristers set up the problem at the beginning of the trial; the video stops and the computer gives the student the opportunity to predict possible causes of eye-loss by the teddy bears, guiding them towards the concept of 'environmental stress'; returning to the trial, this point is reinforced as the prosecution makes the case that the cause could have been environmental stress, but the defence counters by claiming that the changes made in the washers were irrelevant to this; back to the computer-controlled simulation of experiments to check the validity of the claim, using some video still-frames; and so on .... Thus the student experiences a continual alternation between video sequences lasting four to five minutes, and computer-controlled exercises lasting ten to fifteen minutes.

The software used to control the disc incorporates facilities taken from the STAF2 authoring language, which allows open-ended questions to be put to the student, who then has to construct their own answer by typing it in from the keyboard, or typing in a numerical answer to a calculation. A sophisticated answer-matching routine ensures that, for the majority of cases, the computer can handle the student's input in a sensible way. The computer-generated text is displayed as teletext overlay on the disc-generated video. [The hardware used for this implementation was: an Apple II with two disc drives and a language card; a Philips Laservision player, VP705; a California Computer System 7710A serial interface card; a Pye television with Teletext facility.]

5.3.2 Evaluation methods

The educational evaluation of the interactive videodisc package had two main aims: (a) to find out what kinds of improvements could be made to the software, and (b) to describe students' experiences of this kind of learning method.

The evaluation was conducted at the Open University summer school for the Structure of Materials course. Two work-stations were available for students to use in their free time, which, given the heavy scheduling of the summer school amounted to evenings only. Students used the package in ones or twos, on a voluntary basis, returning for further sessions if they wished. Instructions for the operation of the disc, and advice on what was available, were given both at the beginning of the disc, and in text form on the wall next to the work-station. The sessions were usually unsupervised, and students were not required to submit any record of their work. Information about the availability of the videodisc package was given to students at the start of the summer school, and it was emphasised that this was optional work.

The evaluation methods used were:

Observation — recording students' actions and conversations, and the timing of these, recorded on pro-forma sheets,

Interviews — informal discussions with students after they had finished using the package, recorded in note form,

Questionnaires — designed on the basis of initial student comments, filled in by students after their work on the disc (see Appendix 1).

Pre- and post-tests were not used, because an assessment of actual learning gains was not the aim of the evaluation. Altogether 40 students were observed, in groups of one and two, 9 students were interviewed, and 20 completed the questionnaire. The results below are based on this information.

5.3.3 Student experience

One of the best ways of assessing students' perception of the value of a learning method is to establish how much they used it. From observation and questionnaire data, students used the package, on average, twice, with a range of one to six times. Given that students are extremely careful about their use of their very limited time for study, this repeated usage is a tribute to the perceived quality of the disc. What they liked was the form of the method, the continual interrogation and the variation in presentation. The questionnaire asked students to mark those descriptions of the package they particularly agreed with, and threequarters said: 'It made you think about things your weren't sure you knew', and 'It was a good way to learn, combining questions with short breaks for video'.

We can conclude, therefore, that whatever its actual value, the perceived value of the method was high.

The observation study showed that one advantage of this type of method is that it holds the students' attention for a considerable length of time. Most of the open-ended comments on the questionnaire made the point that there was too much material on the disc, and that the package took too long to complete. The observation study recorded an average time to complete the package of two and a quarter hours, with a range of one to three and a half hours. This is a long time for students to spend on optional work and moreover it was concentrated work — the interrogative form of the package promoted a lot of discussion, and the gradual progression towards a solution kept the students working steadily, often beyond the time they meant to stop (namely closing time!).

The response from students is encouraging. It suggests that at least the method is a feasible one in the sense that students find it enjoyable and feel they are learning something.

5.3.4 Forms of interaction

In this section we consider the design features of disc and software that were successful in encouraging students to think about their subject, and to practise the reasoning processes and procedures that they need to become competent in their field.

Several different forms of interaction were used on the disc, where interaction is defined to refer to the interval between two consecutive key presses by the student, i.e. the time taken to read the question, decide on the answer, and input the answer, or to watch a section of video, read the instruction and press return to continue.

The following types of interaction were used. They are listed roughly in order of frequency of occurrence, together with a description of their value to students:

Information testing (e.g. 'Which class of polymers fail in a brittle way?') — it was this form of interaction that made students aware that they did not always know what they thought they knew.

Information giving (e.g. 'Glasses have random molecular arrangement and exhibit no step change') — this type of feedback on their answers gave students remedial tuition where necessary.

Tested observation (e.g. 'What do you notice about yield stress after plastic deformation?') — this type of question gave students most trouble, because many of them required the interpretation of pictures such as micrographs (pictures of metals photographed under a microscope). Students often needed help in recognising which parts of the picture were salient, and in identifying what they meant. In some cases this help was offered in the form of a hint, using teletext overlay, labelling the relevant part of the picture. This was a very useful, and often necessary device.

Untested observation (e.g. 'Look at the end-on views of fracture surfaces') — this form of interaction made extensive use of the still-frame and slow-motion operations on the videodisc. Students were left to view these at their own pace, either by cycling round a set of stills by pressing return, or by requesting a repeat of a motion sequence. In most cases, students were unsure what they were meant to be looking for, and so treated these interactions in a rather cursory way. There was no encouragement for them to do anything particular with their observations, so they had little apparent educational value.

Hypothesis-framing (e.g. 'What is the cause of the eye-loss?') — questions of this type gave students the opportunity to marshall their knowledge and understanding of the subject and bring it to bear on a real-world problem. These questions provided the overall framework of the package and helped to bridge the gap between theory and practice. In the questionnaire, half the students agreed that the package helped them to 'see the need for the theory involved'.

Procedural information (e.g. 'Ultimate tensile strength can be read off the vertical axis') — feedback to students who gave incorrect answers took several forms, of which we have already seen 'information giving'. Procedural information was used where it was necessary not just to give the student the answer, but to help them to see how to get there.

Hints (e.g. 'Think about the specimens you have already seen') - a third form of feedback guided them towards the answer without actually giving it.

Instructions (e.g. 'Be more precise, try again) — it was important sometimes to recognise that unexpected answers may not be wrong, and the students should simply be encouraged to use the scientifically correct term.

Simulations (e.g. 'Halt the test at the yield point') — this type of interaction made best use of both video and computer together, as the computer would check, for example, how many frames into a video sequence the student went before stopping. It is possible to allow the student to carry out 'surrogate' experiments in this way, where, to some extent, they operate and control what happens and when. The simulations were given added realism in comparison with the typical CAL simulation by the use of video. In the questionnaire, half the students agreed that 'the pictures made it much better than the CAL tutorials'.

It is difficult to give an exact assessment of the relative learning gains provided by these various forms of interaction. It would require detailed testing, which would interfere with the flow of the educational interaction, and in any case would not necessarily isolate the exact learning gain due to one type of question, rather than the accumulation of learning from a series of questions. Evaluation studies that attempt to prove that one form of learning is more efficient, or better than another, are doomed to failure for this sort of reason. The descriptions above serve to show the kinds of learning experience these different forms of interaction provide, and the relationships deduced have been further supported by evidence from the interviews and questionnaires.

In addition, the observation schedule allows us to compare the time taken for different forms of interaction, and to assess what kinds of student response they promoted. Overall, the average time spent on one interaction (the time between consecutive key presses) was approximately one minute. In general, less time was spent on hypothesis-framing and information-receiving, and more time was spent on observation and testing. The latter frequently promoted discussion and argument among the students, which in some cases had the beneficial effect of making students explain their answers to each other, before having them checked by the computer.

The time spent on procedural information, instructions and hints was variable, but depended more on the amount of reading to be done than on thinking time. Similarly, the time spent on simulations depended more on the running time of the video.

To summarise, the various design aspects of this videodisc make it educationally useful because it can

(a) Encourage students to think constructively about the subject.
(b) Provide feedback that guides students towards the right answer.
(c) Help students relate theory to practice.
(d) Give students some control over surrogate experiments.
(e) Promote academic discussion.
(f) Focus attention on the subject matter for long periods.

5.3.5 Design problems

There were two main aspects of the design of the package that created problems for students: the format and the structure of the interaction, and of the information.

The use of an open-ended question format together with a sophisticated answer-matching routine meant that it was possible to design a quite challenging dialogue which was a genuine test of students' understanding of the subject. As reported above, this aspect of the design was appreciated by students, but it was not without its problems. The information-testing form of question promoted three types of discussion among students, in addition to deciding what the *content* of the answer should be:

(1) how to phrase it,
(2) what keywords the computer might look for,
(3) what level of answer is appropriate (e.g. at microscopic or macroscopic level).

These are all similar to the problems of communication between teacher and student in any tutorial situation. It is common for the classroom teacher to expect a particular form of words in an answer, and to accept nothing else. It is not pedagogically sound to inhibit students' thinking in this way, but the computer is doing nothing worse than behaving like a normal teacher. More serious are the problems that occur when the computer misinterprets a student's answer.

When a student inputs a correct answer that is not recognised as such by the computer, three different types of student reaction results:

(1) they experience mild indignation, which is not serious in itself, but can accumulate to undermine the student's confidence in the value and authority of the program,
(2) students learn to 'play the game', and begin to focus on beating the computer, rather than on the subject matter itself,
(3) students accept their own ignorance and search for an alternative (i.e. wrong) answer.

These are all pedagogically unsound, especially the last, and are inevitable consequences of an imperfect answer-matching format. The pilot run collected all student input, and stored it on diskette for later analysis, so that more alternative correct answers could be programmed in. The disadvantage for the pilot students decreases for later students, but there is always a risk that further alternative correct answers will be thought up.

The computer never gave a wrong answer as right, but sometimes students were told they were right when they had only guessed. This meant that they were branched away from the remedial tutorial they needed.

This point raises the tricky question of what should be done about student versus program control. The advantage of *student* control is that the student knows better than the computer does whether or not they need remedial help. In the questionnaire, half the students agreed they should be 'branched to remedial tutorials if they keep getting things wrong' — which shows that they are not reluctant to be helped when they know they need it. The advantage of *program* control is that the student can maintain continuous concentration on the subject matter, uninterrupted by tedious questions about what they want to do next. Perhaps the solution is to combine the virtues of both by having an 'override' option that the student can use if they wish to avoid a section. This was, in fact, provided in the form of a 'skip' option, but students were very uncertain how to use this — they did not know how far they were skipping, and had no way of telling how far they needed to skip. The precise format of helpful user interface features such as this is an issue worth considerable attention if interactive video is to become a user-friendly medium for learning.

We consider now the structure of information on the disc. Because the disc was designed around an existing television programme, the framework this provided was inevitably linear. There was little opportunity for students to take their own route through the material, and there was no information to help them to do this.

It was also clear that using a videodisc creates orientation problems for students. It is difficult to know at any one point where they are in relation to the material as a whole, how much they have done, how much there is yet to do. Since the original design, several specific changes have been implemented to assist students in finding their way around the information on the disc:

It is possible to stop the video at any point and choose the next action from a menu of options.

The students can find out at any point where they are in relation to the material as a whole.

Students are given an estimate of how long each section might take them.

The contents list has been expanded from one to fifteen lists, in order to provide more detailed information about what is available.

Students can call up the contents lists at any time to change their route through the material.

The amount of control given to a student in their use of a videodisc is a matter of choice of teaching strategy. The strategy used in this disc was mainly program control, which made it highly didactic. This is not a necessary feature of interactive videodiscs — they could embody a more student-controlled, exploratory strategy. Then the accessibility of information on the disc becomes crucial. But even in this relatively controlling programme, it has still been found to be important to give students sufficient information for them to have a degree of control over what they do and when.

5.3.6 Summary of evaluation case study

The main points to have come out of this study which should be relevant for future developments are as follows:

(a) Students found the continual interrogation and the varied presentation a good way to learn.
(b) These features also kept students working in a concentrated way for long periods.
(c) The most educationally successful forms of interaction were information testing, hypothesis framing, and simulations.
(d) Observation by students and testing of students took the most student time, the latter because it often promoted discussion.
(e) Student-constructed input, with an answer-matching algorithm, sometimes makes it difficult for students to know what kind of answer is expected, and discussion is about this, rather than the substantive issue.
(f) Students need some control over the presentation of information.
(g) A 'skip' option needs to be backed up with information on how to use it and what its effect is.
(h) A 'contents' list should be accessible at any time, and should be detailed enough for a student to be able to make sense of it.

The total time spent on the evaluation study was as follows:

Preparation — discussions with designers, design of observation and interview schedules, logistic arrangements, negotiating with students and tutors	2 days
Observation — 25 sessions	approx. 2–3 hours each
Interviews — with 9 students	approx. half an hour each
Questionnaire design and distribution	10 days
Data analysis and report	3 days

The total of 15 days for the evaluation compares with a total of 370 days spent by the principal members of the production team. The results led to an extra 10 days work by the programmer to implement the structural changes to the interactive program, but this relatively minimal effort produced a significantly different experience for the user, giving them, for example, much more control over their use of the disc.

5.4 PEDAGOGICAL DESIGN ASPECTS

The chief advantage of evaluation data is that it can enhance our intuitive models of the student at work, in such a way that it makes the very difficult problem of going from the definition of objectives to the formulation of suitable learning activities and hence instructional design, easier to handle. Using the framework of the first section, we have to decide, given our chosen objectives, what kinds of learning activities — cognitive processes, types of thinking, conceptual manipulations, etc. — the students should do in order to achieve those objectives, and what kind of interaction format will support the kind of thinking we want to encourage in the student. It could be seen as a basic law of interactive design that 'quality of interaction determines quality of thinking'. Let us look at this idea in more detail.

The interaction between a student and any computer-based medium will consist of a series of alternate actions by student and computer program, determined by the internal processes of each. An interaction event should therefore consist of something like the components shown in Fig. 5.1.

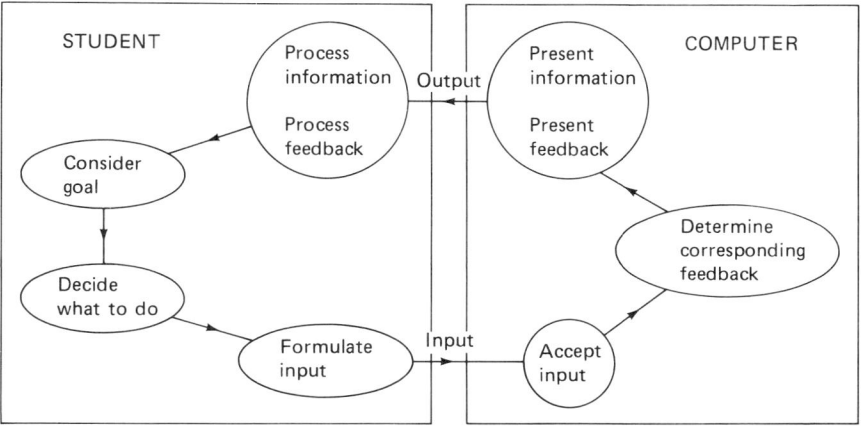

Fig. 5.1 — Components of an interaction event.

In designing the format of interaction for interactive media, the instructional designer has to go through a process of analysis to determine, for each type of interaction event, how it will support the various types of processing the student could be expected to go through. It is the quality of these that will then determine the quality of learning that takes place.

To see what such an analysis might consist of, consider the interpretation of those putative processes for two types of interaction on the Teddy Bear disc, described in the previous section, namely 'simulation' and 'tested observation'. One example of a simulation is the interaction event where the student is asked to 'Halt the test at the yield point'. The videodisc displays a real time film of the load/extension graph being produced during a tensile testing experiment. The student has to press an interrupt key when they believe the metal specimen has reached its yield point. They have the opportunity to try again if it is wrong and are told if it is too soon or too late. An example of tested observation is the interaction event where the student is given three photographs of specimens which have failed in either a 'ductile' or a 'brittle' manner, and is asked to select which of them failed in a ductile manner. If they get it wrong, they are told so and asked to try again. We can interpret the cognitive processes going on during these interaction events as follows:

Student activity	*Simulation*	*Tested observation*
Process information	Familiar phrase 'yield point'; familiar graph	Familiar phrase 'ductile'; unfamiliar picture
Consider goal	Where is the yield point?	Which specimen(s) failed in a ductile manner?
Decide what has to be done	Stop at point X on graph/Press key sooner or later	Use familiar phrase to choose specimen/Guess
Formulate input	Press key at chosen point as graph is drawn	Select option
Process feedback	Know, because told, that key press was too soon or too late	Told right or wrong; eliminates possibilities

Given this analysis, the instructional designer has to consider whether each interaction event is well-formed. For example, is the information presented to the student meaningful? For the simulation, yes, both graph and language are familiar; for the observation the language is familiar, but the pictures are unusual for these students ('Nice picture but it's totally meaningless to me', 'What am I looking at here?' — quotes from observation sheets). Secondly, is the goal of this event apparent to the student — in both cases yes, it is explicit in the question put to them. Thirdly, given the information and the goal is it possible to decide what should be done? For the simulation, yes, both goal and information are sufficiently meaningful that it is easy for the student to determine what they have to do, and doing it correctly depends upon their understanding of the meaning of 'yield point'. For the observation, the students have to rely on the familiarity with the language to help them interpret the pictures — 'Must be number 2 because it's got smooth surfaces', 'You expect brittle things to be sharp corners, not smooth' — and this enables them to decide what to do without merely guessing. Fourthly, is the formulation of the input straightforward and unambiguous? It is in both cases here — it is clear, for example, which key has to be pressed. Finally, is the feedback meaningful — does it help the student to determine in a constructive way what they should now do to achieve the goal? For the simulation, yes, they know they have to press the key sooner or later; for the tested observation yes, they now have fewer specimens to choose from.

From this anslysis we can see the importance of the 'decision' activity, because this is where the quality of thinking is determined. If the student has to decide merely that 'it is not this one so it must be that one' then the quality of thinking is fairly low-level — it involves only logic and very little interpretation of analysis or recall of information. Being thus almost content-free, it is unlikely to make much impact on what the student knows about the subject or on how they think about it. This is probably what is most likely to happen in the observation case above, when the student's initial input is wrong. The feedback allows them to do little more than guess — it is meaningful, but not constructive. They have learned only that it was specimen number 2. To improve this interaction event as it stands, we would have to reinforce that learning by adding a further event where the student was again asked to name the specimen that failed in a ductile manner, and this time the question would encourage a decision that would analyse the similarity between these new pictures and the previous ones to determine both which features related to ductility, and what the correct answer should be.

Similarly, although the simulation example gives meaningful and constructive feedback, the quality of thinking it encourages is still rather low-level. The student learns only that the yield point is in a different place, not what it is. To encourage a more complex level of analysis and interpretation, the feedback should point to the fact that the specimen has not yet started 'necking', or that it has already started 'necking', in order to help the student relate the meaning of the term 'yield point' to its counterpart in the real world.

Both these interaction events are successful at meeting the criteria of ensuring that some student activity does occur, even if on further analysis the quality of that activity seems rather low-level. By contrast, some interaction events, such as a 'goal-free observation' for example, fail even to ensure that any student activity occurs. The 'goal-free observation' is quite common in interactive video because many teachers like to take the opportunity to show students slides or pictures that they would not otherwise see, or that they only ever see one example of. The student is invited to browse through a selection of such pictures, with no particular goal other than the implicit one of becoming aware of the variety, or complexity of the collection. In such a case, the information being presented to the student would be unfamiliar and therefore relatively meaningless, the goal is absent, there is no decision to be made, the input is simply to press continue, and there is no feedback to process. Any cognitive processing the student does during such an interaction is entirely self-motivated, which means it can easily be nothing at all. The aim of the kind of analysis outlined here is to design the kind of interaction events that improve the chances of some valuable cognitive processing being carried out by the student. For the two examples above, it cannot be guaranteed, and they may still be guessing, but at least they are invited to do something more.

This detailed level of analysis can also be used to demonstrate why student-constructed input should be used where possible instead of multiple-choice questions (MCQs). MCQs are pedagogically unsound because (a) they encourage guessing rather than thinking, and (b) by offering wrong answers, they also encourage thinking about *incorrect* answers. It is part of the technique of designing MCQs that plausible wrong answers must be offered. Therefore it is likely that a student will spend some time considering what a wrong answer means, what it might be like in practice, and the conditions under which it could be true. And it is hard to erase the memory of the processing. At a later stage, they are likely to remember the mental image they created more easily than they will remember which answer was the right one.

Student-constructed input can be done by the student typing in keywords, with an answer matcher that allows spelling mistakes, and says something like 'don't recognise that — try again' for the first unrecognised input, and thereafter offers hints, or the right answer. As with MCQs it is possible to predict the most likely wrong answers and create suitable replies for each of those, but at least they are not offered to the student. They could be seen as 'concealed multiple-choice questions'. There is still the problem of non-recognition by the program of some student input, but the pedagogic problems are fewer than with straight MCQs.

These examples illustrate the complexity of the analysis that must be carried out in designing the various interaction events for interactive media if the material is to encourage effective and efficient learning. The principal advantage of an interactive medium is that it has the capacity to encourage student activity, and this is frequently cited as the most important reason for using it. Instructional designers cannot therefore avoid the responsibility of specifying in some detail what that activity should be, and precisely how it will help the student meet the relevant learning objectives. The quality of interaction they design determines the quality of thinking, and therefore the quality of learning the student will achieve.

5.5 SUMMARY OF INSTRUCTIONAL DESIGN POINTS

This chapter has argued for the design of interactive media materials to be carried out within an educational technology framework such as that suggested in the first section. This puts particular emphasis on an analytical design process, and on evaluation as the means to assist that process. From the evaluation case study described earlier, we can derive the principles of design for the most fundamental aspect of the design process that an interactive media designer must consider, namely the quality of interaction:

Information and pictures presented must be meaningful to the user.

The goal of each interaction event should be explicit, or the user should be invited to make it explicit.

The decisions to be made on the basis of the information, the goal, and the feedback, determine the quality of thinking being done, and must therefore encourage or elicit a high level of cognitive processing, i.e. avoid guessing, MCQs, merely linguistic analysis, etc.

Formulation of input should be straightforward and unambiguous, i.e. it should be clear which key has to be pressed, and when, whether to press return, what kind of input is acceptable, etc.

Feedback should be both meaningful and constructive to enable further decisions to encourage a high level of cognitive processing.

Users should be given information about what is on the disc, and where, and where they are at any point to assist their orientation and their control.

Interactive media in education will stand or fall by the quality of interaction they provide because that is their unique feature in comparison with every other kind of teaching medium. Practitioners must build design principles to work by, to ensure that these media fulfil their potential and make a genuine pedagogical contribution.

ACKNOWLEDGEMENTS

The videodisc and the interactive software of section 5.3.1 were produced by a collaboration between Paul Blenkhorn, (then ACS), Stephen Brown (then IET), Phil Butcher (ACS), Robert Fuller (then IET/Physics), Keith Williams (Technology) and Martin Wright (BBC/OUP).

APPENDIX 1: QUESTIONNAIRE ON T252 VIDEODISC

Your answers to these questions will help us decide how the disc could be improved and how it should be used.

1. How many times have you used the disc?

2. How much time have you spent on it altogether?

3. The following statements are all quotes from students who have used the disc. Please tick just those statements you particularly agree with.

   (a) It made you think about things you weren't sure you knew

(b) It was a good way to learn, combining questions with short breaks for video
(c) The pictures made it much better than the CAL tutorials
(d) It helped by bringing a lot of things together to relate to a real problem
(e) It helped me see the need for the theory involved
(f) I got very interested in the problem
(g) There was a tendency to lose track of what you were doing
(h) Too often it did not understand my answers
(i) I wanted to be able to do more actions myself, not just answer questions
(j) You should be branched automatically to more remedial work if you keep getting things wrong
(k) There is not enough labelling on the pictures
(l) I needed more information to be able to use it as I wanted (e.g. did not know when I had finished a section, could not escape at any point, no index, etc.

4. Any further comments?

NAME (optional)　　　　　　　　THANK YOU FOR YOUR HELP
Diana Laurillard, IET, Walton Hall.

6

Why do instructional designers need Conversation Theory?

Gary Boyd and Gordon Pask

6.1 INTRODUCTION

This chapter is concerned to show when and why, and how Gordon Pask's Conversation Theory can and should be used as part of interactive video learning activity systems.

Pask's (1976c, 1986) Conversation Theory provides an altogether radically alternative approach to education and training; one based not on the shaping of behaviour, but rather upon the eliciting of distinctions and agreements in formalised and exteriorised conversation.

6.2 THE THEORETICAL CONTRIBUTION OF CT

Conversation theory arises from a concern to promote enlightenment and an acceptance of the problematic nature of both language, and the notion of the human individual. Enlightenment is possible in so far as we can learn to give good grounds and good reasons for our assertions and beliefs. However, words evoke different processes in different minds, or psychological 'p' individuals. And psychological individuals do not always correspond on a one-to-one basis with individual human bodies: the same person is capable of envincing more than one type of response (exhibiting more than one person) in a conversation.

Language is a construct, partly biologically evolved, partly socially evolved, partly arbitrarily made. Different participants in a conversation may be employing quite different interpretive and generative frames. And this as Basil Bernstein (1971) has shown can interfere with learning. Children using and understanding language as 'restricted code' do not properly grasp what is going on when teachers use language more flexibly as 'elaborated code'. If one instructional designer conceives of 'evaluation' as a cost/benefit determination operation and another conceives of it as formative revision-oriented then they may readily come to blows as to where in the sequence of project activities the 'evaluation' block belongs. People who believe that they are speaking the same language often have greater difficulty with subtle understanding than do foreigners who know that there is a problem of context which always must be checked out.

The difference between an educational conversation and any old conversation is that an educational conversation promotes *abstractly understood co-operative potency*. Pask's Conversation Theory is a general representation of conversing entities co-operating to reach agreements and distinctions, i.e. *understandings*, of an *abstract* nature which can bring them and the conversational medium together into a new collective identity with, possibly, an enhanced *potency*. Some abstract understanding of a co-operative nature is always achieved in the Conversation-theoretical mapping or projection of a Conversation; whether any enhancement of the participants, potency actually occurs depends on other constraints which must be added.

The highly unusual and most noteworthy aspects of Pask's theory are that it takes both the identity of the individual participants and the genre of discourse as being problematical.

Consider the first aspect: the identity of individual participants in an educational conversation. The awareness that psychological individuals don't necessarily or even usually correspond to biological individuals in one-to-one enduring relationship is well known to psychiatry, and to some playwrights (e.g. Pirandello) and some philosophers (e.g. Cassirer versus Strawson), but is not usually acknowleged in educational technology's writings. But the ability of individuals to hold more than one point of view about the same topic, for example, is acknowledged in Conversation Theory, and this is crucial for educational design: we cannot take it for granted that a concept understood in one context will be understood in the same way in a different context.

In order to meet this problem, the tools of Conversation Theory have been developed to enable the ostensive demonstration of these different frames (or contexts) and procedures (or concepts) which people are using. They are used to compare the results of the cogitations of two participants against the productions of various simulations run on likely models, so that deeper shared world-models can be constructed. Pask's proto-language L_p can be used to facilitate the process. (Both the process, and the language L_p are described in detail in the next chapter.) The shared outcomes are not considered to be the *natural truth* nor are they *the inner truth*; rather they are whatever-it-is which emerges from acting together in partly formalised conversation, or debate. The debate should be a discursive unfolding of relations in a discourse where neither side dominates. This is not 'learner-control' *nor* programmer control, but rather mutual control. This ideal situation assumes responsible participants who have learned something about good strategies and tactics for learning. The further the situation departs from this ideal the more teacher guidance must be provided.

Consider now the second aspect of CT: the problematical nature of discourse. When adult learners with pre-constituted schema and narrow habits of language use are confronted with subtle abstract and uncertain knowledge development tasks then much more than programmed learning is called for if a good outcome is to be achieved.

Adult, and older adolescent learners have formed an impression of their whole world and how it works, and how it is to be talked about. Usually this model is misleading, limiting, or just plain wrong in many ways. As a consequence significant learning for an adult usually involves a good deal of un-learning and structural rearrangement of 'reality'. It is as much a matter of changing oneself as it is of acquiring new procedures, or vocabulary. For everyday forms of life vague and sloppy language has a kind of utility, especially if it is basically ideological in the sense of contributing to the formation and maintenance of coalitions.

Social solidarity is often fostered by ignoring precision. What, if I thought carefully, I would define as the core meaning of, for example, 'liberty' may very well be entirely different from what you would define as the essence of liberty. But we can both vote for someone who claims to be promoting our liberty if the word is left undefined. Wittgenstein's caution that each word has a cloud of meanings which is variously employed in actual forms of life, is quite conveniently ignored in the interest of solidarity. But if we mean to *educate*, then the multiple contents of each cloud of meaning must be carefully unfolded. Dewey asserts that this is best done through 'discussion'. Conversation Theory provides a means of regularising just such discussion. However socially comfortable it is to ignore distinctions, such vagueness simply will not do if we are to develop real competence in the remaking of our planetary culture.

In order to understand, and appreciate, and re-create complex cybernetic sub-systems, like Shakespearian drama, or welfare economics, we must use our languages with precisely objectified agreements and distinctions. For such learning neither the ambiguities of common speech, nor the empty precision of mathematics will be adequate without both refinement and formal and procedural elaboration. The tools of CT, captured in interactive video-computers, should prove increasingly helpful in these situations.

If all that you are doing is learning the correct procedure for sharpening a lawnmower, or learning to recognise the proper terms of describing an heraldic blazon, then interactive video without Conversation Theory is probably quite adequate to support your learning. If, however, the classification of skin inflammations in such as way as to optimally inform diagnosis and treatment, or the quintessence of Prigogine's thermodynamical inversion of quantum physics, or an understanding of complex closely-coupled cybernetic systems like the living mantle of this planet Earth is the sort of understanding you wish to promote with interactive video, then maybe Conversation Theory is the best available door to an effective disc.

6.3 CONTRIBUTIONS FROM RESEARCH ON INSTRUCTIONAL TV

A great deal of research has been done on the effective design and use of instructional television, mostly with groups of learners, and much of this research is probably applicable to interactive video. The great strengths of television are: its ability to show human models of mastery with which the learner can identify (Bandura, 1982) and the ability to show with photographic realism and with high fidelity sound, situations otherwise inaccessible, such as erupting volcanoes, and the interior of nuclear reactors in operation. Extraordinary time acceleration, as with the motions of clouds, or the Granada longitudinal study *28PLUS*, and extraordinary film and computer animation of realistic images (e.g. *Warnings from the 21°Century*, NHK, 1986) are possible and instructionally valuable *if* the learner's attention is properly directed, and if orientation and review questions are interspersed.

One problem with the instructional television research, and a problem which is even more apparent with CAL (Computer-Assisted Learning) research is that each experimental situation is very complex and each learner is unique, and un-re-usable so that generalisations are difficult — and perhaps inappropriate. (A vast data-base to select studies nearest to the current design task might be more useful.)

A good recent study of relevant American instructional television and computer-assisted instruction (CAI) research from the standpoint of its applicability to interactive video has been provided by Michael Hannapin (1985). From this work some of the important questions which remain to be researched become apparent, notably:

(a) What important relationships exist among: types of learning, types of learners, and kinds of interactivity?
(b) When is inserted questioning, or overt interactivity harmful to learning? When really helpful?
(c) What coaching and advice procedures are necessary so that learners may make effective and efficient use of learner control of path and pace with interactive video?

6.4 USING CT

In order to explore these and other important research questions it is desirable to have a very flexible laboratory system with extensive recording and analysis facilities. CASTE, Gordon Pask's Course Assembly System and Tutorial Environment, which uses the tools of Conversation Theory, has the needed flexibility and parallelism to serve as the basis for such a laboratory. In general the CAL/IVD languages and authoring systems, which are mostly frame-based tree-branching programmed learning construction kits, are not sufficiently flexible, adaptive, or analytical for research purposes.

A version of the CASTE system C-CASTE is currently being adapted by Mitchell at Concordia University to enable research with interactive video to be conducted (Mitchell and Dalkir, 1986).†

---

† It is possible that the procedure-mesh tutorial system 'G' developed by Meurrens in Belgium, which though independently conceived actually closely resembles CASTE, would also form a good basis for an interactive video instructional research laboratory (Meurrens, 1986).

Ch. 6] WHY DO INSTRUCTIONAL DESIGNERS NEED CONVERSATION THEORY? 95

When it comes to the marshalling of 50,000 pictures or a million recorded sounds to support a learning activity, or even the characteristics of 20,000 organic chemicals, all of which can be recorded on videodisc, then something more than conventional verbal description with pointers to the illustrations is really needed. Conventional relational database retrieval techniques can be used but are cumbersome, and must be combined with instructional control routines. Interactive access to the vast quantities of data which optical media can store calls for much more sophisticated and adaptive systems than those of conventional branched programmed instruction, or conventional instructional game and simulation software. Developments in Conversation Theory may be the most propitious route toward the realisation of the systems we need.

Interactive video need not be, and for socially constructive reasons perhaps should not too often be, individualised instruction. Pairs of students, or small groups can often work as effectively, or even more effectively than individuals (Johnson and Johnson, 1975). Conversation Theory and the entailment mesh technology (see next chapter) can accommodate such multiple learner situations.

Individualised instruction does have its uses, but it has been greatly oversold. In most educational situations, other than distance education, there are other knowledgeable or at least helpful people at hand. Educational technology which builds on this fact, rather than trying to deny it, should receive much wider acceptance than programmed instruction or CAI received.

How to use Conversation Theory with interactive video, is dependent on the learners and their needs and other, usually institutional, factors; but clearly one of the most propitious ways is an extension of what Gordon and his associates have already done with their Team Decision System. This is what I called elsewhere (Boyd, 1982) the small group 'personally guided' mode of computer-aided learning. Abstractly-understood co-operative-potency is developed in the group of participants who personally guide the collective learning with the aid of CT-based transcription and transaction facilities which can use computer simulation and video representations as models to be mastered.

In the subject-matter dimension very difficult fields can be explored and learned. All of the social sciences are reflexive and historical. They involve what Von Foerster has called the 'second cybernetics', that of systems which observe themselves. They also involve a relativism of truth to different groups' beliefs and interests which usually comes out as disagreement over what can be considered to be data, and disagreement about the implications of even those observations which can be commonly agreed upon.

6.5 CONCLUDING POINTS

Part of the politics of life is: for me to try to build a model more inclusive than yours, so that you have to use my model. Then, I can model your hypothetical simulations and achieve a kind of domination over even your dreams! This sort of one-upmanship is usually at the expense of our long-term collective viability. No model (not that of natural science certainly) is the *whole* territory.

One can really learn to understand this in a Conversation Theory-based learning system.

The ordinary assumption that the instructional problem is to transfer knowledge and skills from those who already possess them to those who do not is acceptable for mechanical skills and much matter-of-fact knowledge. But education, especially education in times of turbulent change, must also be concerned with helping people build new knowledge for themselves, and helping them to evaluate old knowledge and skills from the standpoint of their affiliations, aspirations and fears. Different presentations, and differing ways of applying rules change who benefits and who pays, and how.

Mutually guided discovery learning is what is needed to make the best educational use of, for example the BBC *Domesday disc*. Here there is a vast wealth of complementary and even paradoxical illustrative material on the evolution of Britain. How does one get from that to a deeply, beautifully coherent understanding such as the one Jacquetta Hawkes (1953) exhibits in her book *A Land*? Not by programmed instruction, rather by guided conversation and personal inspiration.

It does not make human sense to attempt to fully automate teaching and learning where art, science, and ethics are concerned because such teaching and learning is the highest human achievement. If anything can serve as a functional definition of a human being it is that together we learn and teach through Art and Argument.

Part of the Art, and parts for the arguments can be stored and selectively accessed with computer/video technology, but the pieces need to be brought together in well formed conversation to be democratically truly educational.

REFERENCES

References for this chapter are included with those of Chapter 7.

7

Conversation Theory as basis for instructional design

Gordon Pask and Gary Boyd

7.1 INTRODUCTION

Gary Boyd and I have debated Conversation Theory (CT) and its knowledge representations. As a result of this discussion, the previous chapter includes the question '*why* do educators or communicators need such an elaborate system as conversation theory' and, in answering it, brings up and answers the complementary question of '*when* is it useful to employ this methodology'; not, for example, when it comes to inculcating names for a few key facts, or when people are dealing with concepts that are adequately handled by superficially grasped procedures. True, such things do have the status of concepts and it is theoretically important that they are on a par, in the abstract, with all others. But use of the methodology for the purpose of teaching in this context would resemble the use of a steam hammer for cracking an egg. On the other hand, if you want to teach someone, or help someone learn, how to be a manager, the controller of a power station, a physicist or a philosopher, then it is useful and maybe essential to deploy these methods. As to teaching 'physics' or 'management' we are not so sure, chiefly as a result of not knowing precisely what it means to 'teach a subject matter', in contrast to 'teaching how to be a something or other'.

7.2 CONVERSATION THEORY

In this part of the chapter, an initial task is to say what conversation, in the strict sense, *is* and, also, what parts of it can be represented in terms of CT, namely, as entailment meshes manipulated through the protologic Lp. The task is of consequence because *all* learning involves concept-sharing, i.e. conversation, between a pair (or more) of participants, labelled A and B.

An entailment mesh is a formal symbolic representation of the knowledge structure of the relevant subject matter. The symbolism used is a protologic called Lp, which defines the way the formal statements in the entailment mesh may be manipulated and derived from one another. Each topic in the mesh must have associated with it a description, in everyday language, and an explanation, or model, i.e. an embodiment of its meaning in some event such as a simulation or a construction. These are the tools which allow an 'educational conversation' to take place.

Upon analysis, a conversation is a series of transactions, verbal, pictorial, or behavioural, between participants, A and B, who are jointly conscious of some concept named T. Particular significance is attached to those transactions in which A and B share a mutually reproducible (hence, resilient, stable), concept; so that A can reconstruct a concept of T from A's usual repertoire of other concepts, and also from some of B's, usually different, concepts (and vice versa). Such transactions, indicating a resilient or stable shared concept, are called 'understandings' and it is these which are inscribed as 'shared concepts' in entailment meshes.

In order to demonstrate the process of concept sharing, consider a symposium-type experiment, which has often been used in learning about conversation theory.† The materials betokened by the photographs in Fig. 7.1, illustrate a collection of 'unfindable objects', due to, and constructed by, Carelman. All that is needed to get a sensible idea of what goes on is that certain facilities, such as a symposium or the 'Lp machine', do in fact, exist.

Photographic reproductions of some of Carelman's 'Unfindable' (but constructed) objects are prepared in replicas. These are tangible objects but it is very unlikely that anyone has seen them; in any case, their 'function' is equivocal. All of them are, however, fairly small in size and relate to some common field of experience, such as plumbing, travelling or geography. One target object, T, is selected; I have used the many-pronged ladder of Fig. 7.1, as the target, T. This target object also demonstrates exception to the 'very unlikely' rule. A particularly taciturn North American gentlemen said he *had* seen such a thing, in a disused cement factory near to St Albans, in England. He surely told the truth and surmised that it was used for 'cleaning the plant'; which, for all I know, it *may* be.

The people taking part are informed of the intention of the experiment; namely, to construct personal concepts, to form a shared concept in conversation, to represent the result in Lp, and to manipulate the Lp expression in various ways. The experiment proceeds in stages.

(i) One pair of people is deemed to be a participant, A, and are given photographs of the target object, T, together with photographs of other objects selected from some field such as music. They repair to a room and, between them, they construct a personal concept, T(A), of T, using amongst other things, their concepts of the several musical objects other than T. They usually deliberate for less than half an hour.

(ii) Another pair is deemed to be a participant, B, and they are provided with the same photograph of T and also with photographs of objects from some other field, like gaming. They go to discuss the matter of their concept

---

† The editor suggested that an architectural notion be used as the basis for demonstration, which is quite possible. However, there are better tried out materials available in the field of general design.

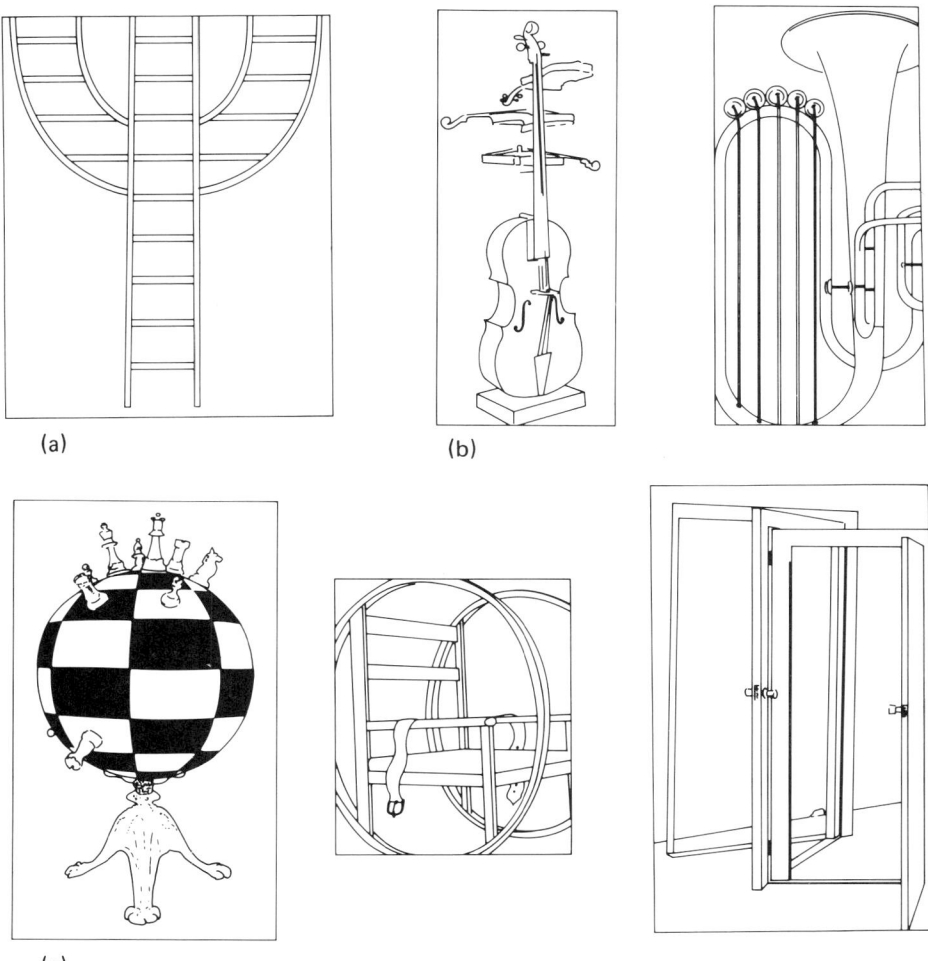

Fig. 7.1 — (a) Target object, T, same for A and B. (b) Objects shown with T, but only to A. (c) Objects shown, with T, but only to B.

of T, namely, T(B), and its derivation from their concepts of the gaming objects, amongst others. Their debate takes place in a different room.

(iii) Once A and B have gone, the rest are free to examine T and the separate groups of photographs available to A and B, distinctly.

(iv) After half an hour or so, when both A and B have established concepts of T and their derivation of these concepts, they return to the symposium and try to reach agreement about a shared concept of T, say T*. This is done by a conversation using verbal, visual and behavioural modalities. Essentially, the conversation is made up of 'how' questions and answers (how T is made or used), the answers being complete or partial explanations of T(A) and T(B) and T*; also 'why' questions which elicit their derivation of their concept of T from concepts of other objects from other A and B concepts. Typically, T(A) and T(B) are quite different, and T*, although related to part of each, is again distinct.

(v) The A and B conversation is observed by everyone and is frequently productive. It is recorded and it is also inscribed in Lp meshes, representing the relations of each shared concept to other concepts, a mesh each for T(A), T(B), and T*. In practice, the Lp inscription requires a portable version of THOUGHTSTICKER, a system for helping a user to assemble an entailment mesh. Such arrangements use a reasonably powerful microprocessor and fast printer. The display and print-out is made visible to the entire gathering, preferably, by making, and projecting Xerox overlay transparencies on the spot. It is convenient to have someone versed in Conversation Theory and Lp (to act as a 'simultaneous translator').

(vi) Once the conversation has stabilised, other members of the symposium are encouraged to join in. The generally visible Lp meshes are also Lp manipulated, by unfolding them (directing thought, automatically, from the point of view, or perspective, of various different topics), and Lp inferential operations, such as 'saturation' are applied. The result of these manipulations is both to display the statements of thought more clearly and to propose further concept relations. These, as well as novel concepts are accepted and are added to the Lp meshes, using appropriate identifying labels, like the notations indicated in Fig. 7.2(a) to (f).

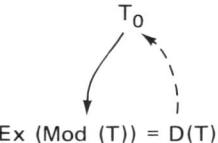

Fig. 7.2 — Mesh components. (a) Shared concept Ex=Execution, Mod (T)=Model of T, D(T) description or behaviour imaging application of T.

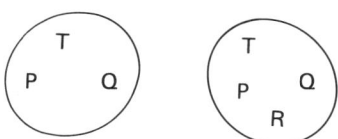

Fig. 7.2 — Mesh components. (b) Collective coherences (concepts that stick together) (letters, T, P, Q, R, S, . . . and so on may stand for the concepts of objects such as those in the symposium experiment).

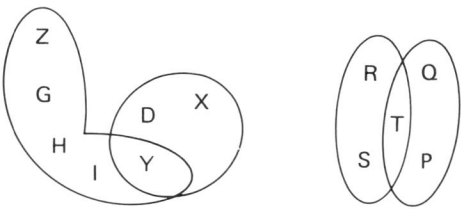

Fig. 7.2 — Mesh components. (c) Distributive forms (concepts that stick together and do so in many ways).

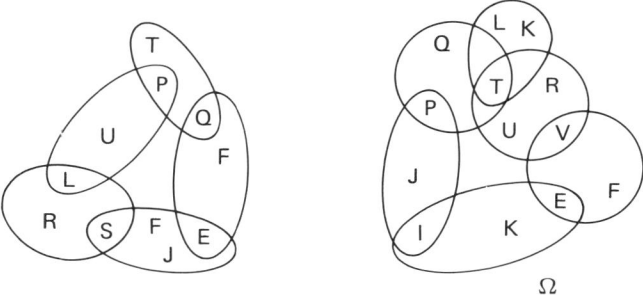

Fig. 7.2 — Mesh components. (d) Meshes.

This experiment demonstrates, at the simplest level, what a conversation *is* and what 'concept sharing' means. The fact that A and B are pairs of people is incidental. It is a useful gambit, in so far as it encourages discussion between members of a pair and it avoids the embarrassment which can arise when expressing ideas that seem to be bizarre, an event that is quite common when agreeing upon a concept.

Much of educational conversation is biased, or asymmetric in the sense that A is a teacher and B is a student (although, the frequency with which such clearcut asymmetry exists is usually overestimated). We have looked here at symmetric conversations between A and B; participants who can both point to, and recognise, some concept named T. Theoretically speaking, the biased case so common in education is a special, and relatively simple case of conversations which are on the whole, pretty symmetrical.

7.3 AMBIGUOUS INTERPRETATION

The trouble with this kind of explanation is not immediate belief, for the observers are, themselves, participants. The trouble comes, as it should do, from doubts that emerge upon subsequent contemplation.

1. [AVERAGE] [MEAN] [MEDIAN] [MODE] [VALUES OF VARIABLE]
2. [MEAN] [SUM] [DIVISION BY NUMBER OF OBSERVATIONS] [ONLY ONE]
3. [MODE] [FREQUENCY] [OCCURRENCE OF VALUES] [COMMONEST FREQUENCY]
4. [MEDIAN] [AS MANY BELOW AS ABOVE] [MAGNITUDE]
5. [FREQUENCY] [EVENTS] [INDEXING] [OBSERVATIONS]
6. [DISTRIBUTION] [FREQUENCY] [CONVERGENCE WITH LARGE NUMBERS TO NORMAL] [AVERAGE]
7. [EVENTS] [SAMPLED] [DISCRETE OR DISTINCT]
8. [EVENTS] [RANDOM] [NUMBER OF OBSERVATIONS]
9. [SAMPLED] [TEMPORAL] [SPATIALLY DISTINCT OBSERVATIONS]
10. [DISTRIBUTION] [NORMAL] [SKEWED] [MULTIMODAL]
11. [NORMAL] [GAUSSIAN] [BINOMIAL EXPANSION] [MEAN]
12. [DISTRIBUTION] [SCATTER] [VARIANCE] [MEAN]
13. [VARIANCE] [SQUARE ROOT] [STANDARD DEVIATION]
14. [EVENTS] [INDEPENDENCE] [NORMATIVE] [DISCOVERED AND LATER EXPLAINED BY MODEL]
15. [STANDARD DEVIATION] [MEAN] [PROPERTIES OF STANDARD DEVIATION]
16. [MORE THAN ONE DISTRIBUTION] [INDEXING] [VARIABLES INDEPENDENT] [CORRELATION] [FORM LINEAR OR NEARLY LINEAR]
17. [CORRELATION] [CAUSALITY] [RELATION]
18. [CORRELATION] [STANDARD DEVIATION] [PROPERTIES OF CORRELATION]
19. [VARIANCE] [COVARIANCE] [CORRELATION] [LIMITATIONS]
20. [SIGNIFICANCE OF CORRELATION] [CORRELATION] [SAMPLE DISTRIBUTIONS]
21. [SIGNIFICANCE OF SAMPLE MEAN] [DISTRIBUTION] [POPULATION MEAN]
22. [SIGNIFICANCE OF SAMPLE MEAN] [SIGNIFICANCE OF MEAN] [SAMPLES OF POPULATION]
23. [STATISTICAL SIGNIFICANCE] [SIGNIFICANCE OF MEAN] [SIGNIFICANCE OF MEAN DIFFERENCE] [SIGNIFICANCE OF CORRELATION]
24. [STATISTICS] [AVERAGE] [STANDARD DEVIATION] [STATISTICAL SIGNIFICANCE] [NORMAL] [PARAMETRIC OR NON-PARAMETRIC] [VARIABLES AS NUMERICAL] [ORDERED]
25. [STATISTICAL SIGNIFICANCE] [ARBITRARY LEVELS] [RANDOM]
26. [STATISTICAL SIGNIFICANCE] [DESIGN] [DISTRIBUTION]

Fig. 7.2 — Mesh components. (e) An Lp mesh for statistics (several authors) shown as print-out.

1. [AUTOMOBILE] [ENGINE] [VEHICLE MANEUVERABILITY] [DRIVE TRAIN] [TRANSMISSION]
2. [ENGINE] [STARTING] [IDLING] [STALLING]
3. [ENGINE] [COOLING SYSTEM] [FUEL SYSTEM] [ELECTRICAL SYSTEM]
4. [VEHICLE MANEUVERABILITY] [SUSPENSION] [STEERING] [BRAKES] [TIRES]
5. [DRIVE TRAIN] [DIFFERENTIAL] [DRIVESHAFT]
6. [TRANSMISSION] [AUTOMATIC] [MANUAL] [CLUTCH]

Fig. 7.2 — Mesh components. (f) An Lp mesh for motor cars (due to Kim Dalkir) as print-out.

One kind of doubt, epitomised by 'yes, but it depends upon how you interpret the dialogue' is best allayed by using a computer-regulated interface. In this case, the 'why' and the 'how' questioning is externalised through a language which is (in principle, at least), non-verbal and non-ambiguous. Explanatory replies are obtained as model-building behaviours, for example in a computer-traced laboratory (several exist, for probability theory, fuzzy set theory, heat engines, genetics, ritual regulation in anthropology) or, alternatively, by program writing (as in LOGO) or by parameterising simulation programs. Under these circumstances, it is easy to ensure that the explanatory models do work; further (of importance when, as later, the system is used tutorially), to ensure that the models are not merely parroted copies of some previous demonstration. By the same token, replies to 'why' you gave this 'how' explanation are obtainable by a rather formalised version of the Lp procedure; using a computer-marked display of the existing mesh and adding to it as required.

Interfaces of this kind were developed in the early 1970s; for example, CASTE (a Course Assembly System and Tutorial Environment) and THOUGHTSTICKER in their original laboratory and (with some difficulty) transportable versions. They embodied a lot of special purpose equipment and owed a great deal to earlier work on adaptively regulated systems in the late 1950s and the 1960s (Lewis and Pask, 1965; Pask, Scott and Kallikourdis, 1973). Quite apart from their tutorial utility, which is discussed later, they were seen as devices for externalising conceptual events in a way that would convince quite naturally sceptical empiricists that agreements over concept sharing and understanding were, in fact, being detected as hard valued psychological events; further, that if a shared concept is understood, then it is substantially indelible.

7.4 LOGIC OF Lp

Another kind of post-symposium doubt refers to the status of participants and the logic of Lp and mesh manipulation (the Conversation Theory protolanguage). For example, regarding participants, they are only in special conditions, correlated with distinct brains and situations; Laurillard calls them 'people in context' and I call them 'P Individuals'. Entailment meshes are claimed to belong to participants, specified in some such manner. Unfortunately, in order to render a statement like this one rigorous, and in order to manipulate entailment meshes and to make inferences about the Lp statements they represent, it is essential to invoke a fair body of theory.

A personal concept is a collection of, usually several, applicable procedures. Any procedure is algorithm-like in character; each explanation for how something can be done, or recognised, or imagined is such an algorithm. Hence, procedures resemble computer programs that are interpreted in a brain (as programs are interpreted or compiled in a computer) with the big exception that a concept is made up of procedures all or some or any of which can be applied coherently and at any given moment. So concept application is a more liberal notion than standard computer program execution. However, in common with program execution there is a process (concept application) and a product (behaviour, recognition, image; or all of them), for whatever concept is concerned.

'Applicability' is one criterion for 'concept-hood'; another is that the concept can be derived, produced and reproduced, from other concepts in the personal (participant's) repertoire. If and only if this is so does a concept have stability and resilience; it is permanent and able to grow by the addition of fresh procedures, rather than being merely evanescent. Thus applicability and reproducibility are characteristic of concept-hood; so, finally, is distinction.

Concepts cohere, stick together, as they do when one is produced from others, yet they remain distinct. If the ladder-like object in Fig. 7.1, is produced and reproduced from concepts of the multiple door and the rocking chair, this does not mean that ladders, doors and chairs form an amorphous splodge; they remain distinct. More formally, if a participant's concept of a circle is produced and reproduced from concepts of a plane surface and of a pair of compasses, this does not mean that geometrical figures, like circles, are confused with instruments, like compasses, and the paper on a drawing-board.

Shared concepts are obtained, in conversation, by an exchange of procedures (usually, as explanations; often as models, such as computer programs) between the participants (essentially the replies to 'how' questions) and the exchange of derivations from other concepts (the replies to 'why' questions). If A and B share a concept, then A can reconstruct $T(A)$ as usual, but also in some of the ways that B is able to reconstruct $T(B)$ and the shared result, T^*, is part of both A's and B's mental repertoire. This shared concept is betokened in Lp, and it is part of an Lp entailment mesh due to the existence of:

(a) An explanation, or working model, T (not just the name 'T').
(b) Both A's and B's derivation of T from other concepts (T's derivations, its entailment relations; in short the logical coherence of the concept T with other concepts). These coherences are the relations inscribed in the mesh. It does not greatly matter whether the coherences refer to concepts of odd-looking ladders (as in the symposium case) or things as abstract and well-defined as circles, derived from a plane and a compass operation or (say) the idea of slicing a cylinder. It is, however, very important that both a model or explanation exist (sufficient to achieve a construction, a behaviour, or a recognition) and that coherence relations exist. It is also essential that these coherences do not obscure previously stated distinctions between the concepts involved.

Given these caveats, there is a logic, Lp, of concepts and their stringing together in memory and thought; some operations are shown in Fig. 7.3. For example, given an Lp mesh it is possible to directionalise it, automatically

Ch. 7]   CONVERSATION THEORY AS BASIS FOR INSTRUCTIONAL DESIGN   105

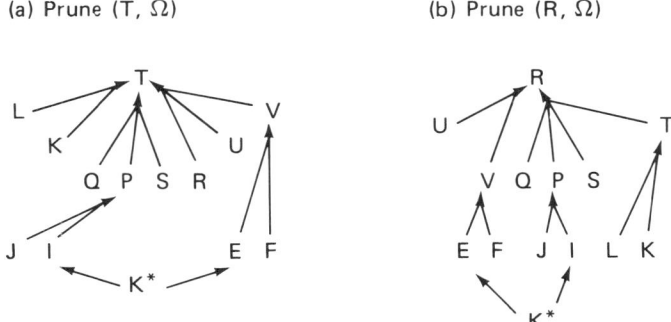

Fig. 7.3(a, b) — Mesh operations (mesh designated Ω of Fig. 7.2(d). Directionalising, unfolding, pruning to obtain all possible learning strategies from concept that is placed at hand. (a) Prune (T, Ω). (b) Prune (R, Ω).

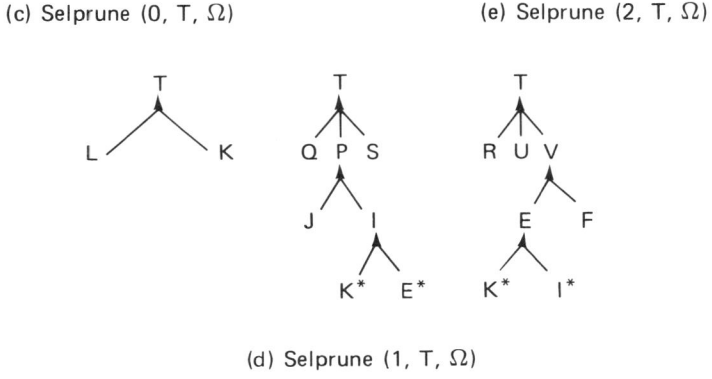

Fig. 7.3(c, d, e) — Mesh operations (mesh designated Ω of Fig. 7.2(d). Directionalising, unfolding, pruning to obtain all possible learning strategies from concept that is placed at hand. Selprune on selective pruning to obtain one learning strategy at once (c) Selprune (O, T, Ω). (d) Selprune (1, T, Ω). (e) Selprune (2, T, Ω).

(but in much the way that we give a direction to thought) by unfolding the mesh from the point of view of any one concept, or several of them. Typically, this operation yields a very large number of derivation paths which, in the context of learning, are interpretable as many possible learning strategies. From this multitude (also called 'pruning' of the mesh, from the perspective of a given concept Fig. 7.3(a), (b)) it is, again automatically, possible to dissect out its constituent tree-like hierarchies, the 'Selprunes' of Fig. 7.3(c), (d), (e), interpretable as particular component learning strategies for the mesh. Also, there are automatic inferences. Given the statement

(f) Saturation

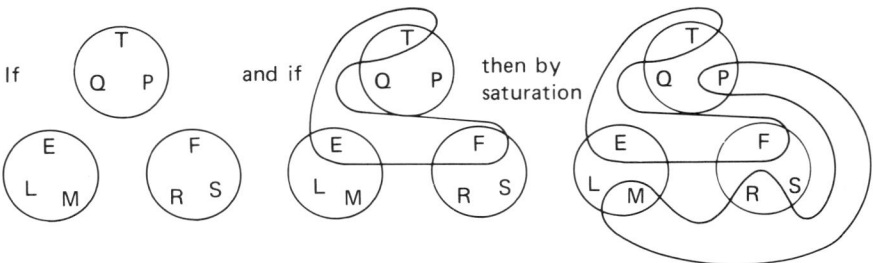

Fig. 7.3(f) — Mesh operations (mesh designated Ω of Fig. 7.2(d). Directionalising, unfolding, pruning to obtain all possible learning strategies from concept that is placed at hand. (f) Saturation.

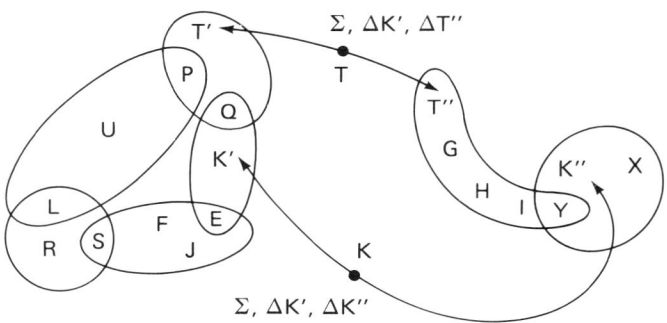

(g) An analogy (Σ is a similarity, Δ are differences) between related concepts

Fig. 7.3(g) — Mesh operations (mesh designated Ω of Fig. 7.2(d). Directionalising, unfolding, pruning to obtain all possible learning strategies from concept that is placed at hand. (g) An analogy (Σ is a similarity, Δ are differences) between related concepts.

of a certain critical number of coherences, a 'saturation' process derives other coherences between concepts that might have been, but were not in fact, stated. These are filtered, so that none of them loses the required distinction between concepts, and are presented to the participants as suggestions, which can be accepted or rejected but, in any case, promote further ideation (Fig. 7.3(f)).

There is a great deal more to Lp. For instance, there are transformation rules. Participants in a conversation are prone to make assertions of coherency when they really intend analogy relations; this gives rise to a loss

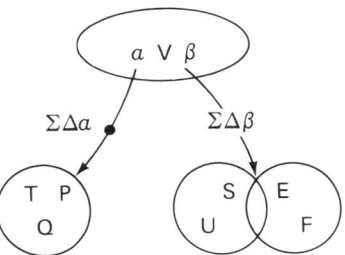

(h) Generalisation
Σ, as before
Δα, unidirectional
Δβ, unidirectional

Fig. 7.3(h) — Mesh operations (mesh designated Ω of Fig. 7.2(d). Directionalising, unfolding, pruning to obtain all possible learning strategies from concept that is placed at hand. (h) Generalisation Σ, as before, Δ∞, unidirectional, Δβ, unidirectional.

of distinction which can be restored by revising the assertion or, much more often, by transforming the assertion into an analogy relation in which concepts rendered indistinct are refined into several analogous concepts (the similarity and difference of the analogy assume 'default' values, later qualified or amplified by information input from the participants as in Fig. 7.3(g)). Much the same takes place in the case of assertions that are really generalisations (Fig. 7.3(h)); they are transformed into generalisations and the concepts, added in order to effect the transformation, are given 'default' values, filled in and amplified, later on, by the participants. Many other matters, notably complex forms of negation and the status of prepositional operators are relevant, well worked out, but cannot be covered here.

A couple of outstanding questions do, however, require some further explanation.

First, it is quite possible to represent one participant's view, or image, of another participant in terms of an Lp mesh. This is not only a practical expedient of educational consequences (one learner's image of another learner, the student's image of a teacher) but follows from the formalism needed to justify, for example, the operation of 'pruning' from the 'perspective' of a given concept. In the light of that comment it is natural to specify participants themselves as especially coherent clusters of concepts which have autonomy but are able to interact in a conversation. Because of that, Conversation Theory is able to speak, even make predictions about, participants who are not necessarily individual people but are, for example, autonomous mental organisations of the type that coexist in one brain when people weigh up hypotheses; or that, at another extreme, are groups or institutions, even, for that matter, inanimate but possibly sentient organisations; the intelligences, if they exist as they probably do, that are nowadays fashionable in computer science.

Next, in this terse account of Lp, I have, perforce, painted a rather static picture. In fact, we know that conceptualisation is dynamic in many more ways than, for example, unfoldment or simple inference; further, the logic underlying the formalism requires that this is so.

The point becomes apparent if we imagine the rather arid illustrations of Fig. 7.2, the basic components of a knowledge structure, combined together to build a multiply-connected 'space' of knowledge describing a whole subject area. The internal structure of any subject matter area must be expected to be highly complex as well as capable of dynamic change, if it is to attempt to represent real thought.

7.5 VIDEODISC AND OTHER TECHNOLOGIES IN Lp

When we talk of 'driving through knowledge' (or navigating in the ocean of thought, 'belief'; or other phrases of the same ilk) we allude to driving or navigating in a cartography of this kind, which cannot be represented in ordinary space, let alone projected with any conviction, onto the surface of a page. That, alone, is a fascinating exercise which videodisc and CD-ROM technology can immensely enhance.

It is a more fascinating exercise when it is recalled that every shared concept must have at least one working model; if it is the concept of a shop on High Street, Bermondsey, that model shows the shop for real and what goes on inside the shop; the Mafia to whom they pay protection money, the old dears who come as customers, the owner's tedium, the sale of bric-a'-brac. Or, if you prefer it, model the concept of Relativity theory (supported, we insist, by enactments of Einstein's personality, Euclid's personality, anecdotes, an opera or so, the history).

It is also exciting to realise that the fluxes going on inside the knowledge structure, the coherencies and distinctions, are kinetic. There is a complementarity, both process and structure must coexist. The process supports (and in mesh development) creates, the structure; the structure constrains (and is meaningful because of) the process and evolution of thought.

7.6 Lp AND OTHER REPRESENTATIONS

Fundamentally, these are the reasons why the protolanguage, Lp, of Conversation Theory and its entailment meshes or Lp expressions, differ from other knowledge representations, most of which are much more facile and may have greater immediate utility, but far less depth or generality. The fact is, our intellectual environment is littered with 'information patterns', structured 'concept orderings' and variegated 'concept maps'; which no doubt, prove very helpful; just as drawing up a menu or an informal action plan may prove helpful. But, those I have seen, which are many, can be subjected to only the most trivial manipulation and are utterly uncommitted to what a concept *is*; that crucial matter is usually 'taken for granted' as 'obvious' which, quite frankly, it is not.

This cavalier treatment of conceptual elements permits, at best, compositions which might be performed in a relational data base or, more often, are subjected to noun-like, unconditional hierarchicalisation. Knowledge is reduced to an immutable edifice of insubstantial bricks, and learning to an 'optimal-path' through the labyrinth. All the rooms have lables, such as 'prerequisite concept cluster for reaction mechanisms; chemistry, O Level', and there are some regularities; for example, 'prerequisite concept cluster for reaction mechanisms; chemistry, A level', is likely to be situated on another floor and to have art nouveau furnishings, if the first one had Bauhaus decor. Factor analysis, probabilistic search and other well known data-base techniques can be (often are) misapplied to respectabilise this collation of labels. It increases the confusion enormously, just as the same operations enormously improve access to an author and abstract indexed library. However, in the case of knowledge, nobody has paid much attention to what a book *is*, let alone what its content or its author *is*, or *how* the contents *are* related in the *learner's* mind.

That diatribe was provoked by another of the editor's very useful suggestions 'say *how* entailment meshes are *not* like concept maps'. I have done so. I am not asserting 'we are right and the rest are wrong'. But I *am* saying that we have developed a useful theory of thought, the Lp calculus of concepts shared in a conversation; that the theory as it stands works with no smudging or avoidance of tricky issues, and is evolving systematically. Few others have tried or, if they *have* done so, then they have obfuscated their findings under the guise of practical expediency. It is prudent, of course, *not* to rock the conventional wisdom, which you *do* by theorising and thinking about thought. The consequences of your theory pinch the corns on too many well established toes. But, maybe videodisc and CD-ROM technology is powerful enough to justify that risk.

7.7 AUTHORING AND LEARNING

Earlier in this chapter, we promised an account of how the computer implemented interfaces used in Conversation Theory and Lp could be employed in a tutorial capacity. The following account is, in a way, simply an elaboration of the outline already given rendering it more specific. Further, the evidence required to ensure that concept sharing is a hard valued event, namely, an explanation of a concept and its derivation, has already been stated. Hence, the main task is to indicate that additional equipment is involved and what tutorial heuristics are used.

There is an authoring mode and a learning mode (ideally, there would be no discernible difference) and this account is focused upon the learning mode where an already authored mesh exists and where each shared concept is associated with an explanatory model. This model can be used, in practical applications, to demonstrate and simulate the concept as well as to evaluate explanations offered by the learner (and to ensure that they are not copies of a previous demonstration). A concept is also attached to graphic and textual descriptive material. An obvious enhancement, almost trivial in the context of this book, is to have several models attached as programs on CD-ROM or random-access videodisc, in place of the descriptive materials at the moment on random access slides or tape. Authoring, incidentally, only calls for a read and write once capability which is available and becoming decreasingly costly; there is no obvious need for erasure.

The learning mode tracks, retains, records, and computes from the behaviours of one or several learners A, B, . . ., the participants.

Several caveats are usually introduced.

(a) Although learners are free to look at any concept they want, to locate it and its coherence, its analogies or its generalisation to related concepts in a mesh, to examine many concepts at once, to unfold them, to maintain the unfoldments as active contexts, they must *learn* the concepts they address. There is no limit to the amount of description, demonstration and simulation they have, in order to do so; nor any restriction upon whether it is taken in sequence, all at once, or after interruptions, due, for example, to studying other concepts. However, at some stage, the learner must offer an explanation which is successfully evaluated with respect to the models in the existing mesh.

(b) In order that a concept is *understood* the evidence for permanent retention and concept sharing must be provided by either of the following heuristics; (1) the concepts in at least one derivation, one selective pruning (Fig. 7.2), of the understood concept must be diagnosed and displayed as learned (or understood), or better (2) the concepts in all derivations of the understood concept, its pruning (Fig.7.2), must be computer-tested and displayed as learned (or understood).

7.8 Implementation and operation

On thinking about (a) and (b) and also about the heuristics of (1) and (2), it becomes clear that implementations of this kind of system require several independent processors. The tutorial jargon includes names like 'aim', for a focus of attention and 'subgoal topic' for a concept that is currently being learned in that context. Obviously, there must be at least one 'aim' machine and at very least one (preferably quite a few) 'topic' machines to allow psychologically meaningful and learner-initiated comparison and contrast. These must be independent, so that a simulation, for example, can be interrupted or restarted while another concept simulation continues or is altered in a different manner; further, these machines must interact and communicate with each other and a machine, again independently acting, that keeps track of them all and contains a representation of the one or several meshes involved. This requirement can either be satisfied by a multimicroprocessor network (Fig. 7.4) or a multitasking design (Fig. 7.5), but 'fakes' like many 'apparent' windows simply will not suffice.

Ch. 7]   CONVERSATION THEORY AS BASIS FOR INSTRUCTIONAL DESIGN   111

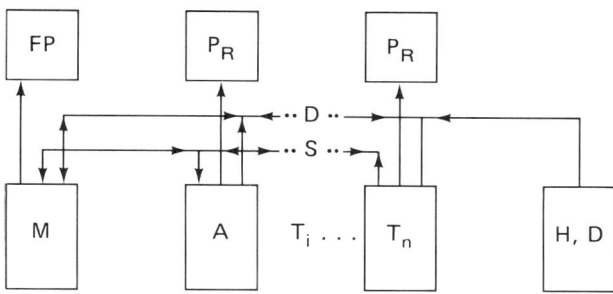

Fig. 7.4 — FP=Fast printer. PR=Random access videodisc or other random access peripheral. D= hard disc link. S=Signal link. M=Master or CASTE machine. A=Aim machine. T_i, T_n=One or more topic machines. H, D=Long-term rewritable store and auxiliary CD ROM.

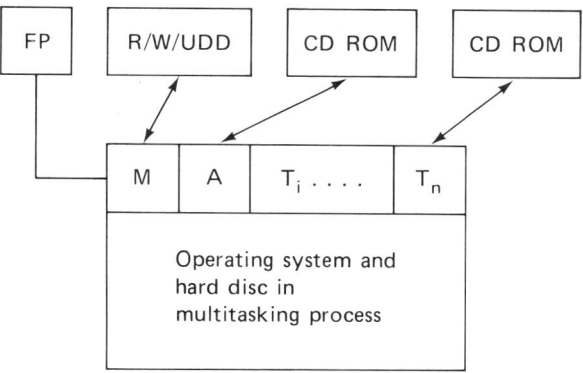

Fig. 7.5 — An alternative CASTE organisation using a genuinely multitasking machine with four or more high definition windows on its display (otherwise, the machine and communication architecture of Fig. 7.4, using a microprocessor network). R/W/UDD is a read-write videodisc unit for mesh location conceived as a trip through what may be known or believed (minimally in terms of entailment meshes but equally with graphic capabilities comparable to Negroponte's Dataspace System). CD-ROM is read only. CD-ROM used for prespecified models and for explanation or demonstration. Otherwise, notation of Fig. 7.4 is used.

The fundamental tutorial heuristics, (1) and (2) differ little if it is required that the learner covers all the concepts in the mesh and understands them. Otherwise, (1) leads, usually, to more rapid learning and (2) guarantees deeper comprehension and, often, far more rapid recall. There are numerous variations. Simple computations from the record of learning determine what learning strategies have been adopted and permit the recommendation of further learning strategies; the provision of such guidance can be optional or mandatory or in many ways conditional. It is possible, also, to regulate the learner's uncertainty, to maintain a balance between overload and boredom. Adaptive techniques are profitably applied at the level of single concept learning.

Perhaps the major enhancement, readily achieved by the deployment of CD-ROM and compact videodisc (using the same equipment, in practice) is to make the currently impoverished computer graphic representations of the mesh and the learner's locations in the mesh far richer and more realistic; eventually to merge them with the concept descriptive and concept demonstrative enhancements, noted previously.

7.9 Transportable systems

The 1970s versions of CASTE, one of these tutorial and authoring interfaces, used computers but a great deal of not-too-reliable peripheral equipment, together with special purpose devices for interfacing them. To implement a transferable form of this system proved quite difficult, due, in large measure, to the need for independence and communication between independent processes. There are, however, several current implementations. At one extreme of size, there is a program suite that runs on a pair of Symbolics 3600 machines. At the other extreme, there are multimicroprocessor versions; some, such as C/CASTE/1.0 designed at the CSRKE, Department of Education, Concordia University, by Charles Small have impressive potentialities and the fundamental design, recoded to run on upgraded hardware, can be readily enhanced to include the videodisc and other technologies which are the foci of this book.

REFERENCES

Alty, J. L. and Coombs, M. J. (1978) Proceedings of the Workshop on Computer Skills and Adaptive Systems, University of Liverpool, Liverpool 21–22 March 1978.

Bandura, A. (1982) Self-efficacy mechanism in human agency, *Amer. Psychologist* **37**, 122–48.

Beckwith, D. (1983) The nature of learners as total systems, *Journal Visual and Verbal Languaging*.

Benstein, B. (1971) *Class Codes and Control,* Routledge & Kegan Paul, London.

Boyd, G. M. and Jaworski, W. M. (1985) PALS, PATHS, PLACES and PRODUCERS: four more appropriate forms of computer aided education. *Proceedings of COMPINT85,* pp. 614–616, IEEE Computer Society Press, Washington, DC.

Braten, S. (1982) Simulation and self-organisation of mind, University of Oslo. *Contemporary Philosophy. A New Survey,* Vol. 2, pp. 189–218.

Coombs, M. J. and Alty, J. L. *General Proposals for the Design of a Knowledge-based Consultant: Rationale and a Cartoon,* Dept. of Computer Science, University of Strathclyde, Glasgow, Scotland, UK.

Daniel, J. S. (1974) *Knowables, Conversations and Learning: A Summary of Recent Work at Systems Research Inc.*, Tele-University, Quebec, Canada.

Daniel, J. S. (1975) Learning styles and strategies. In N. Entwistle and D. Hounsell (eds), *How Students Learn*, Lancaster, United Kingdom: University of Lancaster.

Entwistle, N. (1978) Knowledge structures and styles of learning: a summary of Pask's recent research, *British Journal of Educational Psychology*, **48**, 255–65.

Frye, N. (1957) *The Anatomy of Criticism*, Princeton University Press.

Gaines, B. R. and Shaw, M. L. G. (1983) *Is There a Knowledge Environment?*, Dept of Industrial Engineering, University of Toronto and Dept. of Computer Science, York University, Canada.

Gerrit, C., van der Veer, Jos, J. Beishuizen 'Learning Styles in Conversation — A Practical Application of Pask's Learning Theory to Human–Computer Interaction'. Vrije Universiteit, Amsterdam, Netherlands.

Glanville, R. (1975) 'A Cybernetic Development of Epistemology and Observation, Applied to Objects in Space and Time (As Seen in Architecture).' Ph.D. thesis, Brunel University, Dept. of Cybernetics.

Hannapin, M. J. (1985) Empirical issues in the study of computer assisted interactive video, *Educational Communications Technology Journal*, **33**, 4, Winter, 235–48.

Hawkes, Jacquetta (1953) *A Land*, The Cresset Press, London.

Hounsell, D. and Entwistle, N. (1975) *How Students Learn. Readings in Higher Educaton*, 1. Lancaster, Institute for Research and Development in Post Compulsory Education.

Jaworski, W. M. and Hinterberger, H. (1981) Controller program design by use of the programming concept ABL, *Angewandte Informatik*, pp. 302–310, July 1981.

Johnson, D. W. and Johnson, R. T. (1975) *Learning Together and Alone: Cooperation, Competition and Individualization*, Prentice-Hall, Englewood Cliffs N.J.

Laurillard, D. M. (1981) Interactive computer simulations in undergraduate teaching. *Proceedings, Second International Microcomputers in Education Congress, London, 1980*, Harvester, London.

Laurillard, D. M. and Marnante, G. J. (1981) *A View of Computer Assisted Learning in the Light of Conversation Theory*, Milton Keynes, United Kingdom: Open University, Institute of Educational Technology.

Lee, (1984) *The Practice of Conversation Theory: Understanding and Encouraging Innovation*, US Army Research Institute for the Behavioural and Social Sciences, Great Britain.

Lepore, E. (1986) *Truth and Interpretation; Perspectives on the Philosophy of Donald Davidson*, NY.

Lewis, B. N. and Pask, G. (1965) The theory and practice of adaptive teaching systems, in R. Glasser (ed.), *Teaching Machines and Programmed Learning* (Vol. II), National Education Association, Washington, DC.

Lindstrom, B. (1983) *Learning Styles and Learning Strategies: Conversation Theory. The Work of Gordon Pask*, Gothenburg, University of Gothenburg, Department of Education, Sweden.

Luria, G. R. (1961) *The Role of Speech in the Regulation of Normal and Abnormal Behaviour*, Pergamon Press, London.

Luria, G. R. (1968) *The Mind of a Mnemonist*, Basic Books, New York.

McKenzie, J. Interactive computer graphics for undergraduate science teaching, *Comput. and Education*, 2, 25–48.

Meurrens, M. W. F. (1986) An intelligent approach to computer aided learning: G, in F. Percival (ed.), *Aspects of Educational Technology*, XX, Kogan Press, London. (In press.)

Mitchell, P. D. and Dalkir, K. (1986) C/CASTE and artificial intelligence based on computer aided learning system, in J. Brahan (ed.), *Proceedings of the Fifth Canadian Symposium on Instructional Technology*, NCR, Ottawa. (In press.)

Ogborn, J. (1987) *Conversation: Theory; Epistemology; Heuristic?* (In press.)

Papert, S. (1980) *Mindstorms; Children, Computers as Powerful Ideas*, Basic Books, NY.

Pask, G. (1961) *An Approach to Cybernetics*, Hutchinson, London, reprinted 1968, 1972.

Pask, G. (1972) A fresh look at cognition and the individual, *Int. J. Man-Machine Studies*, **4**, 211–216.

Pask, G. (1975a) *The Cybernetics of Human Learning and Performance*, Hutchinson, London.

Pask, G. (1975b) Conversation, cognition and learning, *A Cybernetic Theory and Methodology*, Elsevier, Amsterdam.

Pask, G. (1976a) Conversational techniques in the study and practice of education. *British Journal of Educational Psychology*, **46**, 12–25.

Pask, G. (1976b) Styles and strategies of learning, *British Journal of Educational Psychology*, **46**, 128–48.

Pask, G. (1976c) *Conversation Theory: Applications in Education and Epistemology*, Elsevier, Amsterdam.

Pask, G. (1977) Knowledge, innovation and 'learning to learn'. *Proceedings, NATO — ASI "Structural/Process Theories of Complex Human Behaviour, Banff Springs, Canada*, Noordhoff, Alphan aan den Rijn.

Pask, G. and Scott, B. C. E. (1972) Learning strategies and individual competence, *Int. J. Man-Machine Studies*, **4**, 217–53.

Pask, G. and Scott, B. C. E. (1973) CASTE: a system for exhibiting learning strategies and regulating uncertainty, *Int. J. Man-machine Studies*, **5**, 17–52.

Pask, G., Scott, B. C. E. and Kallikourdis, D. (1973) A theory of conversations and individuals (exemplified by the learning process in CASTE), *Int. J. Man-Machine Studies*, 5, 443–566.

Pask, G., Kallikourdis, D. and Scott, B. C. E. (1975) The Representation of Knowables, *Inter. J. for Man-Machine Studies*, **17**, 15–134.

Pask, G., Ensor, D., Scott, B. C. E. and Pask, E. (1977) Cartoons. Tests for

Lindstrom, B. (1983) *Learning Styles and Learning Strategies: Conversation Theory. The Work of Gordon Pask*, Gothenburg, University of Gothenburg, Department of Education, Sweden.

Luria, G. R. (1961) *The Role of Speech in the Regulation of Normal and Abnormal Behaviour*, Pergamon Press, London.

Luria, G. R. (1968) *The Mind of a Mnemonist*, Basic Books, New York.

McKenzie, J. Interactive computer graphics for undergraduate science teaching, *Comput. and Education*, 2, 25–48.

Meurrens, M. W. F. (1986) An intelligent approach to computer aided learning: G, in F. Percival (ed.), *Aspects of Educational Technology*, XX, Kogan Press, London. (In press.)

Mitchell, P. D. and Dalkir, K. (1986) C/CASTE and artificial intelligence based on computer aided learning system, in J. Brahan (ed.), *Proceedings of the Fifth Canadian Symposium on Instructional Technology*, NCR, Ottawa. (In press.)

Ogborn, J. (1987) *Conversation: Theory; Epistemology; Heuristic?* (In press.)

Papert, S. (1980) *Mindstorms; Children, Computers as Powerful Ideas*, Basic Books, NY.

Pask, G. (1961) *An Approach to Cybernetics*, Hutchinson, London, reprinted 1968, 1972.

Pask, G. (1972) A fresh look at cognition and the individual, *Int. J. Man-Machine Studies*, **4**, 211–216.

Pask, G. (1975a) *The Cybernetics of Human Learning and Performance*, Hutchinson, London.

Pask, G. (1975b) Conversation, cognition and learning, *A Cybernetic Theory and Methodology*, Elsevier, Amsterdam.

Pask, G. (1976a) Conversational techniques in the study and practice of education. *British Journal of Educational Psychology*, **46**, 12–25.

Pask, G. (1976b) Styles and strategies of learning, *British Journal of Educational Psychology*, **46**, 128–48.

Pask, G. (1976c) *Conversation Theory: Applications in Education and Epistemology*, Elsevier, Amsterdam.

Pask, G. (1977) Knowledge, innovation and 'learning to learn'. *Proceedings, NATO — ASI "Structural/Process Theories of Complex Human Behaviour, Banff Springs, Canada*, Noordhoff, Alphan aan den Rijn.

Pask, G. and Scott, B. C. E. (1972) Learning strategies and individual competence, *Int. J. Man-Machine Studies*, **4**, 217–53.

Pask, G. and Scott, B. C. E. (1973) CASTE: a system for exhibiting learning strategies and regulating uncertainty, *Int. J. Man-machine Studies*, **5**, 17–52.

Pask, G., Scott, B. C. E. and Kallikourdis, D. (1973) A theory of conversations and individuals (exemplified by the learning process in CASTE), *Int. J. Man-Machine Studies*, 5, 443–566.

Pask, G., Kallikourdis, D. and Scott, B. C. E. (1975) The Representation of Knowables, *Inter. J. for Man-Machine Studies*, **17**, 15–134.

Pask, G., Ensor, D., Scott, B. C. E. and Pask, E. (1977) Cartoons. Tests for learning 'style'. Forms III, V, VI. (Computer administered versions are also issued.) Systems Research Ltd, Richmond, Surrey.

Petri, C. E. (1978) *Concepts of Net Theory and Concurrency,* GMD, Bonn.

Reichardt, J. (ed.) *Cybernetics: Thought and Ideas.* Studio Vista, London, 1971. Also 1963, 1966, 'Fun Palace' and 'Proposals for a Cybernetic Master', reprints with Lewis, B. N., Littlewood, J., and Price, C.

Rescher, N. (1973) *The Coherence Theory of Truth,* Oxford University Press.

Van de Geer, J. P. (1957) *A Psychological View of Problem Solving,* Leiden.

Van der Veer, G. and Van der Wolde, J. (1980) *Psychological Aspects of Problem Solving with the Help of a Computer Language,* Vrije Universiteit, Amsterdam.

8

From Trigger Video to Videodisc: a Case Study in Interpersonal Skills

Nick Rushby,
Centre for Staff Development in Higher Education

This chapter traces the development of a training package based on a videodisc, which had the aim of helping bus crews to deal with difficult passengers. The case study is set into the context of a research programme that began with the use of trigger video, and is heading towards a simulation of an extended conversation using videodisc, voice input and a natural language interface. Unlike the more usual kind of training video, the trigger technique uses very short, subjective camera, video sequences to stimulate-trigger-group discussion. The trainees are intimately involved in the incident they see on the screen and, in the ensuing discussion, are encouraged to examine their attitudes and beliefs. The use of trigger video and a model of transaction analysis form the basis for the training package. What is now becoming clear is that triggers can not only be used as components within linear video case studies, but can also be a point of departure for extended conversation in interpersonal skills training, blurring the distinction between linear and interactive video, and increasing the flexibility of the technique.

8.1 INTRODUCTION

There are two common perceptions of interactive video. Those who come from film or video see it as a way of resequencing linear material to make it more interesting or effective; while those whose background is in computer-based learning or training see it as a way of enhancing the computer-based courseware with audio and high quality, animated, colour graphics. The reality is that interactive video is a new medium whose potential we are only just starting to appreciate. Some of the characteristics of interactive video have been available to us in linear video, although we have rarely made use of them. Videocassette players have controls which can be operated by the learner to stop or freeze the action, to restart it, to fast forward or to rewind. Yet, with one or two exceptions (for example, some of the self-study material produced by the Open University) these facilities are seldom used.

This chapter examines a technique called 'trigger video' which uses linear videocassette in a semi-interactive form and traces its development into a videodisc-based technique, used for training in interpersonal skills.

8.2 TRIGGER VIDEO

It was a combination of enthusiasm for the potential advantages of video and dissatisfaction with existing material that provided the stimulus for the first series of 'trigger' videos produced by the Centre for Staff Development (entitled 'Call Yourself a Manager?'). The content and development of these videos is described by Schofield (1982).

The approach introduced two innovations to the use of video in managment training.

First, unlike most materials, the programmes are not recorded in a documentary or fictional form, but instead as a series of very short scenes, each depicting a different type of organisational problem. Typically, some fifty such scenes will be included in a single (linear) video-tape. Appropriate scenes are selected by trainers to meet particular training objectives, and are then shown singly to trainees, who are asked to respond in a number of ways. Typically, one scene may lead to one or two hours of discussion and analysis, and so the materials are extremely cost-effective.

The second innovation is that the viewer is placed on the spot: dropped into a problem to which he or she has to respond immediately—just as in real life. In all the episodes, what is said is aimed directly at the viewer who, imagining himself or herself as the person addressed, has to respond to the issues presented. In developing such programmes considerable emphasis is placed on the need for immediate responses, bringing a reality to the material and allowing users to identify readily with what they see on the screen. Research undertaken on the effectiveness of previous programmes emphasises that it is this perceived reality by users which leads to the high face validity of the material (see Weil and Schofield, 1984).

By using such material participants readily discover significant differences in the way they perceive the behaviour they see on the screen. These differences permit the further exploration of strategies to manage the problems that they face, and to come to terms with the influence of their own interpersonal behaviour on the required decision. The method shares much in common with management simulations but, because of the richness of the visual medium, becomes a more powerful force for learning than many such traditional methods.

8.3 THE ROLE OF THE TRAINER

Many existing training methods do not bring out the importance of interpersonal behaviour and relationships. Conversely, some methods which attempt to do just that may be unpopular with trainees who will sometimes strongly resist taking part. Many people do not like to discuss openly their feeling about other people or difficult situations. The short video episodes can trigger a response in the viewer which can be taken and discussed in relatively supportive surroundings, but even so the trainer should be aware that there will still be problems in getting people to identify their real feelings. Different episodes affect different emotional levels. In most cases the initial feelings will be exposed and discussed without too much difficulty: however, the process becomes more difficult the further one tries to dig down into peoples' emotions. For that reason, feelings should be discussed only to the extent which is legitimate for the particular training purposes and which the trainer can manage. The use of the episodes can thus provide a basis on which individuals can identify and understand feelings which are relevant to their role, and also develop an adequate vocabulary, which is frequently lacking, to express emotional reactions. As we will see later, this has implications for the extent to which it is advisable to package trigger-based training material for delivery in the absence of a skilled trainer.

Some questions for trainees that apply particularly to using the triggers for focusing on interpersonal issues are:

—how did I feel?
—what did I think?
—what would I probably do?
—what would I really want to do?
—what did I think the person was thinking about me?
—what did I think the person wanted from me?
—what did I feel about him or her?
—has a similar thing ever happened to me and what did I do then?

By use of these episodes, and with appropriate interventions from the trainer, individuals can come to appreciate the important distinctions between how they feel and what they think (and also to expand their often limited vocabulary to identify feelings); between what action they would take and what they would really want to do, and so on. For example, a particular incident may make them feel very angry but expression of that anger may be inappropriate in the situation, and an important learning point is the need to identify those personal feelings, to understand both the reasons for them and their effects on the other people involved.

The triggers can also be used as miniature case studies. Here the emphasis is different: as well as asking individuals for their feelings about what they saw, they may also be asked about more cognitive issues in the situations. Thus the group might describe the main points arising in an episode and identify the organisational issues, analyse the communications between manager and employee, or determine and examine the behaviours identified, and so on. The subject groupings on the tape may often form the basis of the use of the episodes as miniature case studies. The main advantages of using the episodes for general management training in this way is the way that they do bring reality to issues: participants can see the behaviours exhibited. The episodes are deliberately 'short' on information, and the trainer may wish to supplement this, depending on the group concerned.

The successful series of seven sets of triggers for management training was followed by three sets focusing on adolescence in order to meet staff development and training needs in the teaching and caring professions and, more recently, by a programme on racism in organisations. This line of development is now being extended into the area of cultural awareness with materials for training teachers working with overseas students.

8.4 TOWARDS INTERACTIVE VIDEO

As we have seen, the trigger video technique can be a powerful tool for the trainer experienced in its use, but is incomplete as a resource for self-study. It relies on the trainer to lead the discussion, to elicit feelings, and to challenge attitudes. This led to the intriguing question of whether interactive video could be used to mediate trigger video and to act as a surrogate for the live trainer. Intuitively, technology based training may seem inappropriate for learning interpersonal skills because of the impersonal nature of the human computer interaction. However, if the trigger technique could be packaged in some way, then it may be possible to show that it is adequate for learning at least some aspects of interpersonal skills.

We can think of the single trigger, to which the trainee (or trainees) respond, as being the first half of a dialogue as shown in Fig. 8.1(b). As such, it is an advance on the more traditional cameo style video, shown in Fig. 8.1(a), in which the viewer is a passive observer—a fly on the wall—and which does not prompt a response. Our aim in using interactive video was to move towards a more sustained conversation between the trainee and the learning materials as shown in Fig. 8.1(c).

8.5 'WHO DO YOU THINK YOU'RE TALKING TO?'

'Who Do You Think You're Talking To?' is a trigger-based interactive video programme to train bus crews to deal with potentially difficult passengers. The aim of the training is not only to improve customer relations, but also to reduce the number of consequential assaults on bus crews. (A recent report noted that there were 1200 such attacks in 1985 on London Regional Transport buses alone!) The disc was designed and produced by the Centre for Staff Development (CSDHE), for the Local Government Training Board, who have a responsibility for training bus crews throughout England and Wales. It consists of eight episodes, each based on a typical incident (an indignant passenger who has been waiting for too long, a passenger who is lost and does not speak English, a rowdy group of young people annoying other passengers, two 'punks' looking for trouble, a drunk, etc.). The driver is asked how he or she would respond if the incident actually happened to them, and then a follow-up scene is shown, to illustrate the likely consequences of their action.

8.6 DESIGN

As is often the case, this project had several aims. In addition to the overt aim of producing an effective package to meet a perceived training need, there was a political aim of being concerned about training for public

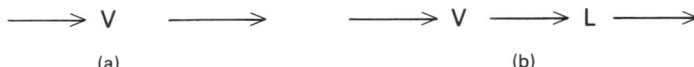

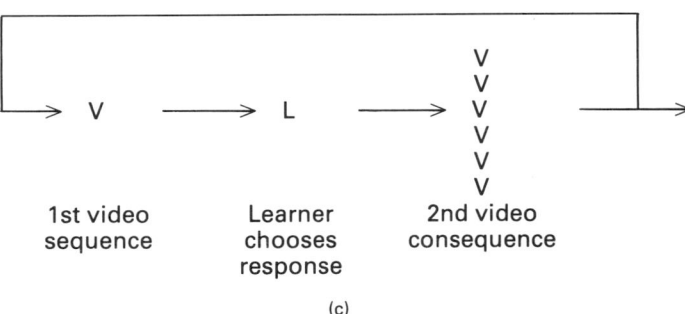

Fig. 8.1(a) The single step cameo video (the passive learner watches a video sequence with no interruption). (b) The two-step dialogue of trigger video (the learner watches a short video sequence and then is immediately required to respond to it). This sequence can be repeated so that the learner can explore the consequences of alternative responses. (c) Three-step dialogue on videodisc (the learner watches a short video sequence and then is immediately required to respond to it. A further video consequence is then selected by the system and shown as the third step in the dialogue).

transport (an area for which the Local Government Training board (LGTB) had recently taken over the responsibility) and an internal staff development aim of familiarisation with videodisc technology in training.

The perceived training need was to help the drivers to deal with potentially difficult situations so as to improve their customer relations and to reduce the number of assaults on staff. The underlying message is that most awkward passengers are not born—they are made by the situation in which they find themselves, and that the drivers and conductors can often talk themselves out of trouble—or at least avoid talking themselves into it!

The initial proposal from the LGTB was that the CSDHE should be involved in a project that would start with the production of a linear video training programme for the drivers of one-man buses. This linear video would then be transferred onto videodisc where it could be resequenced under computer control. Although at that time our experience with interactive video was very limited, everything we had seen led us to believe that this approach would be less than satisfactory. Although it may be possible to make linear video more adaptable by interactive resequencing, a package that really exploits the power of interactive video must be designed from the outset for that new medium. We can find an analogy in the early use of closed circuit television (I deliberately use the old name) to make recordings of lectures which could later be used as surrogates with other groups of students. Thus was born the 'talking head' programme that made the lecture available to a much wider audience, but lost much of the charisma, excitement and motivation engendered by the expert performing in person. Live lectures and linear video are different media and require different techniques.

We therefore persuaded the LGTB that the two stages should be reversed: that the first version should be an interactive videodisc and then, if they wanted, there could be a videocassette, using material shot at the same time, edited into a linear sequence. The video component would be supported by a booklet giving some background information and containing the minimal operating instructions needed to use the videodisc.

A further requirement grew out of the discussions about whether to use a videodisc player on its own, or add a computer to control the presentation of the package. We decided with confidence (the feeling you get before you fully understand the problem) that it should be possible to design a disc that could stand alone as well as being used under computer control. This placed various constraints on the structure and sequencing of the disc which might have been avoided if computer control was assumed. (For example, each video sequence was made into a 'chapter' on the disc, which could be selected by the trainee using a two-digit code, and the chapters were separated by special sequences on the disc that caused the player to stop automatically. In the computer-controlled version, these sequences are ignored, and there is more freedom to move between sections.) The conclusion to be drawn is that, although some control can be built into the disc itself, the addition of a computer can simplify the design process and the human–computer interface.

The end product was to be a flexible package that could be used in a variety of ways in the many passenger transport undertakings in the UK. This part of a driver's training is supervised by bus inspectors and so they would want to use the package as a resource under their control. In other circumstances, it might be used for self-instruction either by individuals or by small groups. One criterion for success would be if the staff were motivated to use it in the canteens, during their breaks!

The package was designed on the assumption that an extension of the trigger video technique could be used to illustrate typical problems faced by drivers and conductors, and to help them to explore a range of possible responses. Although the trigger technique had been proven in many other applications (see for example, Boud and Pearson, 1978, 1979; Kagan, 1975), its success rested on presenting a series of typical incidents with credible outcomes, in such a way that the driver felt they were (or could be) real. The perceived validity of the incidents is one of the keys to using trigger video, whether on linear cassette or disc.

8.7 STRUCTURE

The training programme consists of eight episodes, each depicting a potentially difficult situation for the bus driver. There is a gentle introduction to the sequence, and a conclusion which reiterates and brings together some of the ideas that have been introduced. The detailed structure of each episode is shown in Fig. 8.1(c). It starts with a trigger followed by a list of six possible responses that the trainee could make if the incident really happened to them. The trainee is invited to choose the response which is nearest to the one he or she would make in real life and then sees a likely consequence to that response. The dialogue thus consists of three stages: a trigger, a response and a consequence. The episode concludes with a commentary on the specific choice and an invitation to repeat the episode (to look at another response) or to continue with the next episode. The pace is initially quite slow in the expectation that the users will be unfamiliar with the technology: later in the programme, particularly in the computer-controlled version, it becomes rather faster.

This structure brings us to the question of how the incidents and the responses were selected and scripted—the model underlying the dialogue. The number of incidents was restricted by the amount of time available for the trainees to work through the package and the length of the disc. Our intention was that the trainees should work in small groups, discussing possible responses among themselves and watching the possible consequences. With a target package time of about 60 minutes and allowing for an introduction and conclusion, eight episodes seemed to be about right. This number was also feasible (just) within the 60 minutes of video available on each side of a VHD disc. With a LaserVision disc offering 37 minutes of video per side, the package would have been restricted to about four or five episodes. The eight episodes were defined by interviewing bus drivers and inspectors to get examples of typical problems, involving the rules governing bus crews, courtesy, and physical violence. The interviews also yielded typical responses to these problems. It soon became clear (somewhat to our relief!) that most of the problems could be covered adequately by the eight episodes and for each of these there were only about six likely responses: other problems and outcomes could be considered to be variants of this basic set. Life on the buses seems to be quite predictable in this respect.

The final set of eight problems were:

(1) An angry man who has been waiting for 45 minutes for the bus to arrive;
(2) A young mother with shopping and a dangerous folding pushchair who needs help getting on the bus;
(3) A foreigner who does not speak English and does not seem to know where he is going;
(4) Two aggressive skinheads late at night;
(5) An old age pensioner who does not want to show her bus pass;
(6) A youth who asks for a half fare but is not obviously under sixteen;
(7) A group of rowdy punks disturbing other passengers;
(8) A drunk on a late-night bus.

Unlike basic driving skills, this aspect of training is not usually handled by full-time trainers, but by the bus inspectors as an incidental part of their job. It was necessary that the underlying model of behaviour used in the package should be easy for the inspectors to understand and to explain to their staff, and so the sets of possible responses were fitted to a simplified transactional analysis model (for an introduction to Transaction Analysis see Harris, 1972). For each episode, six responses were devised, corresponding to the driver adopting the role of:

—a critical parent;
—a nurturing parent;
—an adult;
—an adapted child;
—a free child; and
—an avoiding action.

The order of these choices was scrambled in the selection menu presented to the trainees. The likely consequences of the responses were again based on the suggestions and experience of the bus drivers themselves, and a commentary on the response and consequence was added in the form of a voice over a caption of the three or four major points arising from the episode. An example of the design and script for episode 4 is shown in Fig. 8.2.

These example dialogues illustrate how the passengers' responses are influenced by the driver's actions. In most of the episodes there is no single 'correct' action: each alternative has some advantages and disadvantages. However, the advice underlying the feedback is that behaviour that can be characterised as that of a 'nurturing parent' can often calm a potentially difficult situation, while an avoiding action does little to help and a childish response can make it far worse.

The final package can be used in two ways. The basic version, used by most of the public transport undertakings because of its low cost, does not involve a computer to control the disc, but relies on the user pressing a sequence of five keys on the remote control unit to move to the next place in the programme. This sequence of keys is explained at the start of the programme and is repeated in the printed notes that accompany the package. Because the disc player on its own is not able to keep any record of preceding steps in the package, the commentary after each episode is limited to that one choice, and the conclusion is limited to generalisations about the need to practice these skills and to avoid inappropriate responses.

In the more sophisticated version, the disc player is controlled by a small microcomputer (an Acorn BBC micro or VHD Commander) which not only simplifies the interaction, but also maintains a history of the training session so that the final debriefing can take the overall pattern of responses into account. Even in the computer-controlled version, care has to be taken not to be too specific in praise or criticism, because the trainees are encouraged to explore alternative responses. The debriefing only suggests that the kind of responses given are those which might ease the situation if it happened in real life—or alternatively, might exacerbate it! In the latter case, the trainee is advised to seek further guidance from a more experienced colleague or from an inspector.

Scene	It is night and the bus pulls up at a stop. Two skinheads are standing on their own at the stop. The bus doors open and both jump in pushing and shoving each other, and shouting some abuse. They ignore the driver and move to go down to the back of the bus. As they pass the driver the second skinhead turns round and gives him a V sign.
Casting	Both male, white, 16–19, dressed as skinheads.
Camera	Camera in the positon of the driver (so that the viewer sees what the driver would see) slowly turns with them as they go down the bus.
Options	1. 'You ignorant so and so's. Why do you want to make trouble for me?' (Adapted child) 2. 'Two what?' (Free child) 3. Say nothing but adopt the recognised emergency procedure (Avoiding) 4. 'Now you two. Come back here and pay your fare properly' (Critical parent) 5. 'Don't be like that lads. Come back and pay and there won't be any problems' (Nurturing parent) 6. 'Hey you two. I'm not driving on until you come back and pay' (Adult)

Follow-up to response 1.

Camera	Mainly a long shot but tight enough to give some impact. No zoom as it might make the viewer think he/she is walking towards them. As the skinheads walk towards the driver the camera pulls back but in a very unobtrusive way.
Action	There is general giggling. One says, 'Did you hear that?' Second one says, 'Yeah.' They both get up and walk slowly down the aisle towards the driver. They come up very close and one says, 'Now what did you say?'
Commentary	Your reaction demonstrates weakness and the youths have responded rather like an aggressive dog when it detects signs of fear in a stranger and goes into the attack. You have now drawn their unwelcome attention on yourself when it would have been much safer to have ignored them and driven away from the stop. In your present situation you should be prepared to defend yourself from an assault, and only attempt to collect their fares if they settle down and show clearly that they have been joking and have no violent intentions. If the situation gets further out of hand, however, you should operate the agreed emergency procedure without delay.

Fig. 8.2 — An example design and script for Episode 4.

8.8 PROTOTYPING AND DEVELOPMENTAL TESTING

Videodiscs are quite expensive (the total budget for this project to develop a 60-minute package, covering the training, video and CBT components totalled just £33 000) and the videodisc, once edited and mastered is unalterable. So it was crucial that the design and dialogue was right first time. The developmental testing therefore assumed major importance. The draft scripts were trialled with the bus inspectors and drivers, and then a computer-based prototype was produced. This took the form of a computer-based training package which simulated the video and audio from the disc together with the user's responses, working at the same pace as the final disc, so that we were able to obtain a feel for the final version. Thus, even before any video recording had been made, it was possible to know what would be on the disc, with the length and order of each component. This prototype was exposed to typical consumers as well as the clients (that is, to bus drivers as well as the Local Government Training Board). A key feature of developmental testing is that the material is used with typical trainees, representative of the population for whom the training is intended.

After the disc had been produced, a second phase of developmental testing took place on a small section of the computer program, to verify that the computer-based dialogue was easy to use and did not rely on inaccurate assumptions about the trainees' knowledge of computers. For example, it is often (but not in this package) the case that inputs to the computer should be ended by pressing the return key. Only when we were certain that we were working along the right lines, was the rest of the software completed.

The evaluation is still continuing, with drivers and inspectors being interviewed to find out how the package is being used, whether they like it, whether the incidents seem real—and whether they feel that it is improving their skills in dealing with difficult passengers. The results so far, are encouraging. Typically, the package is used by a small group of drivers, in their rest room or cafeteria, during their off-duty time. The drivers treat it as a kind of game, discussing among themselves which response to make to each episode and trying to predict the likely consequences. The option of repeating the episode to look at alternative responses is frequently used. The more experienced drivers find it easy to recognise the incidents and relate them to their own anecdotes. The package might therefore be described as a catalyst for peer group training, rather than a prescriptive tool.

It is too soon to know what long-term effects the training package is having: this can only be measured in terms of the number of complaints received by the bus companies and, in a more dramatic way, by the number of drivers who are assaulted by passengers.

8.9 TECHNICAL ASPECTS

The decision to reject interactive videocassette in favour of disc was clear-cut, both in terms of cost and presentation.

It was the LGTB's intention that the package should be made widely available in locations such as canteens where, although television sets might be found, there were no existing videocassette players. The cost of a VHS cassette player together with an intelligent controller would have been considerably greater than the cost of a stand-alone VHD disc player. The total additional costs of some fifty workstations would have been prohibitive.

On considerations of presentation, it was felt that, even allowing for clever sequencing of the video material, the access time from cassette would be unacceptably slow. In order to retain the drivers' enthusiasm, the package had to have some of the qualities and pace of a game, and this was not feasible with a cassette-based system.

The choice between the two alternative disc systems was also straightforward. The LaserVision system offered 37 minutes playing time per disc side, with the capability of showing still frames at random and, since it is a non-contact system with no disc wear, infinite disc life. The Thorn VHD system offered 60 minutes playing time per side but required that any still frames should be planned in advance. VHD is a contact system (there is a stylus that is in physical contact with the disc) and so it was assumed that discs and styli would have to be replaced from time to time.

We did not envisage the need for selecting still frames at random but, it soon became clear that the quantity of video material would far exceed 37 minutes. Simple arithmetic showed that with eight episodes, each with a trigger, six follow-up scenes and commentary $(8 \times (1+6+6) = 104)$, together with an introduction and conclusion, we would have to be careful to keep the length down to 60 minutes. Even if some sequences could be shared, the savings would not amount to 35%!

In the event, the disc wear inherent in the contact system has not proved a problem. In a year of use, no one has reported a problem with the player stylus or with a worn disc. Even the disc used for software development and frequent demonstration has continued to perform without noticeable deterioration. We conclude that although disc wear may mitigate against VHD in a point of sale application, it does not seem to present problems in this kind of training.

LaserVision may also be preferred over VHD on the grounds of a better picture quality. In fact, both give considerably better results in the field than VHS or U-matic cassette, and are limited by the quality of the monitor or television set which is used.

Finally, on grounds of cost, the VHD system was significantly cheaper than LaserVision, for players, mastering and pressing the final discs. Again, the total additional costs of some fifty workstations would have been prohibitive.

Thus, the stand-alone interactive video package runs on the Thorn VHD disc player with a remote control handset, connected to a video monitor or television set. The computer-controlled variant incorporates an Acorn BBC microcomputer and interface, either as a set of separate boxes, or packaged in the form of a VHD Commander. The Commander is a BBC B+ microcomputer, interface and genlock board in a case to match the VHD player. When used with a suitable monitor it is capable of overlaying the computer generated text and graphics onto the video signal from the player. We will return to this technique of overlay in a moment.

The controlling CBT program is written in an authoring language called

Microtext, which, although relatively unsophisticated (and consequently cheap), is quite adequate for the task of handling this level of dialogue, guiding the trainee through the sequence of eight episodes, and keeping track of their pattern of responses.

8.10 SCREEN PRESENTATION

The videodisc contains all the instructions, menus, and pauses needed for it to be used in a stand-alone mode. However, when it is used under computer control, the instructions and menus, together with some additional information are generated by the computer. All this can either be overlaid—superimposed—on the video picture, or can be presented on a separate screen.

Considerable work has been done to provide overlay facilities at reasonable cost, and this is now the accepted form of presentation. Although it is not significantly cheaper than using two screens (the cost of the additional electronics to synchronise and mix the two signals is about the same as a second monitor), it is more compact and convenient and has the advantage that the trainee has a single visual source of information. However, that single screen is easily overloaded and there may be some circumstances where two screens are preferable from an instructional point of view. There are two versions of the bus crews package, one for dual screen and one using overlays: the two feel very different to the trainee. Neither is perfect in terms of its pacing and consistency of message: both have instances where the trainee is receiving slightly different messages, either from the two screens, or from different parts of the same screen. We stated at the beginning of this chapter that interactive video was a new medium and that our understanding of it is incomplete. We found that mixing video and CBT components on the same screen presents a number of such problems which deserve further research.

8.11 COSTING

Any attempts to give a detailed costing for the project are subject to a continual dating process as the costs of labour increase and the cost of the technology tends to fall. Moreover, since different organisations attribute—or hide—costs in different ways, the precise figures may not be very meaningful. However, it may be helpful to give some indication of the main budget headings and the magnitude of costs. The total project budget was about £33 000 and can be broken down into six heads.

(1) The instructional design and scripting accounted for about £8000 of staff time, or about 25% of the total project budget. This included devising the instructional model, interviewing bus drivers and inspectors, the non-computer related aspects of prototyping, scripting and developmental testing.
(2) The resources needed for project management were minimal—about £2000 or 5%.

(3) The video production including the hire of a film crew, lighting, professional actors, and the initial video editing accounted for a further £10 000 (approximately 30%).
(4) The costs attributable to disc production—premastering, pressing the master disc and making 100 copies—were £5000 (15%).
(5) The software components were responsible for £6000 of staff time (20%). This part of the budget covered the development of the prototype CBT package and its metamorphosis into the final controlling program.
(6) Finally, the costs of the hardware needed—the videodisc player, microcomputer and monitor—were approximately £2000 (5%).

8.12 FUTURE DEVELOPMENTS

Computer control of the disc is the key to future development of this package. The current version provides inservice training in handling passengers, by taking the trainees through a sequence of eight situations and allowing them, singly and in small groups, to explore different courses of action. With small modifications to the computer program, the same package could be used to screen potential recruits, to see whether they are likely to do well in handling difficult passengers. Better selection might mean less need for training.

Somewhat to our surprise, the package is also being used for customer care training outside the transport industry, for example in the training of Post Office branch managers. It transpires that all but one of the eight episodes have direct analogies in the Post Office and that this package stimulates helpful discussion among their trainees. Clearly, there are numerous possibilities for variants of the package, using the same basic technique in different situations.

8.13 INTERPERSONAL SKILLS AND TECHNOLOGY BASED TRAINING

If we ask a teacher or trainer to describe their mental picture of CBL, we typically get an image of a single learner, sometimes in a language laboratory-like environment, sometimes in their own private place of study, working with a personal computer, usually through some drill and practice or package that resembles programmed learning delivered on the screen. Individualised learning has become isolated learning. There are some very effective ways in which this isolation can be overcome: for example, by arranging that a small group of learners (say three or four) work together with one microcomputer, discussing what they are doing, often teaching each other, and arriving at group decisions about what to do next. This approach has the dual advantage of reducing the numbers of workstations required for a given number of students, as well as making learning a more social activity.

Computer-based learning has traditionally concentrated on applications in mathematics, the hard sciences, aspects of business studies, and similar, fairly clear-cut topics with a high numerical content. In part this was due to the early perception of the computer as an arithmetic engine intelligible only to technologists. The association between computer-based learning and programmed learning tended to make materials prescriptive and more effective for those topics that could be broken down into a sequence of small steps. The growth of computer-based simulations also favoured the mathematical model and, although there were a number of discrete, decision-taking simulations in the form of action mazes these too tended to be based on a black and white, right and wrong, model of reality. Most of the applications of interactive video have similarly been in procedural training or in the provision of structured information.

These historical trends, coupled with a real concern about the impersonal aspects have caused educational technologists to shy away from technology-based training for interpersonal skills. Yet, on closer examination, we can make a case for the use of interactive video, not as a whole solution, but as a component in the learning package. Training in interpersonal skills—working with others, committee meetings, supervision, leadership styles, interviewing, racism, and so on—presents many of the same problems as learning in other areas, for example distance learning, just in time learning (where the learning/training is made available just before the student needs to exercise that knowledge or skill), and privacy of risk. Some components of the overall training could be delivered through technology, if it were possible to humanise the interaction, and enrich it with the non-verbal cues that are a crucial part of interpersonal communications.

However, there is an inherent danger. As we saw earlier, different trigger episodes affect different emotional levels and, while in most cases the initial feelings can be exposed and discussed without too much difficulty, the process becomes more sensitive the further one tries to dig down into peoples' emotions. We know from practical experience of using linear trigger tapes with groups of trainees, that the technique has a capacity to hurt. For example, the trainee may experience an unpleasant emotion and recognise that it was caused by the kind of behaviour that they have shown to others in the past. This recognition can be very distressing and the trainer then has a responsibility to repair the damage. There is, therefore, a risk in using packaged interpersonal skills material of causing hurt which cannot be put right by the package on its own, or by the trainee's immediate colleagues. This danger has caused us to avoid trigger episodes which might stir any deep emotional levels, in the bus crews package and in the designs for other interpersonal skills discs.

The success of the bus crews package indicates that, with imagination and careful scripting, and with video to provide the non-verbal cues, an interactive video package can provide some of the feel of a human interaction and can increase the trainee's awareness that there are different ways of dealing with interactions between people. However, some colleagues find the suggestion that interpersonal skills can be taught or learned by such impersonal means extremely dubious, and the wider application of this technique is still open to debate.

A dialogue with a person seen and heard on a video screen, where the user is communicating by speech in a subset of natural language is much more natural than one that is carried out in telegraphese through a keyboard and a display screen full of text and crude graphics. It is not even necessary that the dialogue be precise. Listen carefully to two people engaged in a dialogue and you will see two phenomena. Firstly, that they are in fact engaged in two interleaved (and possibly unrelated) monologues when each waits only for the other to pause for breath before continuing with their own monologue. Secondly, that where they are interacting, they are remarkably tolerant of ambiguities: if one does not understand what the other has said (perhaps due to inattention) or does not wish to respond, then they will continue with the response that they would like to make anyway. This provides the instructional designer with a way out of awkward situations where, because of the limitations on our ability to process and understand natural language with machines, the user's input cannot be recognised or where there is no relevant response that can be made. However, it should not be taken as a legitimate excuse for poor response matching. Agony aunts advise those who seek success in attracting the opposite sex, that they should try to become good listeners, to concentrate on what their partner is saying, and to respond to their interests. In interactive video, as in real dialogue between two people, there is nothing as fascinating as a partner who listens and really tries to understand.

ACKNOWLEDGEMENTS

Thanks are due to the Local Government Training Board for supporting the development of this training package, and to my colleagues who worked on its design and implementation, particularly Allan Schofield, George Delf, Tony Hardwick and Steve Cadwagan.

REFERENCES

Boud, D. and Pearson, M. (1978) *Bringing Reality into the Classroom: The Use of Trigger Films in Introducing Socio-emotional Aspects of Learning in the Health Sciences,* Tertiary Education Research Centre, University of New South Wales, Australia.

Boud, D. and Pearson, M. (1979) The trigger film: a stimulus for affective learning, *PLET,* 16(1).

Harris, T. A. (1973) *I'm OK—You're OK,* Pan Books, London (previously published as *The Book of Choice,* Jonathan Cape, London, 1970.)

Kagan, N. (1975) Influencing human interaction—eleven years with IPR, *The Canadian Counsellor,* 9.

Schofield, A. (1982) Call Yourself a Manager?—a new approach to using simulation in management training, in L. Gray and I. Waitt (eds),

Perspectives on Academic Gaming and Simulation 7: Simulation in Management and Business Education, Kogan Page, London.

Weil, S. and Schofield, A. (1984) *Integrating Theory and Practice: the Use of Triggers in Professional Education and Training,* Centre for Staff Development in Higher Education, London.

9

The creation of an integrated IVD training curriculum

Richard C. Smith

Industrial and governmental decision-makers are moving toward interactive videodisc as a solution to specific training problems which exist in the organisation. Those problems often include high worker turnover rate, lack of standardised training throughout the organisation, and dissatisfaction with current job performance. The State of Florida's umbrella social work agency recognised all these problems in the early 1980s, and within three years was implementing statewide a 160-hour training curriculum which wove together interactive videodisc, elements of computer-based training, and printed workbooks. We discuss here the University of West Florida's creation of that curriculum and also review the design strategies and lessons learned from the experience.

9.1 INTRODUCTION

The Office for Interactive Technology and Training (OITT) of the University of West Florida was organised in 1981 to create a 160-hour interactive videodisc training programme for Florida's Department of Health and Rehabilitative Services, the single largest agency within the state government. The training was to be for newly hired workers in the federally-funded Aid to Families with Dependent Children (AFDC) programme, itself the largest (annual disbursements approximately $230 million) programme administered within the state.

The training was to be the first within HRS to use new technology, and one of the major initial tasks was to devise a plan for the introduction of the equipment in offices traditionally staffed by people rather than machines.

The AFDC project was completed in September 1983, within the delivery of nine videodisc sides, eight trainee reference manuals and more than fifty minidiskettes of computer software (Smith, 1983; 1984a; 1984b; 1984c). All of the design work, scripting, programming and printing was done in-house within the University, while the video production was contracted elsewhere. The project can best be characterised as a CAL project, but the use of interactive videodisc as an integral component gives it a different flavour. We pay particular attention in this chapter to the video components of the training.

Other programme offices within HRS, notably Children's Medical Services (CMS), have also installed a hardware base for the delivery of interactive videodisc training, and as of 1986 has contracted for, and is using, a dozen or more shorter training programmes. Many of the experiences and suggestions within this chapter reflects OITT's experience in developing CMS courseware as well.

9.2 PLANNING

An IVD training programme is subject to the same curriculum development cycle that applies to any training segment. The inclusion of videodisc, however, with its attendant technical aspects, adds to the burden of development. The following points illustrate some of the additional problems to be considered.

1. If IVD training is new to the trainee, then there must be a basic introduction to the equipment itself. This is often accomplished with a separate curriculum, which may already exist. Several operational details must be covered, such as: the location of the on/off switch; the desired sequence and precautions for loading the videodisc and computer diskettes; what to do in case of trouble. This introduction is keyed to the particular equipment being used for training delivery; different equipment combinations will require different instructions. There may be practice exercises included to help newcomers overcome initial hesitancy (if not outright fear) at approaching a computer keyboard.

2. If the new training is a follow-on to an existing sequence of courses, then care is needed to ensure that the new training follows the same response rules as previous training. If, for example, previous work has accustomed the trainee to use 'single keystroke' responses (with no ‹enter› or ‹carriage return› required), then the designer of new training should avoid imposing new habits. Likewise, if the trainee is accustomed to asking for help in a certain way, for example by pressing a particular key, then that facility should be incorporated in the new training. IVD is unique among training media in its high degree of interactivity, and a trainee's habits are formed and hardened at each training session. Designers of IVD training ignore these habits only at the expense of their training's effectiveness.

3. Course management procedures should be carefully considered. IVD is an individual exercise, usually self-paced, which raises a variety of questions. Where should the materials be kept? How does the trainee obtain and return them? Who monitors student progress, and to what purpose? Often the materials are checked out to the trainee by a learning centre supervisor, who can maintain the required use logs. In other situations, the trainee is allowed unsupervised access to the materials, in which case it is

often the responsibility of the computer materials themselves to record time-on-task, lesson progress and other management details.

4. Throughout all the initial planning, the course Prescriber (the agency which specifies and uses the training) and the Provider (the group which designs and produces the training) must constantly be on guard against using key phrases or jargon which may have different meanings to each planning participant. The Prescriber of one early curriculum for which OITT was the Provider had specified early in the discussion that the curriculum was to be 'menu-driven'. OITT planners thought they understood this requirement clearly, and designed a series of lessons which could be selected at the trainee's choice, with return to menu at the conclusion of each lesson. It later developed that the Prescriber meant 'an organizational system just like the one we used in curriculum XYZ, which included menus'. This previous system (with which OITT was unfamiliar) included not only menus, but a rigid hierarchy of lessons and sublessons from which there was no escape until the trainee had viewed each and every segment, and had satisfactorily completed a segment test on each. 'Menu-driven' was clearly a phrase which had precise, but different, meanings to each member of the planning team.

5. It is much too easy to pass through the planning stage casually and with an incomplete written record of what has been agreed. It is too easy to lapse into a mind state of 'we'll straighten that out when we get there'. Six months later, 'when we get there', it is long forgotten that there is an important unresolved question, with the eventual result that either the Provider or the Prescriber is surprised and displeased, both of which are undesirable results.

6. A major cause of such misunderstanding is that, while the Provider is usually under 100% contract to work on the project, the Prescriber is simply sandwiching the project into a day which is already too full with other responsibilities. The Prescriber's representative may allocate a morning conference to joint planning with the Provider, thinking that this is a major time commitment, while in reality the planning described above may take several full days of intensive work. This situation has been described (Wright, 1986) as the 'I'm ready to play now' syndrome, in which the Prescriber, having casually agreed to decisions made early in the project, returns six months later to confess that only now has he or she actually read the material, and that it cannot be done as agreed upon, the required changes bringing with them enormous costs in time and money.

These examples serve to point up the crucial need for committed communication between Provider and Prescriber, not only at the beginning of a project, but throughout the work as well. Such communication can take place in face-to-face meetings, telephone conversations, written correspondence. In all cases, however, the Provider must undertake to maintain a written record of what was decided, when and by whom, and to maintain this information in a retrievable form. It is not enough simply to record that 'After much discussion we agreed to use a Menu system', but rather the discussion must be summarised, relevant points recorded, and a full description made of the agreement. It is true that this 'stenographic' work requires effort which otherwise might be applied to producing the training materials, but a Provider needs only one experience of long evenings and weekends correcting a major misunderstanding in order to see the advantage of exhaustive communication.

9.3 SPECIAL IVD CHOICES FOR THE PRESCRIBER/PROVIDER

Any training curriculum requires early agreement on course content and instructional design. An IVD project requires in addition co-operative specification of equipment and computer.

It is rare that a Provider is permitted to specify the delivery hardware for the curriculum. In those cases the instructional design can proceed with only a minimum of external constraints, and the hardware can then be chosen to implement the design. In this best-of-all-possible-worlds the instructional design drives the entire system, which is chosen simply for its effectiveness in delivering the training at hand.

It is seldom, however, that this happy arrangement can occur. It is more often the case that the Prescriber already has IVD hardware installed and some courseware running. The Prescriber has already purchased the equipment, the units are already installed in a training room, and it becomes the Provider's task to produce training which can be delivered on the existing installation. In these early days of IVD development, there is no agreement as to a standard equipment configuration. One videodisc player will have a longer search time than another. The screen resolution of one custom installation may exceed the resolution of another installation. One system may have graphics printers available at all instructional stations, while another may have alphanumeric printers, and a third may have no printers at all.

These capabilities all form constraints which limit the instructional design and its implementation, and therefore a first task of any design team must be to understand fully the hardware capabilities and limitations of the delivery system.

Our experience at OITT indicates that many course Prescribers cannot understand why we must ask so many questions about the hardware, thinking perhaps that all hardware is roughly equivalent. Questions about the gross characteristics are obvious: Is there a keyboard? Touchscreen? Light pen? How many disc drives? Is there a hard disc, and if so, what is its capacity? What videodisc player is used? How is it interfaced to the computer?

There is somewhat more latitude in the specification of a computer language or authoring system, which can often be made independently of the equipment. On the other hand, an experienced Prescriber may already have several courses running which are written in one language, and may specify that language for new courses as well, in order to keep maintenance time and costs to a minimum. Naturally the Provider must know the details of the language to be used, not simply at production time but at planning time as well. If the specified language does not easily scan open-ended answers for keywords, then clearly that feature must not be included in the instructional design. Perhaps the language provides for branching only at the moment of response, when the designer may want to programme a later branch depending on current response. Perhaps the designer wants to base an entire exercise on a multiple-matching capability, but discovers too late that the language does not support this.

It is the business of the Provider to explore all these topics at the beginning of a project, and to instruct the project team carefully concerning the overall capabilities of the delivery system. Thus a primary rule begins to emerge: *Develop courseware with a specific delivery system in mind.*

9.4 INTEGRATED COURSE CREATION

OITT has had good success with an integrated approach to the process of course creation. In this approach, the coursewriter is given full responsibility for the entire segment of course being developed. The same person creates the training situation in the mind, visualises the talent and props to be used, hears the words being spoken, sees the view angles and knows how the trainee will interact with the screen. If a computertext screen is to be used, then the writer determines the words, the spacing, the rhythm of presentation. As choices are developed, the writer determines the branching specifications as well as the form of remediation to be used.

The writer must have clearly in mind the consequences desired as a result of a particular learner response. Thus if a keyboard response is one choice, then the programme flow must be clear in the writer's mind; alternative choices generate alternative responses. We have never been successful in splitting the writing responsibilities among specialists in narrative, screen design, branching, etc. Nor have we achieved success in writing a first, rough, linear script with the idea of coming back later to convert it to a branched interactive script.

Being committed to the idea of asking scriptwriters to see the entire project in the imagination, it becomes necessary to provide a mechanism, a common communication medium, for moving those ideas out of the mind to a place where others can see it, respond to it, correct it. This mechanism is a preprinted form, which we have called a scriptpage and others a Super StoryBoard, on which are provided ways to describe the mind's eye as it might appear to the delivery system. The scriptpage is designed to reflect all the capabilities of the delivery system, and therefore the page form will be different for each system. A particular scriptpage design will certainly include areas for description of visuals and dialogue. It includes page identification and a template for branching specification. It must include a place for specification of delivery mode (computer, videodisc, graphics, etc.) and any other system characteristics which will be used by the training.

If the software system calls for data in a particular way, then the scriptpage should call for the specification in a similar way. Fig. 9.1 is the scriptpage used for the simple Apple delivery system used in the AFDC project, while Fig. 9.2, is a page developed for use with the IBM InfoWindow system. The two pages clearly differ in complexity, which reflects the difference in complexity of the delivery systems themselves.

In each of these two examples, the page specifies what is to appear on the trainee screen, whether computer-generated or from the videodisc, what is to be heard, whether synthesised computer music or spoken dialogue, and the page numbers which immediately precede or follow. Branching is specified fully. The master script book is thus built a page at a time, and copies are made from it as needed. The system is not 100% effective at keeping people from working from outdated scripts, but it comes close. What is really needed is a word-processing system which operates on the script as a common data base. The script could be updated by designer, writer or programmer, and by definition the only script version is the current one. At the present time (1986) a few proprietary authoring systems are beginning to appear with these characteristics.

If course writers are to be given the responsibility of integrated course preparation, then they must have a familiarity with the delivery system which allows them to see the course unfold in their minds' eye. They must be able to visualise text appearing on the screen in the proper place and in the proper size and colour. If there is to be windowed video material simultaneously present, the writer must have that capability clearly in mind. If user response is required at a certain point, then the writer must know which types of response systems are available for specification. In a given instructional situation, the same writer would probably conceive a different script for a different delivery system. We find that this approach gives writers a sense of ownership and global responsibility for the curriculum.

The writers themselves must be carefully trained in the capabilities of the delivery system. They must be taught details of branching, be given an understanding of what is and is not possible. Full training of a novice videodisc writer can take a week or more. Nevetherless it is our experience that good writers are highly creative individuals, and from them come some of the best instructional strategies.

9.5 COMPOSITION OF STAFF

Probably the minimum number of persons which can produce computer/videodisc material is three: a designer/writer, a programmer and a video producer. The in-house professional staff for our project hovers around ten, which does not include any of the contracted video production work. The communication links between and among these workers must be designed and nurtured, and it is a difficult job. There may be many instructional modules in a particular training package, with three or four under active

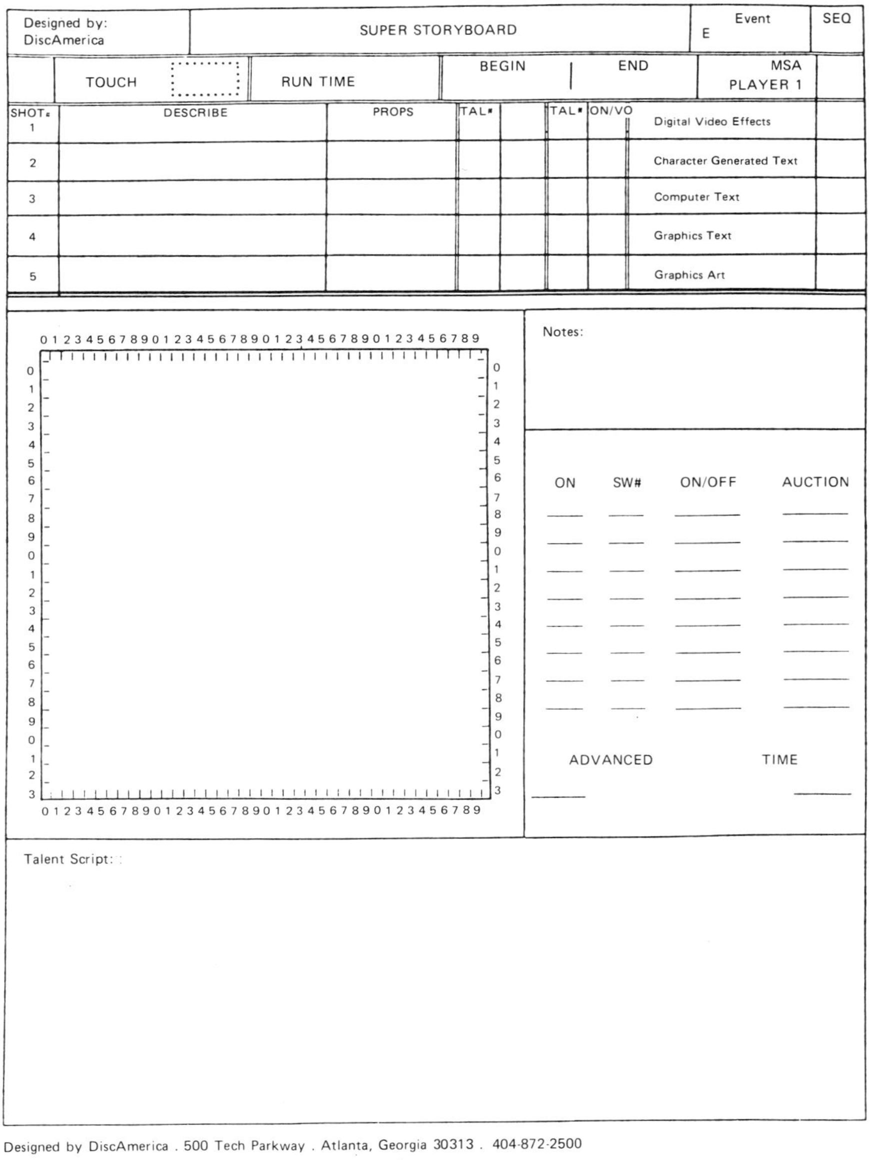
Designed by: DiscAmerica
SUPER STORYBOARD
E
Event
SEQ
TOUCH
RUN TIME
BEGIN
END
MSA PLAYER 1

SHOT#	DESCRIBE	PROPS	TAL#		TAL#	ON/VO	
1							Digital Video Effects
2							Character Generated Text
3							Computer Text
4							Graphics Text
5							Graphics Art

0 1 2 3 4 5 6 7 8 9 0 1 2 3 4 5 6 7 8 9 0 1 2 3 4 5 6 7 8 9 0 1 2 3 4 5 6 7 8 9

Notes:

ON	SW#	ON/OFF	AUCTION

ADVANCED
TIME

Talent Script:

Designed by DiscAmerica . 500 Tech Parkway . Atlanta, Georgia 30313 . 404-872-2500

Fig. 9.1.— Scriptpage developed for an Apple delivery system.

development at any one time. The designers are working on the beginnings of the latest module, the writers are producing script for another, the video producers are working on a third, while the programmers are at work on a fourth. And all the while the client is making changes everywhere. It is

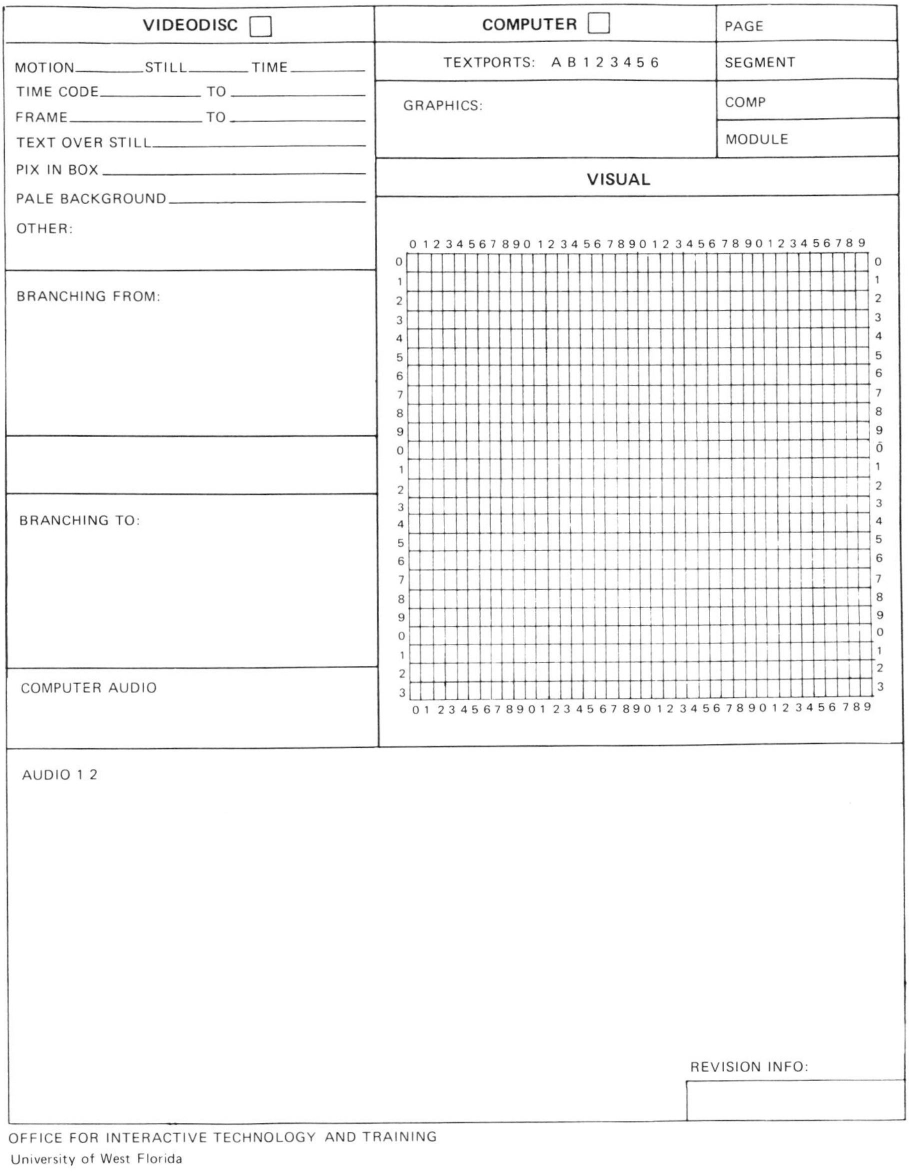
VIDEODISC ☐
MOTION______STILL______TIME______
TIME CODE__________ TO __________
FRAME__________ TO __________
TEXT OVER STILL__________
PIX IN BOX __________
PALE BACKGROUND__________
OTHER:
BRANCHING FROM:
BRANCHING TO:
COMPUTER AUDIO
COMPUTER ☐
TEXTPORTS: A B 1 2 3 4 5 6
GRAPHICS:
PAGE
SEGMENT
COMP
MODULE
VISUAL
0 1 2 3 4 5 6 7 8 9 0 1 2 3 4 5 6 7 8 9 0 1 2 3 4 5 6 7 8 9 0 1 2 3 4 5 6 7 8 9
AUDIO 1 2
REVISION INFO:
OFFICE FOR INTERACTIVE TECHNOLOGY AND TRAINING
University of West Florida

Fig. 9.2 — Scriptpage developed for an IBM delivery system.

crucial to know what (and where) the current version is, and to define and use a common medium of communication. Fred Brooks (1975) devoted an entire chapter to this communication problem in his classic book of essays, *The Mythical Man-Month*.

9.6 SELECTION OF MEDIA MIX

It is important to remember that a decision to use interactive videodisc for training does not require the designer to abandon all other media. In fact, there are many kinds of content which are best suited to that 400-year-old technology: the printed page. The best example of this sort of content is factual reference material, the kind of content which asks to be underlined, taken home, clipped in a reference book, or otherwise owned by the trainee. Even in those cases when most of the instruction is presented interactively at the computer console, there can be advantage in having printed reference or summary material available to the learner for parallel reference. Where printed material is included in the training, reference should be made to it in the video portion so that the two media are seen as separate parts of the same training curriculum.

The interactive video delivery mode provides other types of media as well. One 'medium' is Audio Channel 2, which we have found to be a valuable resource not only for music and sound effects to accompany computer text or animation sequences but also as a highly engaging job simulator, particularly in cases when telephone or other audio practice is part of the training to be accomplished. For example, the screen may be held motionless with only a title on it, while aural information is presented to the trainee, slowly at first, then more rapidly, so that the trainee gains experience in active listening.

The point to be made here is that there are many media available to the designer: video motion, video still, stand-alone audio, computer, text, graphics, animation, the printed page, and all should be considered for delivery of a specific training point. In special defence of the printed page's role, we note that even computer programmers insist on having hard copy to work with; should non-technical trainees be asked to get along with less? This need has been recognised earlier, and the MIT Movie Manual (Lippman and Backer, 1982) project is one example of a technological response.

9.7 THE RELATIONSHIP BETWEEN PROVIDER AND PRESCRIBER

The relationship between courseware Providers and the approving Prescriber is one which deserves considerable attention. The need of the Provider to educate the Prescriber has been addressed earlier. The need, however, is ongoing and not completed in the early planning stage. Our experience has been that Prescribers often have little understanding of the time and budget constraints imposed by a videodisc development project. Thus we sometimes hear requests such as 'Let's do that scene on location in the mountains', or 'Can't you make that lead-in video sequence a little fancier with swirling and twisting special effects like I saw on television last night?' when such a modification would consume the entire video production budget. Our best response has been simply to quote the estimated price and ask for a decision on how the available funds should be spent.

9.8 PROJECT SCHEDULING

Perhaps the most common approach to project scheduling is to start at the beginning and go as fast as possible until it is finished. This approach has one advantage: it is simple and everyone understands it. Unfortunately, it can be used only where there are not time or resource constraints, and most of those projects have already been done. A greatly preferable alternative is to use the heavy artillery of the Critical Path Method (CPM) or its cousin, Performance Evaluation and Review Technique (PERT). These approaches are well known to industrial engineers, general construction contractors, and to large corporations, but their use does not seem to be widespread in the design of training projects (Smith, 1984d). It is perhaps appropriate here to review the concept of the Critical Path Method and the reasons for using it.

CPM (not to be confused with CP/M, Control Program for Microcomputers) requires project managers to specify, in advance, which activities must come before which, and how much time should be allowed for their completion. The chain of sequential activities which together requires the longest time is said to form the Critical Path, since a delay in completion of any of these activities will delay the entire chain and hence the project. The graphical representation of all linked activities is called the project network. Deadline dates can be superimposed on the network, and it becomes clear which deadlines can be met and which cannot. The activity network for the large AFDC project included almost 400 separate but interlinked activities, and more than thirty separate deadlines.

An important queston is, 'What do I do if I discover that the deadlines can't be met?' There are several alternatives. You can reassign staff from non-critical to critical activities; you can agree to do less in the available time; or you can request a time extension. Probably the one thing you ought not to do is hire more people to do the work. Fred Brooks (1975) has considered this question from the point of view of training the new people and establishing and maintaining the increased number of communication linkages, and as a result formulated Brook's law 'Adding manpower to a late software project makes it later'.

9.9 PRODUCTION DATABASE

One task which our development team tries to undertake is the compilation of the production database, an assembly of information which is often left to the video producer. The Production Database is the compilation of all information needed by the video producer. It includes such esoterica as shotlist, props required by shot, actors used in a given shot, whether they are to be on-camera or off-camera, and other details. The scriptpage of Fig. 9.2 shows spaces for the specification of such items. It is our belief that the generation of this information comes naturally while the script is being created by the writer, and that this stage is a natural one for the compilation of the information. This is information which can be handed over to the producer, without which the producer would have to develop one at increased cost and time. Given that the goal of the training creator is to minimise expenditure of time and money, it makes good sense to do this operation where it is cheapest. The process works best where the video producer is an active early member of the design team.

9.10 CONCLUSION

This chapter has addressed some of the techniques that OITT has found useful in producing workable and effective IVD training curricula, among them the integrated scriptpage, the use of Critical Path scheduling methods, and the early integration of the video producer into the training team. Perhaps even more important than these specific details is the need to build and maintain high communication levels, not only between the Prescriber and the Provider, but within the development team itself. It is essential to develop shared ownership of the training product, so that all are willing to do what is necessary to finish the job on time and within budget, and to ensure that no one is surprised by any feature of the project as it is finally delivered.

REFERENCES

Brooks, Jr., F. P. (1975) *The Mythical Man-Month,* Addison-Wesley.

Lippman, A. and Backer, D. S. (1982) Personalized aids for training: an assault on publishing, *Proceedings of the Fourth Annual Conference on Video Learning Systems,* Society for Applied Learning Technology, Warrenton, VA.

Smith, R. C. (1983) Development of computer assisted learning videodisc based training for newly-hired workers in Florida's umbrella social work agency, *Proceedings of the Conference on Interactive Instruction Delivery,* Society for Applied Learning Technology, Warrenton, VA, 9–11 February 1983.

Smith, R. C. (1984a) Full scale pilot testing of Florida's videodisc training project, *Proceedings of the Second Conference on Interactive Instruction Delivery,* Society for Applied Learning Technology, Warrenton, VA, 15–17 February 1984.

Smith, R. C. (1984b) First results from Florida's interactive training program, *News,* **6,** 1. Videodisc Design/Production Group, University of Nebraska, Lincoln.

Smith, R. C. (1984c) University of West Florida training project, *Videodisc Monitor,* **2,** 12–14.

Smith, R. C. (1984d) Management of a microcomputer-assisted learning project, *Comput. Educ.,* **8,** 1, 197–201.

Wright, E. (1986) The Jello Plan and other pitfalls (unpublished).

Part 2

Exploiting the technology

In the early days of the use of a new technology it is important for practitioners to focus on what the technology can do if it is to be fully explored and exploited, even though this inevitably leads to charges of the innovations being technology-led, and therefore user-irrelevant. All the authors in this book have addressed themselves to the user's needs in their development of interactive media materials, but we cannot deny the fact that the technology both leads and constrains. The chapters in Part 2 confront this issue and consider both the potential offered by interactive media — such as the capacity for storage and access of pictorial information, the enhancement of video by computers, the enhancement of computers by video — and the constraints they impose — such as their economic feasibility, the need for organisation and planning, the limitations of existing hardware and software.

What is the potential of interactive video? Rupert Dowling and Bert Camstra chart the domain of hardware for interactive media systems, relating the requirements of education and training to a classification of levels of interactivity, and to the types of systems and formats available. Martin Wright and David Nelson bring their experience of the video production side of interactive video to an analysis of how the new tools on offer can be exploited by the producer to dramatically enhance the user's experience of video-based information.

And the constraints? Andrew Hart considers the pedagogical benefits of interactive video against the background of a higher education system that is progressively losing resources and finding it more difficult than ever to redirect existing resources towards the kind of front-end development that these packaged materials require. Is it economically feasible for education? Hart concludes that generic discs may provide the only solution, whereas Colin Mably, considering IV from the even more impoverished viewpoint of the school system, suggests that both logistic and economic realities point towards the stand-alone commercially-produced disc as the most likely educational usage.

The realities of production, both the successes and the difficulties, are recounted in the final two chapters. Peter Armstrong vividly recreates the battle to persuade the technology to meet the pedagogic ambitions of the Domesday disc. One of the virtues of the videodisc is that it can make vast quantities of information accessible to the user at the touch of a button, but behind these glib phrases lies the reality of trying to handle that volume of information in a way that conforms to the needs of both the technology and the user. Similarly, Colin Jackson takes us through an implementation of the excellent idea of trying to combine two existing and apparently compatible technologies, interactive video and videotext, and exposes the resistance the technology puts up to any such liaison. Practitioners must expect that no matter how much the potential of the technology beckons, the constraints it imposes will always curtail their most imaginative ideas.

10

A question of delivery — an outline classification of interactive video delivery systems

Rupert Dowling and Bert Camstra

10.1 INTRODUCTION

The evolution of interactive video has been marked by confusion on the part of would-be practitioners when faced with an endless choice of video formats, computers, interfaces, programming languages and authoring systems. Furthermore, no taxonomy yet exists which could effectively describe the potential of this powerful new medium (Lindsey, 1984). As one reviewer put it,

> The result of this muddled situation is that interactive video programmes must be tailored at the production stage to suit a specific package of computer and video hardware and software . . . the programs for one system will often not run on another. In the circumstances it is surprising that interactive video has had any success. (Fox, 1985).

The reason why IV has survived this stage is that, while the choices still remain wide, popular acceptance of, for example, laser disc players with an RS232 interface has led to many *de facto* standards within the industry. At the same time, the contemporaneously emerging microcomputer industry has settled to see the predominance of the IBM PC and compatible machines, and many IV products have been able to concentrate on this market. This is not to say that IV no longer exists, or should exist, on other systems, or using media other than laser disc; it is simply that the choice is now clearer, and a standard default can be said to exist.

More than anything, this standardisation has given clarity to people's perceptions of what interactive video is. Many early developers saw the potential of IV as an enhanced form of computer-based training (CBT), and predicted that it would eventually replace CBT altogether. Others saw IV as essentially a video medium with simple user functions provided through a key-pad. This uneasy marriage of self-paced branching (CBT) and a carefully edited linear image (video) led to many different hardware and software combinations, often with different goals.

> Too many schools still follow a well-established recipe for disaster; first policy-makers choose the hardware, then decide on the software. They then teach teachers and other staff how to use the system, and finally, everybody tries to figure out what the goals of system utilization are to be and whether the system already in place can help meet these goals. (Chorover, 1984).

IV is no longer such an ill-defined medium, nor does it depend on CBT for definition. Instead, IV has matured as a unique field, with many applications outside training, and with its own disciplines and style. CBT has, if anything, benefitted from IV — as the successes and failures of each has crystallised people's understanding of CBT's own features and capabilities.

The development of hardware systems and the acceptance of standards has continued hand-in-glove with the constant search for a definition of what interactive video *is*, each contributing to the other. This chapter looks at some of these systems and attempts to outline the range of logistical solutions that have been used, and are being used, to deliver interactive video programmes. (We have attempted to give these in a roughly chronological order, though the practice has been somewhat more haphazard than it may appear below.)

First let us look at two things to consider when classifying any IV programme — how it is to be used and the level of interactivity involved.

10.2 INTERACTIVE VIDEO APPLICATIONS

Bayard-White (1985, p. 2) has defined four broad categories into which 'the current uses of IV fall':

— Training/Education
— Information Storage
— Point of Sale
— Games

This chapter will concentrate on the perspective of interactive video in education and training. There are three reasons for this. Firstly, it is in this field that IV has excited most attention, as witnessed by the growing number of governmental and state-sponsored reports on the subject, some of which are given in the Bibliography. Secondly, it is this application which has demanded most of the emerging technology, in terms of rapid and complex branching structures, 'intelligent' question and answer mechanisms, ease of transportability across systems and interfacing with other hardware 'add-ons' for example for complex or unusual simulations. Lastly, the lines between the categories above often become blurred, and Training and

Education may be seen as an umbrella category which often encompasses design features and technological requirements common to one or more of the other three.

To illustrate this last point, let us look briefly at each category in turn.

10.2.1 Information storage

The Public Archives of Canada (Mole and Laugham, 1982) has estimated that a single laser disc is capable of holding 40 000 pages of text, 5000 photographs, twelve minutes of moving footage, eight hours of narrated film strip (presented at two frames per minute) and 1000 microcomputer programs.

Early applications of CD-ROM have shown that it is possible to store several complete *Encyclopaedia Britannicas* on one compact disc.

This massive storage capacity, with any part accessible within seconds, has obvious implications for databasing. However, it has also permeated a wider consumer market. The US National Gallery, for example, has produced a videodisc with still-frames of all its paintings — providing the user with an interactive 'tour' of the gallery. McDonnell Douglas found that the maintenance and repair manuals for their aircraft had grown to over one million pages. They now use videodisc based manuals accessed via a radio mounted in a helmet fitted with video/audio monitors. This allows maintenance staff access to information while on the job, keeping their hands free to perform their task.

Here the line between simple information storage and training applications already begins to blur. Many applications exist in art, such as a videodisc database of da Vinci's drawings (produced by IBM Italy). Whether these are delineated as information storage or education clearly depends on their usage.

10.2.2 Point of sale

Many large stores, such as Sears Roebuck in the US and Mothercare in the UK, use videodisc to provide their customers with interactive access to product information in the store. Here again, trainers have been quick to spot the simple crossover from this to product training for sales staff and dealers. IBM have used a disc designed for sales training to demonstrate the capabilities of interactive video at exhibitions. Another example is Istel Ltd, a service company owned by British Leyland, who use the same discs with different controlling programs for point-of-sale, dealer training and cataloguing applications (Hutt, 1986).

10.2.3 Games

It is interesting to note that, where open learning (nowadays given the contrived acronym PBL for 'paper-based learning') is seen to be the precursor of CBT and interactive video, in the field of computer games the clock has turned backwards. The popularity of arcade games has seen a resurgence of 'Make Your Own Adventure' books, based on the branching techniques of open learning.

IV producers have successfully tackled this large consumer entertainment field with programs such as VIDMAX's 'MysteryDisc' series. However, just as an increasing educational note has crept into many of the arcade games, so much of the home entertainment field of videodiscs is concerned with 'Teach Yourself' topics such as golf, gardening, keeping fit, etc.

If educational objectives do seem (to the more fun-loving and frivolous of us) to have insinuated their way into computer arcade games such as 'TrivBusters', where education *is* the objective, the style and the technique of video games can often enhance motivation and enjoyment. Visitors wishing to improve their knowledge of London can use a videodisc-based program called 'The London Game', on permanent display in London's Trocadero centre.

Larry Wilson, of Wilson Learning Corporation, describes watching his son's growing addiction and application to a computer game:

> The biggest problems that schools have are boredom, fear of failure, and lack of relevancy. These games, on the other hand, were exciting, held the promise of success through learning from error, and had their own kind of intrinsic relevancy. The video arcade was an environment where natural learning thrived. (Wilson, 1983)

Finally, within the single application area of education and training, Bayard-White (1985, p. 7) further identities for 'modes of use' for interactive video programs.

— As a class teaching tool, operated by the teacher/trainer
— As a group learning medium, studied and operated by groups of two to four people
— As an individualised tutor
— As a visual archive

Clearly, each of these usages involves different demands and constraints on the program and the delivery system. Many proponents of interactivity would claim that individualisation is a necessary effect of true interactivity and that therefore only the third mode is fully interactive. This then raises an important question for the beginning of any IV project. 'What level of interactivity is required?'

10.3 LEVELS OF INTERACTIVITY

The most commonly accepted classification of IV systems is that developed by Rod Daynes and the Nebraska Videodisc Design/Production Group. The Nebraska scale distinguishes between the interactive capabilities of different systems. It is therefore independent of considerations such as the video medium used (disc or tape), the hardware configuration, or the application of the program.

The scale describes five 'levels' of interactivity:

Level 0 No interactivity — what Parsloe (1983) calls 'Do Not Pass Go'. This level refers to simply watching a 'movie' straight through, from start to finish.

Level 1 This is the kind of manual 'interactivity' provided by video-tape players and domestic disc players, with no computer program involved. Freeze frame, scan, slow motion and step frame facilities are provided in forward and reverse mode, as well as random access (search) by frame number. These facilities are user-chosen, usually by means of a remote-control keypad.

Level 2 This is the first level providing true interactivity, in a limited form. As well as the features of level 1, level 2 systems offer a certain amount of programmed branching. This is by means of an onboard microprocessor in the video player, which can be either pre-programmed by the user or used to download instructions digitally encoded on videodiscs. Typical examples are the 'industrial' standard videodisc players, which have faster access times than 'domestic' players.

The simplicity and ease of use of level 2 systems — a videodisc player, monitor and keypad — make them ideal for applications such as point of sale and information storage. However, the limited memory of the onboard microprocessor (usually 5K) and the difficulty in updating a computer program stored on videodisc makes level 2 unsuitable for most educational applications.

Level 3 Level 3 describes true and versatile interactive video. This is achieved by interfacing a level 1 or 2 video player with an external computer either in response to a student's choice or according to paths predetermined by the designer. The most rudimentary systems at this level use two screens to display the video and computer images. At the upper end computer text, graphics and animations can not only be interposed with the video signal, but also overlaid upon it.

The external computer allows programs and information (such as student records) to be permanently stored in an easily changeable form. The larger processor memory lends itself to far more sophisticated branching and answer handling. Furthermore, a single video disc or tape may be used with several different driving programs. With careful planning this can greatly economise on video production costs.

Level 4 This level has been described variously, largely because it has been a 'sci-fi' ideal covering everything yet to come — that which realises the full potential of interactive video. Level 4 systems will contain the complete hardware and software environment necessary for authoring and delivery, complete with 'intelligent' tools for the inexperienced programmer. With the trend towards suppliers offering not just specialised interfaces or disc players, but integrated kits of compatible hardware and software, the reality of level 4 has moved much closer. However, many limitations still exist to the tools available. These are discussed in section 2.

To illustrate the applicability of the Nebraska scale, we can try to match it against the application areas defined above.

Basic information storage and retrieval applications may lie in the area of level 2, using a simple branching program loaded into the microprocessor of a videodisc player to allow the user to choose what he or she wants to see. Where complex branching decisions have to made, a level 3 system could be used to access a disc or tape through a database management system in the external computer.

Point of sale applications may also be level 2 or level 3. The nature of the user (customer) and the need for a simple, easy-to-use system, has made level 2 systems more popular, though the possibility of linking an external computer which can take orders, check stock, make reservations, etc. makes this an interesting level 3 application area.

Although games demand a high level of interactivity, most applications so far (such as the MyteryDisc series) have been at level 2. This is because of the lack of a standard 'domestic model' level 3 system. Once a system appears widespread in homes, this may be a major IV market.

Because of the demands they make of an IV system, listed above, training and educational applications usually occur at level 3. It is this field which is likely to push first to the realization of level 4 systems. Level 2 have been used successfully for some training programmes. British Airways used the Sony Responder system to train operators in the de-icing of aircraft. This system allows a basic controlling program to be read from the video-tape (U-Matic). (British Airways have also used disc-based systems for projects requiring 'complex branching' (Bayard-White, 1986).)

10.4 VIDEO EQUIPMENT

One obvious classification of existing IV systems is by the video medium used — disc or tape. Unfortunately, this is not as simple as it seems. There are several different formats of both mediums, not necessarily, and in fact rarely, compatible with one another. However, while standardisation has not yet been reached, practice has seen certain formats find more favour than others. It is enough here to briefly outline the different types, describing in detail the characteristics of those which have proved effective in application.

First, a brief mention of the different broadcast standards used in video recording and transmission, as we will refer to these.

10.4.1 Video formats

Essentially, there are three different sets of broadcasting standards in use around the world. These are

— NTSC Used in North America, Japan, the Bahamas and the Philippines. Developed in the US by the National Television Standards Committee.
— PAL (Phase Alternating Line). Used throughout most of Europe, South America, Australia and in parts of Africa and the Middle East.
— SECAM Used in France, USSR and parts of Africa and the Middle East. (The name is shortened from *Sequential couleur à memoire*.)

Although a SECAM video will only run on a PAL player in black and white, they are otherwise compatible, and therefore are usually linked together. Neither system is compatible, however, with NTSC. Most disc and tape players are only capable of handling one system — either NTSC or PAL/SECAM. This is often an important consideration for European producers, requiring videodisc mastering and pressing facilities in the US.

For a more detailed description of the different systems, see Parsloe (1983, pp. 43–53).

10.4.2 Videotape formats

Although shooting for videodisc is usually done using 2in or 1in tape formats, delivery of interactive video programs always uses videocassette. These come in two sizes: ¾in and ½in.

In terms of quality, the best of these is the ¾in — Sony's U-matic format. Systems which use this include Sony's RESPONDER and the FELIX system.

The availability of ½in domestic video-tape players, such as JVC's VHS and Sony's Betamax, has led to their use in many IV projects, using systems such as Scicon's CAVIS and Apple Super Pilot.

Video-tape formats have several disadvantages for IV. Although slow motion and step frame are often possible, they do not allow such fine control as a videodisc player with variable speeds. Search times can be extremely slow (30 seconds is not uncommon) and videocassette recorders (VCRs) are noisy, as the playback head disengages and engages again with the tape. Attempts at freeze frame and still frame give very poor picture quality and no audio.

VCRs do not typically have an onboard microprocessor, so tape-based IV systems only exist at levels 1 and 3 of the Nebraska scale.

Against this, videotape formats can be cheaper because video is often already available (Floyd, 1982). Using existing video in its existing form, however, compromises the IV designer seriously. A program that does not achieve the objectives set for it is never economical. Duke (1983)

suggests that although 'valuable experience' can be gained with tape-based systems, they should be thought of as 'stop-gap solutions with a do-it-yourself emphasis'.

10.4.3 Videodisc formats

Two different, incompatible, videodisc technologies exist — capacitance and laser. Capacitance disc players contain a stylus (there are different types) riding on the surface of the disc. The video signal is encoded as a series of pits in the disc's spiral track, causing a difference in capacitance between the stylus and the disc. Laser discs encode the signal as an analogue pattern of small pits, which are used to modulate the intensity of a laser beam reflected off the disc's surface.

RCA's early 'SelectaVision' discs and players did not allow still frame or frame addressability, and therefore were unsuitable for interactive applications, but the VHD system developed by JVC has been used, particularly in the UK, where it marketed by Thorn-EMI (Bayard-White, 1986, Directory, pp. 133–77). This is a 10in diameter double-sided disc. Fast and slow motion, in forward and reverse, are possible but, since each revolution of the disc contains two video frames, there is no freeze-frame facility. Still frames can be achieved by laying a frame down twice in one revolution.

One disadvantage of capacitance discs is that, since the stylus and the disc come in direct contact with each other, they are susceptible to wear. As Duke (1983, 6.6) points out,

> although a minimum disc life of 10 000 plays may appear reasonable, this equates to some few minutes only of playing time in still-frame mode.

Laser disc technology was introduced by Philips in 1972, and adopted as a standard format (known as LaserVision) by MCA, Pioneer, Sony and Hitachi.

For long-playing video, the disc can be mastered and operated at a constant linear velocity (CLV). In CLV mode there is one frame per revolution at the centre, and increasingly more towards the edge of the disc (LaserVision discs, unlike capacitance discs and audio records, play from the inside out). The playing allows almost two hours of video per double-sided disc, but no slow motion, still-frame or frame addressability (tracks are addressed by a time code instead).

Discs played at a constant angular velocity (1500 r.p.m. for PAL, 1800 r.p.m. for NTSC) contain about 30 minutes — 54 000 frames — of linear video per side. One revolution of the disc covers one frame of video. These CAV LaserVision discs have now become the popular standard for interactive video. 'Industrial' standard players of this type have all the features of a level 2 system — active play at variable speeds both backwards and forwards, freeze and still frames and rapid access of any frame — and many hardware and software packages exist to connect them to a range of external computers.

The one drawback still remaining in laser disc technology is the question of compatibility. While PAL VHD discs will play on an NTSC VHD player, and vice versa, this is not true with LaserVision. All the major manufacturers (Philips, Pioneer, Sony) produce both NTSC and PAL versions of their disc players, but publishers wishing to sell in both the US and Europe must master discs in both systems. So far, the response to this problem has come not from the hardware industry, but from the software sector. Recent IV authoring systems allow computer overlays on any video signal, irrespective of whether it is NTSC or PAL. This is discussed in more detail below.

It should also be noted that, while laser disc players made by different manufacturers are all able to play any laserdisc, differences in the onboard microprocessors used may cause compatibility problems if the controlling program is being down-loaded from the videodisc (in level 2 systems).

10.5 INTERACTIVE VIDEO SYSTEMS

Any typical interactive video system contains a video player (tape or disc), a monitor and a keypad or keyboard. Level 3 systems also contain a computer and a means of interfacing the computer and video player. Other components may be included, from computer peripherals such as a printer, mouse or touch screen to the complex control mechanisms of a flight simulator. The way in which these components are put together, and particularly the emphasis which is placed upon each, distinguishes between the usage and capabilities of different IV systems. To understand this let us recall how interactive video came about.

IV is the product of two technologies — computer and video. More particularly, it is the product of the impact of laser disc technology, with its faster and more accurate access times, upon the field of computer-based training. As video was standing at levels 0 and 1, and CBT was looking for more realistic ways to simulate real life, the two technologies met.

The point of this story is that two very different disciplines are involved. Video producers and CBT designers are both in the business of conveying information, but each in their own different way. Video producers initially found it hard to adapt to a medium where scenes carefully edited together could be 'remixed" (Worcester, 1983). Likewise, CBT authors were not used to the effective domains of video, or the use of audio tracks instead of the written word for commentary.

This dual-pronged approach on the new medium often led to a detectable difference in perspective from one application to another. At one end were the level 2 programmes, where short sequences of linear video, as well as stills, were organised using basic CBT branching and question and answer techniques — the latter usually simple, usually multiple choice. At the other end were CBT programs which treated video as an extra, outside, resource — as a pictorial database or an improvement on computer animation — but steered clear of the inherent affective domains involved. The greatest dilemma arose in that, while the claim of CBT and open learning had always been that the pace of the program was always controlled by the student, video by its nature is self-pacing — according to the wishes of the producer — even within a thirty-second sequence.

As these two perspectives influenced the development of IV systems, and in particular level 3 systems, three types of system emerged:

(1) 'Building block' systems.
(2) Dedicated systems.
(3) Software/Hardware 'slotable' systems.

10.5.1 'Building block' systems

Going back just a few years, we find that much of the discussion around interactive video concerns the hardware configurations available: whether tape or disc is most suitable to a particular need; choosing an economical, and readily available, microcomputer; finding an interface device that will make the two compatible. Computer programs at this time were often written in standard programming languages, such as BASIC or FORTRAN.

This 'building block' approach resulted in many combinations of the various video formats, micros, and interface devices being used. Video designers and trainers looking for an alternative to CBT first chose an appropriate video format and then looked for a computer and interface that would provide them with just enough control, at the right price. CBT programmers looked for players which could be interfaced with the programming environments they were used to, using proven authoring languages. Interactive video as a separately identifiable mature medium was still, as L'Allier (1983) called it, 'an elephant in search of a definition'.

CBT software had already begun to meet this problem. On the one hand were experienced programmers, who wanted powerful and versatile capabilites for authoring, akin to those they were used to in high level languages, but specifically appropriate to the CBT task. On the other were trainers and subject-matter experts who wanted to produce their own programs, quickly and easily, but without need of an extensive programming knowledge.

The results of this were authoring languages and authoring systems. Authoring languages are high-level programming languages which facilitate complex answer handling, branching, graphics and diagnostics, but which require programming expertise to use. Authoring systems are interactive packages which allow a non-programmer to create pages of text, questions and graphics, and to dictate simple branching structures and question and answer sequences.

Versions of both of these exist in interactive video. Authoring languages have extended to accommodate the range of commands needed to control videotape and disc players. Examples are Microtext, TenCORE and Microplato. Authoring systems allow branching programs etc. to be generated on floppy disc, or on a videotape as with the RESPONDER system. The authoring system with Scicon's CAVIS can also be used to generate videotex screens which can be presented separately or overlaid on the video image from a tape or disc. Many such systems are available. Some, like WICAT's WISE and BCD Associates' 'The Instructor' (marketed as IVL in Europe), have been developed for IV. Others, such as Apple Super Pilot, Mentor II and Microtext, are enhancements of CBT authoring systems. Some videodisc player manufacturers produce systems that may be used with the videodisc player's own microprocessor (level 2). Examples of these are Philips' ILVAS and Pioneer's P-Basic.

Because of the range of hardware combinations possible, IV systems of this type are usually referred to by the authoring system used.

'Building block' systems also include systems put together for 'once-off' specialised applications. Examples of these are the American Heart Foundations's CPR training programme, which uses a manikin with sensors wired to the computer to teach laypersons cardiopulmonary resuscitation, and MIT's Surrogate Travel programme, which has two monitors, a choice of four user input devices and three videodisc players (Floyd and Floyd, 1982).

10.5.2 Dedicated systems
Several manufacturers have produced integrated level 3 systems in one package — a computer interfaced with a video player, together with authoring software. Ideally, this provides a complete environment for the development and delivery of IV, on proven-compatible hardware.

Some of these systems, such as CAVIS and FELIX, use diverse players and computers, with a purpose-built interface and authoring system (FELIX combines an Apple II and a Sony U-Matic VCR, housed in a special cabinet).

Digital Equipment Corporation's IVIS system offers a more coherent solution. Using a Pioneer or Sony videodisc player linked to DEC's own Professional-350 workstation, the backbone of the IVIS system is its advanced authoring language — VAX Producer. Producer consists of two elements: a graphics editor which allows easy creation of text and graphics 'frames'; and a programming language which provides complex branching capabilities for linking these frames, as well as control of response handling, data collection, and cells to the videodisc. Thus the advantages of authoring language and authoring system are combined, where a non-programmer can quickly learn to create screen displays and employ a skilled programmer to write the more complex control program.

As a delivery system, IVIS's design and appearance make it attractive to use. Screen resolution is very good (960 × 600) and up to eight colours from a palette of 254 can be used at any one time. Computer screens are overlaid over the video picture with a transparent or opaque background, allowing various combinations of video and computer generated images, together and separately, with or without audio.

For the designer, there are two major disadvantages to this otherwise excellent system. First, although IV delivery can be on a stand-alone system, for development the PRO-350 must be connected to one of DEC's VAX series of mainframes. Second, since IVIS and Producer were developed with interactive video specifically in mind, they lack several facilities which CBT authors may consider essential. Screen plotting is extremely slow, making computer-generated animations unacceptable, except at the simplest level. Except for viewing a single DRAW frame, it is not possible to run uncompiled code. To compile a program may take some time (given low priority on a busy mainframe) and error messages are cryptic and none-too-friendly. Only low level mathematical functions are catered for, making many a potentially 'tidy' loop unnecessarily long.

Another dedicated IV system is MicroTICCIT, a product of the Hazeltine Corporation. This is a networked IV environment, where IBM PC workstations are linked to one of Data General's MicroEclipse systems, operating as the host. The system is the same for authoring and delivery and can accommodate both videodisc and video-tape. The ADAPT authoring system used operates in three levels, each providing more complex authoring facilities and requiring more experience to use. The idea is that non-programmers can start at a basic level of interactivitity, extending their knowledge as their objectives grow more ambitious. An instructional management system is included to keep track of individual student progress records.

Given the obvious advantages of a system specifically designed to aid in the performance of a particular task, it is perhaps surprising that dedicated IV systems have not caught on more. That tape-based systems should have begun to be considered antiquated is explainable — the limitations of video-tape for IV have long been realised. But, while they themselves still use IVIS for internal training applications, DEC have reported little success with it in the market-place. MicroTICCITT has fared slightly better, but partly due to its previous reputation as a CBT authoring system.

The reason for this is that even though the cost of an IV system may be only a fraction of the production costs for an IV programme, it is usually difficult to justify buying an expensive system for the delivery of just a few training programmes and the range of programmes available is not yet large or wide. Also, many users already possess one or more of the components of an IV system and this has encouraged the use of 'building block' systems. Luckily, the growth in standardisation of these components referred to at the start of this chapter has begun to herald 'across-the-board' compatibility between IV programmers. This is due to the appearance of a new type of IV system — packages that combine development software with a hardware interface, which can be used with existing computers and videodisc players.

10.5.3 Software/Hardware 'slotable' systems

Two examples of this new kind of IV screen, developed on opposite sides of the Atlantic, are Teletape's MIC and the VISAGE system. Both are designed for use on an IBM PC, XT or AT using almost any standard videodisc player. Each system consists of a controller board which slots into the PC's expansion slots. The board sends and receives commands to and from the videodisc player, and combines the video and computer display signals before transmitting them to the monitor. To do this the computer signal is first converted to the appropriate analogue RGB format — NTSC or PAL. MIC does this automatically, by interrogating the videodisc player at the start. VISAGE has a toggle switch on the board which must be set. Hence programs running on either system can be easily ported across video formats. With the MIC system, computer text and graphics are not overlaid on the video picture but 'hard keyed' into it — this is as if holes were effectively cut out of the video picture to match the computer-generated image, giving a harder, crisper, display.

These systems also contain their own software. The 'open architecture' approach of both systems means that the software is capable of interfacing with a range of popular programming languages and authoring languages. Hence programmers and CBT authors can write IV program without having to learn a new language, and existing programs can easily be made to run on the new system. The software of both systems enables one feature new to IV — the computer programming of 'soft edits'. This allows the author to program fades in and out of video or computer images, even where they do not exist on the disc, offering a saving on editing time and costs.

Henley Distance Learning Ltd developed a training programme in information management using Microtext, with the intention of later delivering this on the MIC system (Bayard-White, 1986, pp. 85–107). The only authoring language so far supported by both systems is TenCORE, produced by Computer Teaching Corporation. TenCORE has quickly become one of the most popular languages among CBT authors, largely because of its combination of power and versatility with ease of use. Although it is strictly a programming language, it is extremely user-friendly, with graphics and text editors and precise and meaningful error feedback, as well as several tools for response handling. There are over 250 commands available, and mathematical operations and veriable handling are good (there are a number of system-defined variables whose values can be checked and used — useful when debugging). Finally, uncompiled 'source' code can be run, allowing continual checking of the program as you go (Johnson, 1984).

The VISAGE software also contains a number of its own development and authoring tools (e.g. the V:Paint graphics editor) in an icon-driven environment. These will continue to be added to — offering a complete IV environment in one package.

10.6 CURRENT DEVELOPMENTS

So far these 'slotable' IV systems, with their wide compatibility in a range of user issues, offer more for the widespread growth of IV than any other systems. With their continued extension to incorporate new tools and peripherals, there is promise of us coming closer to the truly interactive IV environment for production and delivery envisaged in Nebraska's level 4.

The standardisation and compatibility IV delivery systems thus appearing has prompted the first real wave of generic IV programmes which can be produced and marketed independently of hardware configurations. Up until now OEMs and system manufacturers have been in the position of a gunsmith without bullets. In the future choosing an IV system will enable the user to pick from a wide range of off-the-shelf products. This should do much to encourage the widespread acceptance and application of IV.

Technology, meanwhile, continues to advance. As new developments appear our perceptions of interactive video must expand to include and absorb them. One development which may well be the next chapter for interactive video is the advent of CD-ROM and CD-I. Audio CD players are already common in homes, and the standards proposed by the High Sierra Group in June 1986 would enable CD-Audio, CD-ROM and CD-I discs all to perform on a single standard player. It is predicted that these standards may be with us by 1988 (Minutes of the Second Optical Disc Forum, 1986). Could this be the technology to bring high-level IV into the domestic market for the first time? It seems likely.

REFERENCES

Bayard-White, C. (1984) *An Introduction to Interactive Video*. UK National Interactive Video Centre and the Council for Educational Technology.

Bayard-White, C. (1986) *Interactive Video Case Studies and Directory*. UK National Interactive Video Centre and the Council for Educational Technology, pp. 27–42.

Chorover, S. L. (1984) Cautions on computers in education, *Byte*, **9**, 6, 223–227.

Duke, J. L. (1983) Interactive Video: Implications for Education and Training. CET Working Paper, Council for Educational Technology, 5, 7.

Floyd, S. (1982) Thinking interactively, in *Handbook of Interactive Video*, S. Floyd, and B. Floyd (eds) Knowledge Industry Publications, p. 22.

Floyd, S. and Floyd, B. (eds) (1982) *Handbook of Interactive Video*, Knowledge Industry Publications, pp. 133–135, 150–154.

Fox, B. (1985) Light at the end of video tunnel vision, *Electronic Times*, 10 October 1985.

Hutt, G. (1986) Using interactive videodisk, *Interactive learning International*, **2**, 4, April, 26–28.

Johnson, C. G. (1984) TenCORE and PC PILOT — a comparison of two authoring languages, *Interactive Learning International*, **1**, 2, Oct-Dec., 27–30.

L'Allier, J. J. (1983) Interactive Video — An Elephant in Search of a Definition, *Performance & Instruction Journal*, Nov., 4.

Lindsey, J. (1984) The challenge of designing for interactive video, *Instructional Innovator*, Sept., 17.

Minutes of the Second Optical Disc Forum (1986) Commission of the European Communities, Luxembourg, May 1986.

Mole, J. and Langham, J. (1982) *Pilot Study of the Application of Video Disc Technology at the Public Archives of Canada*, Ottawa, p. 6. (DSS catalogue number SA2-139/1982.)

Parsloe, E. (1983) *Interactive Video*, Sigma Technical Press, p. 14.

Wilson, L. (1983) Interactive video — a step toward natural learning, *Performance & Instruction Journal*, Nov., 32–33.

Worcester, C. (1983) Interactive Video — a New Video, *Performance & Instruction Journal*, Nov., 14–16.

Other references

Elliott, I. (1986) A Specification for an Interactive Video Tutor. Paper presented at GIREP Conference, 18–23 August 1986, on 'COSMOS — An Educational Challenge' in Elsinore, Denmark. European Space Agency, November 1986, ESASP-253.

Mathews, W. (1986) Report of the Courseware Committee. Irish Dept of Industry and Commerce, Feb 1986. Published by Her Majesty's Stationery Office.

11

Interactive video — a producer's medium

Martin Wright and David Nelson

11.1 INTRODUCTION

We see interactive video much more as computer managed video than as an extension of CBT. The power of interactive video is user control, via the computer, of screen images. Much interactive video fails because it does not exploit sufficiently the very heart of the system — the video image.

The videodisc introduces two relatively simple devices over and above conventional video, the freeze frame and random access. These two features and the precision with which they can be controlled, open up a whole new world to the video producer.

This chapter will look at various devices — tricks if you like — which go beyond conventional video grammar to show just how far interactive video can go as a producer's medium. Much of the chapter is about video technique and, detailed examples are given in order that an appreciation can be gained of how far the interactive technology is capable of moving video from its conventional roles.

11.2 CONVENTIONAL VIDEO TO VIDEODISC

Video — that is sequences which are to be played at 25 frames per second (30 frames per second in the American NTSC system) — takes on a different perspective in the videodisc context when compared with conventional video. In the latter, a movie sequence is for observation only. Video control is limited to stop, start, fast, slow and possibly crude freeze frame facility. Random access such as search and skip is cumbersome. With these limited controls interaction too is limited. However, there are of course applications for this kind of unsophisticated video control, e.g. sequences which act as triggers for computer-based teaching. If this is the sort of interactive video needed then computer controlled videocassette can be quite adequate without the expense of videodisc production. However, beyond such applications cassetted video is of limited use.

Once on disc, movie sequences gain new dimensions. Play-back can be fast, three times normal speed with the option of sound from two audio tracks (or stereo, of course), and slow (any speed down to still frame).

Given the degree of control possible with videodisc equipment, how can video producers exploit the new medium? Clearly they have a new set of tools at their disposal over and above the tried and tested grammar of conventional video. We will start looking at these new tools from the producer's point of view and follow that with the user's perspective on how they are applied.

11.3 THE NEW TOOLS

11.3.1 Use of movie sequences

Video sequences can be presented for much more detailed analysis than has previously been the case with video as the following examples illustrate.

Example 1 Motion analysis — sequences of high-speed film of some dynamic situations can be pressed into a videodisc for analysis of the motion involved. With computer overlay and appropriate computer software it is possible to analyse the filmed action in some detail. As well as being a powerful teaching technique this use of IV could prove to be a useful research tool.

Example 2 Behaviour analysis — By being able to slow down or speed up a particular sequence, it becomes much easier to observe certain phenomena. For example, the number of times an animal expresses itself, turns its head in one direction or another, blinks its eyes, emits a particular noise. It can also be applied to the analysis of human interaction for more observation of non-verbal communication. With multiple perspective recording and interleaving of the perspectives (discussed later) it is possible to observe a two-way interaction from different perspectives. This would work well in, for example, a package on interviewing skills.

Example 3 Experiments — Certain critical phases of, for example, chemical experiments (e.g. colour change in titration), reactions between chemicals, for example burning metals in oxygen, benefit in many cases from being slowed down to more accurately determine what is happening. This is clearly particularly important where the reaction takes place quickly. On some occasions high-speed filming will be necessary. However, we have been surprised how even for violent reactions, a considerable amount of otherwise non-capturable detail from the user's point of view can be gleaned from sequences shot at normal speed and replayed slower on the videodisc player. A simple chemical explosion filmed even at normal speed is quite dramatic and breathtaking when slowed down and/or reversed.

Example 4 Perhaps the most common use of video in the large number of training videodiscs being produced at present is the trigger video. This can consist of anything from a few seconds clip of an observed situation through to a fully fledged drama. Either way, there are no new special techniques involved, and much will depend primarily on well considered production values. The function of any such 'trigger' should be clearly defined and the video producer should have a full appreciation of its subsequent use. Otherwise there is a risk of video 'wallpaper' or otherwise meaningless video clips. More effective use of 'trigger' material can be made if the clips are accompanied with a second audio track, used to revisit the action and observe it in a different way. The revisit can be used for analysis, reinforcement, or alternative perspectives.

11.3.2 Still frames/image compression

Unlike videotape or transmitted programmes a videodisc can store up to 54 000 single frames each of high quality pictures which can be accessed with precision. This is one of the major advantages of a videodisc. Furthermore, with the LaserVision videodisc (in particular) there is no limit to the length of time a given single frame can be held. Heads and tapes would soon wear out if this were attempted on videotape. However, although a single image held for a long period will have no effect on the disc, it will tend to leave its mark in the phosphors of the TV screen!

A slide collection of 54 000 is equivalent to between 500 and 1000 slide carousels — a very large slide collection. To be able to exploit this single frame capacity of a videodisc economically in production terms, considerable ingenuity and planning is necessary.

The use of videodisc for still-frame data storage is based on the absolute reliability with which a single frame can be accessed, the relative speed with which this can be accomplished and the duration for which it can be held.

One of the largest applications to date of mass storage of single frames is the Domesday Project described elsewhere in this book (see Chapter 14).

Two key areas of decision-making in the production of these data bases arise. The first is how to assemble the data. The other is how to give the user access to the data. Methods of assembling the single-frame information into the master tape are varied — one route is to use a film rostrum camera, another video rostrum camera, another slide transfer, etc. Which route is best depends on the nature of the subject matter and in what form the original image exists. For example, does it still need to be photographed, or is it a slide, flat artwork, etc.?

In the end, the decision on method comes down to cost and quality — how to achieve one without sacrificing the other.

The design of the user access depends on the use to which the data base is to be put, and becomes a problem of data-base management.

The feature of the videodisc technology now taken as read is the absolute reliability with which a single frame can be accessed, and relative speed as well as the fact that the frame can be held indefinitely.

Whether large or small, still-frame files require careful management. Once a still frame file exceeds fifty frames a good computer data base needs to be defined to go alongside the images. Such a data base can provide all the logging during transfer to video-tape as well as providing the date base for

subsequent programming. We have planning productions whe
shot list has formed the basis of the final computer data base.

A small micro on location during a large stills shoot is an advantage. On a smaller scale the inclusion of limited still-frame files as part of a large package of moving sequences and computer software can offer a range of possibilities.

A file of two or three consecutive images can provide surprisingly effective animation of, for example, a cyclic motion such as an arm bending and flexing. This technique has been used to great effect on the Body Disc (1984) and Weight World (1987).

11.3.3 Image compression

Using still frames it is possible to reduce the 'real estate', i.e. the disc space required for an action sequence, and still retain the majority of the vital information.

Example 1 Origame. In one of the first videodiscs produced commercially in the United States and still in our opinion one of the most innovative — the First National Kiddisc (1982) — there is a section making paper aeroplanes. Only one frame appears on the disc for what would occupy perhaps twenty frames for a 'real time' movie sequence. Nevertheless, all the essential construction stages of the planes are still available. In this example, a moving sequence would add little to an explanation of how to make any particular plane. What is more, when a disc sequence is played back at normal speed, accompanied by the music track in this compressed form it forms a pleasing sequence in its own right.

Example 2 Surrogate Walks. The Aspen Disc (1983) was the first 'surrogate' travel disc and comprises a sequence of stills taken at set intervals along the streets of Aspen, Colorado with various prescribed directions of shots being taken at each point to enable the user to select a particular direction in which to travel; at certain locations additional information was also made available such as the contents of some of the buildings along the routes and the services offered by companies within the buildings, e.g. menus of restaurants etc.

During searches from one still frame to another the video screen would normally go to black. However, the 'Aspen Project' was driven by two disc players so that one disc player could search while the other provided the picture and vice versa. Now, with the new generation of players it is possible to skip from one single frame to another without the screen blacking, provided the two frames are within a range of 100 frames of each other. In many envisaged 'surrogate' applications it will be possible to arrange the still frames to enable this instant jump to be accomplished while providing several user choices at any time (see also Interleaving/Instant skip later in this chapter).

Given the possibility of moving sequences and still-frame files the producer can decide where dynamic action is relatively unimportant. The use of stills interspersed with movie sequences enables compression of sequences to be made possible, not only without valuable information being lost but with additional information and clarification of key points being made, for example, in chemical experiments the action can be stylised so that only key dynamic sequences are included. This will include manipulation techniques of, for example, laboratory glassware, weighing and dynamic changes. Where it is necessary to describe lists of chemicals and the equipment required, a still or series of stills with overlay from the computer program giving details of quantities costs and suppliers etc., gives more information than would a moving sequence, and in a manner which is more appropriate and user friendly.

On the Milton Keynes Information Technology disc (1982) we found that a cookery demonstration for a cake which ran in real time at fifteen minutes could only be reduced by judicious editing to approximately seven minutes running time without losing essential information. But by replacing the sections detailing lists of ingredients/utensils, required cooking times at various points, etc., with appropriate stills over which details were overlaid, we were able to reduce running time to four minutes. We reserved the video sequences for illustrating difficult-to-describe cuisinary arts, such as 'the dropping consistency' of the cake mixture and how best to beat the mixture.

11.3.4 Use of camera

It is normal film practice to use cameras as external observers of a scene or phenomenon from an apparently objective position although it can be argued that the camera can never be truly objective. In the context of interactive video where we are creating images with which we want our users to interact we would want our images to be anything but objective. By careful positioning of the camera it is possible to film an event from the position that would have been occupied by the user had they themselves been present at the event. Therefore, the screen presents the observer's viewpoint.

11.3.5 Multiple perspectives

Videodisc technology freely allows a scene to be viewed from several perspectives e.g. Weight World (1973) for which each of 43 exercises was recorded simultaneously with three cameras. While observing a single chosen exercise the users can select:

(1) A wide overview shot of the person demonstrating the exercise, or
(2) A profile to emphasise posture.
(3) An additional close-up to emphasise technique.

The user (with appropriate disc mapping employed - see below) can act very similarly to a vision mixer in a television studio and select the view required.

This will depend on their knowledge of the subject, how they are going to use the weight training material and whether they are reviewing the material, or seeing it for the first time.

11.3.6 Mapping the disc

The major difference between video and videodisc is that whereas video is a continuous seamless garment to be played in one mode, videodisc is essentially a data base of moving sequences, stills and sound tracks, which can be accessed in any order the software allows, i.e. video material — either stills or moving pictures — can be laid down anywhere on the disc, providing in computing terms there is a suitable file structure to provide ready access. In practice, in order to shorten access times, it is sometimes necessary to duplicate certain images. This is particularly the case with still files which may carry different overlays at different stages in the information or training package. Consequently, the producer and the production team or video or film editor must stop thinking in terms of a continuous running image as they would in assembling conventional video. For the producer, the final master videotape assembly can become quite a complex optimisation process balancing access needs against space limitations.

11.3.7 Interleaving/instant skip

Interleaving is a technique that is already becoming established in a simple form in some US disc applications, but has potential for considerable refinement. For example, in the multiple perspective example of weight lifting described in section 11.3.5 — interleaving would enable the user to obtain instant access to any of the three shots available for each exercise without any blackout between the sections. This would be achieved by arranging the frames of each shot sequentially so that the master shot would occupy say frames 1, 4 and 7, etc. The first close-up frames 2, 5 and 8, etc. and the additional close-up frames 3, 6 and 9, etc. Theoretically, there is nothing to prevent many more views being incorporated. (Unfortunately, the technology is not yet available on the PAL system.) However, approaching it is the instant skip facility available on the new generation of PAL players in Europe (Philips' 410 and 415 Series players). This enables instant skip between up to 100 frames at a time without blackout. In Weight World the action of each exercise was compressed to 25 frames. This allows the user to skip from the master shot instantaneously to either of the close-ups without the screen blacking out.

11.3.8 Screen design

Bringing together the techniques of video and computing, interactive videodisc has problems as well as blessings. This is apparent in the area of screen design.

Much work has been done on screen design for computers including numerous papers on topics including modes of presentation — graphs, histograms, etc., use of colour, use of fonts, readability, and so on. Cable companies and broadcasting organisations have also carried out research on these topics, particularly with reference to teletext services such as Oracle, Prestel, etc. In transmitted television and video in particular with the new generation of complex electronic graphics, there has been a considerable development in the presentation of text and graphical information. This applies not only to educational programming but also to current affairs programmes such as election specials, business programmes and the weather.

However, there is a problem of how to marry the dissimilar media of computing and video. Computer text is designed for VDU screens for close-range viewing and video is designed for a TV mode of viewing with a distance of six feet plus, between user and audience. This difference together with different line definition standards causes considerable problems of screen design. Considerable effort has to be made to ensure that the computer text is compatible with the video image and vice versa.

An alternative approach is to try and approach IV with the minimum use of text by means of utilising the source of the 74 minutes of audio available on a disc.

In 'Life and Energy' (1987) much of the audio, surplus to 'action' requirements is used to drive QWERTY, a computer-generated animated chaperone. Most of the interaction on this disc is with screen images of one form or another, but very little text is used.

11.3.9 Summary

The video producer already has a vast array of tools and tricks of the trade available for use in the videodisc medium. It is when the new tools described above are added to the existing array of well established, tried and tested techniques that the possibilities of new and exciting aspects of interactivity can be exploited.

11.4 USING THE NEW TOOLS

11.4.1 Introduction

The new tools as added to established video production grammar have the potential for making interactive video just that — interactive. The major change from linear video is to put many types of control at the user's disposal. The users become responsible for how fast they go through material, how often they review sections, what directions they take, what level of detail they are going to pursue, which sections they are going to leave out, whether they want to be tested or not.

However, this does not mean that the quality of an interactive disc should necessarily depend on crude measures such as how many user inputs there are per minute. There is no valid reason why as part of an interactive package the user should not sit back and take in information, to be processed and utilised and elaborated upon or viewed differently at a later stage in the package, for a substantial chunk of time. Like every good information package a well put together 'lesson' contains periods of activity and passivity. What is more it is essential that the activity takes various forms — observing, running and experiment, reviewing a section, making choices, constructing a hypothesis, carrying out calculations, writing a report. It is not necessary that all of these activities should be disc-based provided that they are integrated within an overall structure set out on the disc. For example, in the Bulmershe College Primary Science disc (Life and Energy, 1987) the disc will be in part data-base, tutor, hypothesis guider, experiment verifier, pacer, and above all integrator of a range of activities that will take place over a twelve-week term in school. However, throughout, the class teacher is in charge. In other words, they are the manager of the disc resource.

In this section we consider how the new tools of IV can be exploited to give the user this impressive range of interactions.

11.4.2 Activity with images
Videodisc technology enables multiple ways of interacting with the screen.

(1) Using an appropriate light pen/screen writer an electronics project for EETPU uses screen images for electrical circuit testing. This is a fine example of screen simulation (EETPU, 1985).
(2) The South Korean railway simulator (Master Driver, 1984) uses videodisc as its image source. This is 'point of view' filming taken from the front of a cab of a train driven along a stretch of actual railway track. The simulator allows the disc to be 'driven' at variable speeds. Signals and obstacles are provided by high resolution computer graphics.
(3) Route Mapping — The Domesday Disc (1988) allows a user to mark out a route on a screen map. This software distance is then measured via the software either along the route selected or 'as the crow flies'.

Many other examples are in existence. Interactions can be real-time or over a static image, and can be used to improve or check mental as well as motor skills. Interaction can use many devices, such as trackerball, mouse or touch-screen, whichever is most appropriate.

11.4.3 Interaction with a system
There are many tried and tested techniques from the more sophisticateed CBT packages available for use on videodisc, e.g. intelligent response matching such as keyword recognition. In this the user is invited to offer any response to an open-ended question. The response is then compared with a 'lexicon' of likely responses stored in the computer software and an appropriate system response such as confirmation of correctness or further instruction is given. From a pedagogical standpoint anything that makes a user 'work' in obtaining an understanding, is better than giving the user the answers.

Although there is a place for multiple choice answering in some contexts, the use of 'intelligent' responses from the user must engage the user more thoroughly. To what extent keyboard shyness may get in the way is hard to say. This has not so far been our experience.

Example 1   In the Teddy Bear Disc (1983) the user is asked why a particular material (a Teddy Bear's eye) fails! This is in fact a comprehension question. The user is expected to respond by typing in a textual response which is mapped onto a system dictionary.

Example 2   To engage the user in the subject matter in the Stress at Work disc (1987) the user is asked to input a response to 'Last time I was stressed I felt ...'.

In eliciting from the user a considered response we have we hope engaged the mind of the user. This particular response is then interpreted.

Later on the user is asked to input a free format sentence for causes of their stress. This is not interpreted, but saved for use later in the learning package.

11.4.4   Open and closed objectives

Is the videodisc to be run primarily for skills acquisition or for ideas exploration? The answer to this will tend to determine how much freedom is given to the user. If, for example, one of the functions of the interactive video is to teach users how to fill in the latest currency exchange forms, then clearly the objective is fairly closed with defined outputs from the user. These can be tested as pre- and post-entry conditions. But if another function of the interactive video is to create an awareness of customer handling skills, then a lot of rigorous performance measurement may be more difficult and possibly unnecessary. It would be a lost opportunity if the potential for improved communication and learning offered by videodisc technology were put into the straitjacket of a didactic learning model beyond basic 'skills' training.

Videodisc has a potential to allow people to think for themselves by giving them the tools with which to do it, rather than limiting them to the tools and ideas furnished by an individual teacher.

It is also essential that the user feels that he or she is in control of what they are doing, what is available and where they are in the disc package. The package should in computer terms be 'transparent', i.e. the user should be able to work through the system without hindrance, but with advice that certain sections are useful or essential to ensure that understanding of later sections will be possible.

How this is presented to the user will depend very much on the nature of the project. Contents lists and a 'You are here' guide, seem to be vital in order to maintain user confidence.

11.4.5 Production schedules

In planning the total video production, there is a school of thought in IV design that requires a complete watertight design specification before a single inch of film or video is shot. Our experience has led to a contrary view, though broad objectives must be defined. If one is to exploit the images on the disc to full effect much of the interactivity must be designed in the light of the final images produced.

There needs to be an iteration between initial objectives and the design elements, e.g. video and computing. The computing specification can gradually firm up as video production progresses. The final computing specification can only occur upon completion of the disc mapping.

This more dynamic model of IV production is likely to yield more exciting projects. By this we mean — more stimulating, more demanding, and less predictable for the user.

11.5 CONCLUSION

We have attempted to encapsulate our own videodisc production experience. What we would like to have done is to embellish every point with fully interactive examples. But this is print. It is now five years on from the earliest European IV but the industry still has a long way to go on design.

So far much IV has been CBT led. This has had a stifling effect on the input of ideas and the potential of videodisc has not been fully exploited. It has not allowed the V part of IV to come into its own. Good IV producers are going to need leaps of the imagination if IV is going to capture the imagination of users. It is now quality of thought that is needed over and above the wealth of the new techniques that the videodisc medium has in abundance.

REFERENCES

British Garden Birds (1983) BBC Enterprises Ltd.
Milton Keynes Information Technology Disc (1982) First PAL interactive laserdisc produced in UK. Produced by BBC Open University Production Centre on behalf of the Milton Keynes Development Corporation for part of an Information Technology Exhibition in 1982.
The Domesday Disc (1988) BBC Enterprises Ltd.
The Body Disc (1984) Level 1 disc produced by New Media.
Weightworld (1987) A weight training videodisc. The first of a series of discs produced by BBC Open University Production Centre in conjunction with the National Coaching Foundation.
The First National Kiddisc (1982) Level 1 disc NTSC. Published by Optical Program Associates.
Aspen Disc (1983).
Life and Energy (1987) An environmental science disc for 9–13-year-olds.

One of the Interactive Video in Schools (IVIS) projects, 1987 (DTI). Produced by BBC Open University Production Centre in conjunction with Bulmershe College of Higher Education.

The Teddy Bear Disc (1983) A materials science disc produced for Open University Summer School use. Published by Open University Educational Enterprises.

EETPU (1985) *An Introduction to Solid State Electronics.* EPIC.

Master Driver (1984) Seoul Metropolitan Subway Corporation. Designed by Marconi Simulation, Dunfermline.

Stress at Work (1987) An MSC funded project. Produced by BBC Milton Keynes. A Level 3 stress awareness package.

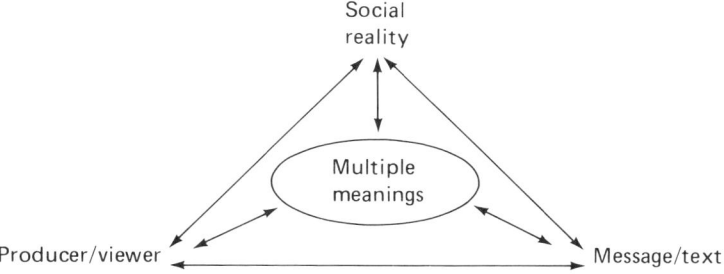

Fig. 12.1 — An interactive model of how meanings are made.

use effectively (Eco, 1979), interactive video may provide the opportunity for more genuine and spontaneous interaction between students and material. This would be very much in line with recent theoretical and practical developments in education.

12.3 COMMUNICATION AND INTERACTION

What specific forms might this interaction take? Which of these forms, moreover, are likely to be valuable in higher education? The study of teaching and learning has traditionally concentrated on communication between teachers and students (Hills, 1979). Educational technology has added a dimension to this approach by focusing on the role of media and materials, in addition to linguistic exchange. Educational uses of information technology demand that we also look at the interaction between students, media and materials and at the interaction between different media within a learning environment. A simple transmission model (which assumes that messages can be transferred down a line effectively, provided 'noise' barriers are overcome) is often used in this context (Shannon and Weaver, 1949; McQuail and Windahl, 1981; Fiske, 1982). This may be enhanced to describe mediated teaching (where a teacher is present) or distance learning (where a teacher is not present). However, if we pursue this line of thought, we will not find a model to describe the range of interactions and their combinations which may occur in the use of interactive video. It is important to bear the various interactive possibilities in mind, since in looking at actual developments, we may find applications which rely on only a narrow range of specific forms. In exploring what we can get from interactive video in higher education, we need to look at all the options. This is especially important since different options have quite different economic implications and educational functions. The case study later in this chapter focuses mainly on the potential for interactive video as a presentational medium within a conventional classroom context.

12.4 COSTS AND BENEFITS IN TRAINING

The current cost of a single basic 'Level 3' system is over £2000. Such a level of unit cost for hardware would seem to make multi-user systems prohibitively expensive. Nevertheless, this book and earlier accounts of interactive video (Parsloe, 1983; Bayard-White, 1985) describe a number of successful implementations within the training world. Accounts of these to date, however, although useful for assessing research and production costs, are mostly unhelpful in identifying the real costs of introducing interactive video. These costs should include (but usually do not) both system hardware and staff time for software development (Bates, 1983). Despite the absence of realistic costings, the enthusiasm for interactive video has been vocal and widespread. Before examining its potential in the context of higher education it is worth looking briefly at their costs and benefits within the training environment, where most innovation has so far occurred.

The training goals which interactive video has sought can almost invariably be expressed in terms of specific objectives. Learning is usually serial and cumulative in development and its outcomes can not only be specified in advance but readily tested (often operationally) until mastery is achieved. The design of such training clearly still has much in common with the discredited programmed learning movement. Its inadequate model of human learning in terms of stimulus/response-based behavioural psychology (Gayeski and Williams, 1984) was responsible for a great deal of unexciting and mechanical teaching which lacked the flexibility and spontaneity of human interaction. Even so, where the content of teaching can be classified, sequenced and related to operational tasks by simulations, and where there are large numbers of trainees whose training needs are very similar, there may be significant economies of scale and savings in expenditure by adhering to such a highly systematised approach. Where there is wide geographical distribution of trainees there can also be short-term savings in time and trial costs (Doulton, 1984).

There are other reasons why interactive video has been so welcomed in some areas of training. Despite the actual complexity of the processes, learning is not only apparently simple but also attractive and stimulating, provided the material is well designed. It requires some physical activity (at least from the trainee's hands) and a kind of alertness which may be superficially contrasted with domestic television viewing. Whilst the design and production process of interactive video is highly complex and systematised and its applications tend towards large-scale uses, the experience of using it can be, by contrast, very informal and personal. In many ways, it restores to the user something of the subjectivity of reading. As one trainer has expressed it: 'Interaction means that rather than looking at a computer as a replacement for a teacher, it is more accurately used as an interactive book' (Palmarozza, 1984; Clark, 1984).

Perhaps the most crucial factor in the popularity of interactive video in training is, however, an economic one. Specific training costs are usually identifiable within a given overall budget. They are, therefore, easier to monitor and audit. They can be measured more realistically and with more accuracy in terms of comparative cost-effectiveness than a great deal of activity within general education. It is important to recognise this, since it is a feature of training which is not shared by higher education and is therefore significant in determining the affordability and acceptability of interactive video in higher education. Traditionally, training has been organised by a very small number of internal trainers who 'buy in' external staff, expertise and resources to provide training for large numbers of employees. The salaried element of the costs of such training is therefore comparatively low, whilst recurrent funds for expenditure are relatively high. What this means in practice is a relatively high degree of flexibility in the use of budgets.

12.5 THE HIGHER EDUCATION CONTEXT

By contrast, higher education is a highly labour-intensive system. Its investment has historically been and continues to be in the expertise of academic staff. Despite a numerical reduction of over 10% in the 48 British universities' UGC-funded academic staff (non-clinical teaching and research) between 1980 and 1985, salaries still accounted for nearly two-thirds of recurrent expenditure in the academic year 1983–84 (CVCP, 1986a). The marginal economies aimed at in the production and distribution of interactive video in particular contexts may seem paltry by comparison. Further, these economies may only apply where an institution already depends on distance learning with a high level of audio-visual communication. In the case of the Open University, which is unique in this respect, it has been argued that existing television programmes can be recycled as part of new interactive programmes more cheaply than the cost of producing a broadcast programme (Bates, 1983). When costs are closely related to the payroll, however, and where staff tenure may exist, it is simply not feasible to shift investment from one kind of resource (staff) to another (learning machines and materials).

Even if this were feasible, there would still be many problems to resolve before interactive video's undoubted potential could be realised in higher education. The main ones can be identified clearly as: professional resistance, modes of learning and specialisation. They do not act independently, of course, but are integrally related to each other as aspects of current teaching and learning practice in higher education.

Professional resistance relates closely to some aspects of academic specialisation. The 'Not Made Here' syndrome has been a powerful deterrent of transfer and exchange of teaching materials between higher education institutions. The differences in emphasis between individuals are no less real than the differences in approach and curriculum content between institutions. Frequently, the very stability and success of one kind of institution's teaching and learning practice prevents the integration of materials from other institutions. Even the use of film and video, which many educators would now regard as routine, still constitutes a major innovation and therefore risk for most academics (Elton, 1977). Resistance to new practices tends to continue for as long as possible until stasis begins to look more dangerous than movement. Even then, change remains piecemeal and patchy unless it is structured by an holistic commitment within an institution. For this reason, any belief in the conquest of learning by means of a technological Trojan horse is misguided.

It has often been argued that new technology is under-used by educators simply because of fear, inertia or conservatism (Moore and Hunt, 1980; Macintosh, 1984). This underestimates the complexity of adaptation and accommodation. It also ignores the importance of other potential deterrents like cost, loss of autonomy, inflexibility, inaccessibility, unreliability, unfamiliarity and lack of appropriate software. A much more powerful explanation can be found in the frequent mismatch between, on the one hand, the possible applications and theoretical cost-effectiveness of learning devices and, on the other, the particular human and institutional contexts in which they need to be used. This mismatch is particularly self-evident in higher education.

In the case of interactive video, professional resistance to innovation in general, to new teaching techniques and to educational media in particular is compounded by the problems of learning modes and academic specialisation. In many subject-areas, the very success of training applications of interactive video provides good reason for their inappropriateness in higher education. Their programme-led sequencing and their traces of behaviourist instructional paradigms make them rather unsuitable for experiential or group learning in the arts, humanities and social sciences. In addition, higher education is a highly specialised system. Even those undergraduate courses which are followed by the largest numbers of students are quite small by the standards of industrial corporations who need to train their employees in specific skills or enable them to master particular sets of information.

Nevertheless, there may well be applications for interactive video in quite different higher education environments than those which are affected by the problems discussed above. The rest of this chapter will be concerned, therefore, with the most immediately likely possibilities in our local context and will look forward to situations which might develop in the more distant future.

12.6 A DEVELOPMENT CASE-STUDY

Southampton University has an outstanding record in the design, production and evaluation of educational media and already has an international reputation for its research and development work in information technology (Hart, 1984; 1985). On this basis, it has certain advantages to offer in the field of interactive video development. The field is already a highly competitive one, and the most desirable way forward may be to concentrate on the development and evaluation of software for generic discs. This may also be the most likely means of securing funding.

Our original proposal to the university in 1985 envisaged a three-year research and development project. We emphasised the existing constraints on innovation by individual departments and by the university's academic support services. We argued that the recent University Grants Committee and Computer Board round of grants to support the use of computers in teaching had concentrated mainly on subject-specific applications and had tended to overlook the necessity of building up an institutional resource to support individual subject-related projects. A series of seminars in Southampton on new media in teaching and learning had provided a useful forum for staff with ideas for work on interactive video. As a result, an interest group was set up to develop its potential. It was both desirable and necessary, we argued, that an impetus should be given to the development of expertise in Southampton in order to realise the benefits which the new technology offered in both teaching and research. These benefits were:

(1) Wide availability within the University of an enhanced teaching and training mode for use in undergraduate, postgraduate and continuing professional education.
(2) An improved service for lecturers and researchers within the University.
(3) The co-ordination of expertise across the University in new educational technology developments.
(4) A base for developing distance learning and continuing education resources for extra-mural exploitation.
(5) The enhancement of the University's adacemic reputation in the areas of information technology and educational media.
(6) A means of attracting extra funding from industrial and training institutions.
(7) A source of additional revenue from sales of materials.

In the short term, the project aimed at the creation of an interactive video presentation system based on the proven success of the existing 'Video-Slide' system (Rees and Robson, 1985); the production of computer programs which should enable videodisc data-bases to be used under microcomputer control for teaching and learning; and the evaluation of video programmes for interactive use in appropriate learning contexts (for example, induction programs for library and computer users). In the long term, the project would act as a catalyst for establishing broader and more far-reaching institutional innovations. It would provide a means of co-ordinating expertise between interested subject departments and the university's academic services to encourage research and development. It might act as a focus for a wide range of simultaneous developments in the design and production of distance learning and individualised learning resources for undergraduate and continuing education with an interactive element. Finally, it might become a centre for research and development which could attract external funds so as to be eventually self-financing. Such aims clearly involve assumptions about innovation processes which demand some explanation.

12.7 TECHNOLOGY AND INNOVATION IN TEACHING

Our strategy was based upon an awareness of three major factors which, some analysts have argued, determine the success of innovation in teaching patterns (Weisgerber, 1968):

— active leadership by those responsible for teaching policy and support;
— emphasis on efficiency as a determinant of teaching quality;
— support for research into appropriate types of teaching.

Elton (1977) echoes this analysis and calls even more specifically for the support of innovation through bodies like the CET, through an adequate system of incentives and rewards for staff who undertake innovative work and, above all, a commitment to staff development and training programmes. Only with this kind of support can new technologies like interactive video and the new techniques of teaching and learning which they demand work in conjunction with new thinking to produce effective innovation.

However, even if all these pre-conditions are fulfilled there is no guarantee of success in introducing new teaching technologies. Too often in higher education a 'top-down' approach which relies on dissemination or diffusion from the centre fails to gain wide acceptance. Keller's Personalised System of Instruction is a classic example of a potentially cost-effective teaching technique which has gained fervent supporters in some places but is by no means generally accepted (Kozma, 1978).

Our strategy was conceived as relying on 'insertion' rather than diffusion. It depended heavily on the co-ordination of existing staff development, educational technology and computing support groups in order to provide a service to the system as a whole. We attempted to work within rather than against the real constraints of current practice. We emphasised the need to develop an appropriate presentation system which could be used by lecturers in routine teaching situations with groups of students rather than as a facility for independent learning. While there were many such systems on the market, we tried quite deliberately to adapt current and local usage in order to build on the success of a computer-assisted teaching software package called 'Video-Slide'.

'Video-Slide' was developed in Southampton to facilitate the preparation and display of screens of information (text and graphics) for presentation in lectures and seminars with the help of a BBC microcomputer. Each screen is referred to as a video-slide and slides are stored on disc in slide-show files. 'Video-Slide' manages the ordering of slides for display so that lecturers can prepare images and text in advance and need only use single key depressions to move on to the next slide, move backwards, or point to information on the screen. The advantage of 'Video-Slide' is that it is designed for a specific purpose — presentation — and is consequently easy to learn and to use. It is also much cheaper than other commercially available packages and has sold well in both higher education and industry.

It was a logical progression to produce an enhanced version of 'Video-Slide' to incorporate interactive video. This would enable lecturers to prepare and display material incorporating text and graphics information as before, but include, at any point in the presentation, video material (a moving sequence or a still frame) and to overlay text and/or graphics onto the video screen. For foreign language and other applications it would also be useful to incorporate a dual sound-track capability into the system.

If such an authoring and presentation system were available, teaching staff could become involved in the process of producing their own computer programs for the control of interactive video teaching material. In this way, with sufficient determination and specialist help, they could not only become familiar with the technology but they could also offer valuable insight into design and evaluation issues from a user's point of view.

This strategy clearly involves a paradox, however. It unashamedly offers interactive video as a presentation system for conventional lecturing and small-group teaching situations. The kind of interaction which occurs remains very firmly under the control of the teacher. Very few people would argue that this is a promising use of the medium and would point to the obvious potential for individualised learning which is being ignored. Developing it in this way, however, acknowledges both the politics and the economics of teaching and learning in higher education. In Southampton, in particular with a large measure of budgetary devolution and scarce central resources, it was perhaps inevitable. Lecturers control teaching and get paid for doing it. They are, therefore, the key features in developing new techniques, technology and thinking about teaching.

Some may find this co-operative, gradualist approach unconvincing. However, it was effective in the initial stages of setting up the project when specific investment funding was not available. Fortunately, the strategy's acknowledgement of the actual problems of introducing change allows for such difficulties. Because it is essentially a 'bottom-up' approach, the energy, motivation and co-ordination are already in existence and it has been possible to proceed in a limited but systematic way. In reality, the strategy has proved extremely successful in that initial funding has now been secured from within the University for a two-year project. This funding allows for expenditure on both hardware and research staff which will enable us to develop several initiatives. A management group has been formed which includes representatives from the central academic support groups and interest subject specialists. Within the Faculty of Science, for example, the Geodata Unit has already had a considerable involvement in interactive videodisc through its work for the Domesday Project, for which it produced the satellite imagery atlas of the British Isles.

In summary, the funded project is based on four main objectives:

(1) mounting demonstrations of established uses and investigating further applications throughout the University
(2) design a new demonstration package based on work in the Geodata Unit;

(3) setting up a system for general access within the Library for use with generic off-the-shelf discs;
(4) devising and planning the implementation of a University-wide standard for interactive videodisc systems, based on the experience of subject-specific studies already under way.

In addition to this work, we have also been successful in attracting substantial external funding for the sort of projects which were envisaged in our original proposal and in which we are now engaged.

The kind of generic material for which we are developing programs designed to meet specialised undergraduate teaching needs is inevitably marketed on videodisc rather than tape. There seems to be little point in exploring tape-based 'Level 3' systems for other than experimental purposes. Such experiments at Cardiff and the Open University have certainly raised awareness about the problems and potential of interactive video but, as has been often pointed out, the inflexibility and technical deficiencies of such systems as the Sony Videoresponder are ultimately extremely limiting and frustrating (Laurillard 1982, Roach 1983).

12.8 A SURVEY OF EXISTING EUROPEAN MATERIAL

At this point, the current dearth of 'off-the-shelf' generic discs in Europe becomes apparent. A recent survey of development by the Scottish Council for Educational Technology reveals more interest than activity (Hills, 1986). Work on videodisc design and production in London, Cardiff and at the Open University has shown that some form of investment funding is necessary even for the initial phase of disc production. Work has also been going on in Cambridge, Glasgow, Heriot-Watt, Birmingham, Nottingham and Leicester Universities and at the Polytechnics of Wales, Central London and Brighton. Apart from the London pilot compilation disc and a similar offering from the Institut National de Recherche Pedagogique in Paris, there is not a great deal of other material available. Cardiff's *Online Storage and Retrieval* is very useful since it is relevant to anyone who wants to retrieve on-line bibliographical information, but it is essentially a training rather than educational resource (Roach 1984). Work on language learning at Brighton Polytechnic seems more promising for users in higher education. Also promising are the Nottingham Zoology image data-base disc and the Cambridge Naga disc.

Discs which have a potentially greater number of users are much more likely to be adapted for use in higher education in Britain during the first years of development. At the moment these are almost exclusively centred on medical education, where there has been intense pressure on a crowded curriculum and increasing staff-student ratios. For example, Micro Scope's *Anatomy* disc, produced in conjunction with Pioneer (Japan) and shown at the World Anatomy Congress in London in 1985, aims to produce about fifty hours of programme time for £15 000 to £20 000. There are at least 3000 worldwide locations which might use it, as it is designed to be accessible at different levels by nurses, radiographers and surgeons, or can be used as a database under specially designed local program control. Similarly, the Göttingen *Cell Biology* disc contains nearly a hundred film sequences of complex cell movements (some of them taken from a film, *The Little Feet* made in Southampton). It also features an audio track in English and German, and occasionally uses electron micrographs to illustrate the structures beneath certain cell movements.

The Rotterdam *Medical Microscopic Morphology* disc uses microphotography to store 3600 indexed images and electronic microscopy for a further 900 photographs. Perhaps most well known in Britain, and of most relevance for our work in Southampton, is the University of London's *The Knee* disc, which contains 92 200 frames of still and dynamic images as a first stage in an ambitious attempt to produce an interactive equivalent of *Gray's Anatomy*. London have used a variety of imaging techniques, from slow-motion film to radiography, thermography and computed tomography. John Pegington of University College London has already developed and used programs for independent undergraduate study and several university medical departments are now also developing their own specialised programs.

The strategy of producing locally designed specialised programs for use with commercially produced generic videodiscs is precisely the one we wish to pursue in Southampton. The reasons, for this, as indicated already, are threefold: technically this enables us to make optimum use of the medium's capabilities; economically it does not involve large investment in equipment or people (most of the generic discs mentioned here retail at less than £100 each); and politically it draws on the collaborative efforts of computing, educational technology and academic subject specialists. What kinds of improvement in teaching and learning can be realistically expected in the future?

12.9 THE EVALUATION VACUUM

We must be wary of being too optimistic even in this apparently promising niche within higher education. Evaluation of teaching and learning must be incorporated at an early stage into research and development programmes. Actual evaluations of interactive video in British higher education are even scarcer than videodiscs. The literature is plagued, however, by bland subjective assertions of effectiveness with no mention of criteria or comparative measures in evidence (Gayeski and Williams, 1984, p. 66).

Diana Laurillard's work at the Open University (discussed on p. 77) appears to be the only systematic work on IV in British higher education in existence. Her findings and other reports from America suggest the need for extreme caution in our expectations of interactive video in higher education. Bosco (1986) has analysed 29 American separate evaluations of use and found that less than half made a positive assessment of its effectiveness. Only eight of these examples, however, were from higher education and in only two cases were the reported benefits supported positively by any statistical test. In general, the use of a statistical test tended to cause conservative revisions to subjective judgements of effectiveness. Another American study (Dalton, 1986) compared video with computer-assisted instruction and interactive video. He found that, although interactive video improved learner attitudes, this may have been due to the effect of novelty and that computer-assisted learning was actually the most effective mode in this particular context. Possibly such measures are not very illuminating and there is more need at this stage to concentrate on learning and teaching strategies in order to find more suitable means of evaluation. Certainly, as Bosco points out, marginal improvements in comparative effectiveness based on experimental designs may be much less important than the need to integrate interactive video within existing organisational and educational cultures. At the same time, there needs to be a focus on the most appropriate kinds of learning interactions. This means looking at students' learning needs and strategies rather than simply at the presentation capacities of interactive systems. It means doing more of the formative evaluation work with actual students which Diana Laurillard has begun with early programmes at the Open University.

Her focus is naturally on the potential of interactive video as a means of independent student learning within an Open University context, rather than as a presentation system for lecturers (Laurillard, 1983). The questions she raises, however, are crucial ones for the design and development of the medium within higher education in Britain. Evidence from the evaluation of written distance-learning materials suggests that students frequently override the routes determined by carefully structured exposition. There is clearly a problem here in the relationship between students' receptive and active modes which has become apparent from studies of how they work through a written text. This problem is also central to the structuring of interactive video sequences. Laurillard proposes, therefore, three basic research questions concerning the balance between student and program control:

(1) How should content be presented and sequenced?
(2) How should student activity be provided for?
(3) How should alternation between receptive and active modes of learning be organised?

The unpopularity of some computer-based learning and the ineffectiveness of a great deal of educational television may be explained by reference to their heavy reliance on program-initiated modes. When students were given the opportunity to interrupt a sequence under their own initiative they apparently tended to allow the 'text' to exert control and followed it in a linear manner. Spontaneous interruption of video sequences was rare unless a specific invitation to do so was built into the program. However, when given a range of choices of content with an opportunity to move around a video sequence, less than half of the students followed the expected sequence. Alternation between receptive and active modes was found to be very unpredictable and depended very much on the individual student's purposes in using the programme (e.g. initial learning or revision). She concludes, that if interactive video is to be effective, students should be given the balance of control but the exercise of such control should be prompted by the program itself.

In a later study, Laurillard found that the linear design and didactic emphasis of the *Teddy Bears* disc (on materials structure) caused problems precisely because it did not incorporate the research findings reported above. Students needed more control over the presentation of information than was offered, the 'skip' option for student-initiated sequencing needed clearer explanation for optimum use, and more mapping of content was needed to avoid students getting disorientated and 'lost' within the program (Laurillard, 1984), features that were subsequently included, following the formative evaluation study.

Our understanding of these learning strategies and their importance for design has been enhanced at a general level by work on human–machine interaction (Barker, 1985; 1986). More detailed work suggests that our models of students are currently too stereotyped to be really useful in enabling a real individualisation of learning through interactive video. McAleese (1986a, 1986b) proposes the development of *intelligent* interactive video which could support the interactional forms of face-to-face discussion and at the same time take into account the learner's prior knowledge. Cognitive maps in the learner's brain can be expressed as concept maps which relate clusters of concepts together in useful ways. Clearly, this kind of approach involved formidable programming problems but may well be a way forward for truly individual interactive learning systems.

For the immediate future, however, we still have the problem of presenting the potential of interactive video in higher education in an acceptable way. Our strategy is based on the premise that this can best be done slowly through existing forms of teaching and learning. It involves creating a presentation system for generic discs and the design of specialised software for micro-computer control of the discs.

12.10 ALTERNATIVE APPLICATIONS OF INTERACTIVE VIDEO

This strategy may make some very specialised uses with small user populations more feasible. For example, a current Department of Education and Science-funded project in Southampton is seeking to provide improved video resources for communication and education within the deaf community. Since conventional video technology has proved so popular and useful for deaf people and teachers of the deaf, we are developing means of teaching the deaf about video production. This involves trying to create a sign-language vocabulary through which deaf people can communicate about video production operations. We are also using conventional video as a means of storing and distributing sign-language communication, since no adequate form of notation exists for sign-language, and some deaf people also have literacy problems. The resources we have created include video production and editing equipment, a full-time Research Fellow and a part-time Media Resources Adviser. Most important, however is a low-cost, video tape-based interactive system of creating subtitles for existing television programmes which stores them on floppy disc and inserts them on an audio track of the videotape.

This system was designed as a result of an earlier Independent Broadcasting Authority project on the subtitling of broadcast television programmes and has been widely used by deaf people and teachers of the deaf. It is, perhaps, interactive video of a very specialised kind and at its most basic, since it merely allows forms of linguistic interaction to occur which would otherwise be impossible for the deaf. It is a good example, however, of many of the other activities which occur within higher education besides the teaching of undergraduates and postgraduates.

There may also be more sophisticated (Level 3) applications of interactive video in this context. Chris Jones, a Research Psychologist in Edinburgh, has produced three discs for teaching English to deaf children. There is a notorious problem in communication with and teaching of deaf children which results from the mismatch between their teachers' and their own experience and facility in using sign language. For deaf children, sign language is habitual and quick but it is deliberate and therefore slower for others. Deaf children's language development is therefore badly hampered by the difficulty of connecting concepts or objects with their names. Often vocabulary cannot be acquired because by the time an interpreter has named an object by signing, the object may no longer be present. Looking in dictionaries is, for some deaf people, a discouraging exercise rather like being shunted around a telephone switchboard. The Edinburgh discs attempt to overcome this problem in a classic way which makes use of the most powerful features of interactive video. The *Interactive Video Dictionary* enables learners to access photographic images or signed equivalents from the disc at any time they wish to while they are reading from teletext sequences produced by the microcomputer program. Other programmes on *Tenses and the Passive Voice* and *Reading and Comprehension* use similar combinations of video and text in ingenious ways to enable independent language learning where the learner's control of the content and sequence helps forge the crucial links between language and action. Similar interactive video programmes have been developed in Rochester and Ithaca in America (Gayeski and Williams, 1984).

This project is really a development within higher education for application outside it in schools. It may be indicative, however, of the changing nature of higher education institutions. While it is easy to see a future for interactive video data-bases for specialised research and library applications in British higher education (provided the software is produced), it is less easy to see what its role might be within new forms and structures of educational provision. It may be worth considering some of the possibilities here, however.

12.11 INTERACTIVE VIDEO AND CONTINUING EDUCATION

Barker (1985) has pointed out that

> Developments in communication technology will undoubtedly provide the means whereby instruction may take place at virtually any geographic location — the home, the office, the factory floor — thereby fulfilling the requirements of a truly open learning system.

While it would be an error to fall into the trap of technological determinism, it is clear that there are infrastructural pressures in the British higher education system which are already causing it to adapt and change. The general issues which arise from these pressures are being pursued by the Society for Research in Higher Education and were the subject of a recent conference (Nicol, 1985). More immediately, the development of continuing education and the CVCP Code of Practice for Academic Staff Training have given some impetus to changing thinking about teaching and the provision of appropriate structures in higher education (CVCP, 1986b). The new Code of Practice at least formally registers the need for academic staff to be provided with systematic help on teaching and learning methods and media. It does little, however, to address the problems of resistance to innovation of the kind which currently inhibit interactive video.

Current accounts of the continuing decline of British industry rarely omit reference to a shortage of qualified scientists and, in particular, of engineers. The Open University currently provides over a quarter of general continuing education in the United Kingdom (Horlock, 1986) and there is apparently a great need for increased provision, particularly in the field of technology transfer in a form 'which enables people to learn at the time, place and pace which meets their needs and requirements' (Holland, 1984). Conventional universities are being called upon to perform a new, third role, in addition to their traditional ones of research and teaching, of providing continuing education for mature scientists and engineers. It is sometimes envisaged that this could occur through multi-media distance-teaching. The Open University's courses in this area are able to break even at the level of 500 enrolled students per annum and at a cost of £3.50 per head for each hour of study (Horlock, 1986). Clearly, there is a potential here for interactive video in a *training* role within higher education for the updating of professional scientists to meet the needs of British industry.

However, there are also many problems. First of all, there is a problem of numbers and scale of operation. Currently, there appears to be little actual demand for such provision, with only just over 1000 places in Masters courses in Britain taken up (Horlock, 1986, p. 7). Further, how many universities could expect to attract 100, let alone 500 professionals for new courses? There is clearly a large marketing task to be done. Secondly, given that many engineering graduates are deemed out of date by the time they graduate and the current average lead-time for the production of an interactive videodisc is around two years, what sort of shelf-life is even the most up-to-date disc likely to have? Granted, new microcomputer programs can be written for new specific applications, but there is an unavoidable inflexibility about what is actually on the videodisc itself for display. By comparison, speech and writing look like fast media. Thirdly, where will the critical funding come from for development costs, materials production and marketing? Finally, we come up against the problem of innovation. Cautious and evolutionary attempts to introduce continuing education at Southampton University, where there is a large and highly successful engineering base, have not led to any real shift in institutional resources. There has been no genuine incorporation of continuing education into the University's normal patterns of teaching and there have been few incentives for staff to engage in it other than some short-term financial rewards. Consequently, as one study has suggested, 'established values are likely to remain relatively intact' (Fleetwood-Walker, 1985).

12.12 CONCLUSION

I have argued in this chapter that interactive video clearly has a potential for effectiveness, since it offers a combination of two powerful media and two distinct modes of learning. At the same time, its flexibility offers forms of interaction with learners which has many of the virtues of personal face-to-face communication. As a result, it has established a particular reputation for training applications, where it may also offer some economic advantages.

However, even in the context of industrial and commercial training, there is a dearth of appropriate learning material. There is also some reluctance at the level of instructional design to learn from the failures of the early programmed learning movement.

In the British higher education context, the economics of interactive video are complicated by particular institutional cultures and politics, especially in the universities. Exploring its potential for development demands an understanding of how change and innovation occur in traditional higher education. Although there are several specific projects which I have discussed, few of them have been able to demonstrate any degree of effectiveness as a result of systematic evaluation of learning.

It may be, however, that the structural constraints which currently inhibit the development of interactive video in many higher education institutions will be swept away. Even within these constraints, there is some space for alternative applications which rely on specialised applications of generic discs. Continuing education may be a catalyst in this respect, since it can be seen as a training function within higher education for which interactive video may be very appropriate. Even so, development, production and distribution costs need to be met on a larger scale than is currently occurring through the Department of Trade and Industry scheme based on Heriot-Watt University.

Radical change is not likely to occur unless it becomes inexorable —

when resisting change is acknowledged to be more catastrophic than deliberate innovation. However, such change is determined not by technological innovations but by the more basic economic and political factors which produce the environment within which innovations may occur. The real and immediate concerns of higher education in Britain are currently with declining income, rising costs and staff–student ratios and deteriorating premises.

By comparison, interactive video may seem somewhat remote. The pressures of structural change are undoubtedly strong but there is no sign as yet of the kind of radical changes which might require distance-learning technology to make new forms of teaching and learning possible. In the meantime, it seems sensible to continue to explore the potential of interactive video in terms of what it can tell us about educational processes. It may be that its chief value will prove to be the questions and insights it provokes in this area. For all its potential flexibility and effectiveness, it may be simply another revolution which does not happen.

REFERENCES

Barker, P. (1985) Information technology, education and training, *British Journal of Educational Technology*, 16/2, May, 103–115.

Barker, P. (1986) The many faces of human–machine interaction, *British Journal of Educational Technology*, 17/1, Jan., 74–81.

Barnes, D. (1973) *Language in the classroom*, Open University.

Bates, A. W. (1983) Selecting media and possible roles for interactive video in the Open University, in R. G. Fuller (ed.) *Using interactive videodiscs in Open University Courses*, I.E.T Papers on Broadcasting No. 218, Jun., 1983.

Bayard-White, C. (1985) *Interactive Video Case Studies and Directory*, Council for Educational Technology.

Bosco, J. (1986) An analysis of evaluations of interactive video, *Educational Technology*, May, 7–17.

Clark, D. R,. (1984) The role of videodisc in education and training, *Media in Education and Development*, 17/4, Dec., 190–192.

Clark, J. (1984) How do interactive videodiscs rate against other media? *Instructional innovator*, 29/6, 12–16.

Committee of Vice-Chancellors and Principals (1986a) *University Statistics*, no. 5. Spring.

Committee of Vice-Chancellors and Principals (1986b) *Code of Practice for Academic Staff Training*.

Copeland, P. (1983) Cavis — from concept to system, *Media in Education and Development*, 16/2, June, 74–79.

Dalton, D. W. (1986) How effective is interactive video in improving performance and attitude?, *Educational Technology*, Jan., 27–29.

Doulton, A. (1984) Interactive video in training, *Media in Education and Development*, 17/4 Dec., 205–206.

Eco, U. (1979) Can television teach?, *Screen Education*, **31**, 15–24.

Elton, L. R. B. (1977) Innovation and the role of educational media, in J. K. Beug (ed.) *Innnovation and Improvement in Teaching and Learning in Higher Education*, Higher Education Authority and Irish Federation of University Teachers.

Fiske, J. (1982) *Introduction to Communication Studies*, Methuen.

Fleetwood-Walker, P., Mathias, H. and Rutherford, D. (1985) *Continuing Education in Universities*, paper delivered at SRHE Conference.

Gayeski, D. M. and Williams, D. K. (1984) Interactive video in higher education, in O. Zuber-Skerritt (ed.) *Video in Higher Education*, 64–74.

Griffiths, M. (1984) Planning for interactive videodisc, *Media in Education and Development*, 17/4, Dec., 196–200.

Hart, A. P. (1984) Not just a bit of an extra, *Media in Education and Development*, 17/3, Sep., 162–167.

Hart, A. P. (1985) Making connections: higher education and cable television in Britain, *Media in Education and Development*, 18/3, Sep., 116–120.

Hawkridge, D. (1981) The telesis of educational technology, *British Journal of Educational Technology*, 12/1.

Hills, L. (1986) *Interactive Video in Education*, Scottish Council for Educational Technology.

Hills, P. (1979) *Teaching and Learning as a Communication Process*, Croom Helm.

Hoffos, S. and Parsloe, E. (1984) *Interactive video*, Sigma Technical Press.

Horlock, T. H. (1986) Continuing Education for Industry. Lecture at the Open University, 17 Feb. 1986.

Holland, G. (1984) Business Growth and Open Learning. Conference report, Open University.

Kozma, R. B. (1978) Faculty development and the adoption and diffusion of classroom innovations, *Journal of Higher Education*, 49/1, Jan., 316–328.

Laurillard, D. M. (1982) The potential of interactive video, *Journal of Educational Television*, 8/3, 173–180.

Laurillard, D. M. (1984) Interactive video and the control of learning, *Educational Technology*, 24/6.

Laurillard, D. M. (1985) 'The Teddy Bears Disc', *Media in Education and Development*, March.

McAleese, R. (1986a) 'The representation of knowledge in authoring environments' in N. Rushby and A. Howe, (eds) *Aspects of Educational Technology*, **XIX**, Kogan-Page, pp. 104–113.

McAleese, R. (1986b) Computer-based authoring and intelligent interactive video, in *International Yearbook of Educational and Instructional Technology 1986/87*, Kogan-Page, pp. 63–81.

Macintosh, P. (1984) Educational technology past and present, *Interactive Learning International*, 1/1 Jul.–Sep., 12–14.

McLuhan, M. (1964) *Understanding Media,* Abacus, p. 264.
McQuail, D. and Windahl, S. (1981) *Communication Models*, Longman.
Moore, D. M. and Hunt, T. L. (1980) The nature of resistance to the use of instructional media, *British Journal of Educational Technology,* 11/2, May, 141–147.
Nicol, D. (1985) New information technologies in higher education, *Media in Education and Development,* 18/4, Dec., 184–186.
Palmarozza, P. H. (1984) Trends in training: an historical perspective, *Interactive Learning International,* 1/1 Jul.–Sep., 9–11.
Rees, M. J. and Robson, D. J. (1985) Video-Slide: a presentation aid for the BBC computer, *Software Practice and Experience,* 15/9 Sep.
Roach, D. K. (1983) Who, What, Where? *Videodisc Newsletter,* 2, Oct.
Roach, D. K. (1984) Interactive video: the Cardiff experience, *Media in Education and Development,* 17/4 Dec., 187–189.
Rosenblatt, L. M. (1978) *The Reader, the Text, the Poem: the Transactional Theory of the Literary Work*, Carbondale, Southern Illinois University Press.
Shannon, C. and Weaver, W. (1949) *The Mathematical Theory of Communication*, University of Illinois Press.
Weisgerber, R. A. (1968) Higher education and media innovations, in R. A. Weisgerber, (ed.), *Instructional Process and Media Innovations*, Rand McNally.
Wells, G. and Nicolls, J. (1985) *Language and Learning: A Transactional Perspective*, Falmer.
Williams, R. (1974) *Television: Technology and Cultural Form*, Fontana.

13

Interactive video as a school resource: Rolls-Royce or Model T Ford?

Colin Mably

13.1 INTRODUCTION

Recent developments in interactive video have been largely led by the technology rather than by education, and centred on building complex systems with little regard for the realities of schools and their teachers and children. Much of what has been produced is very impressive in a technical sense (BBC's 'Domesday' is a fantastic achievement) but often imposes a complex 'prescribed' form of use, tends to be locked into particularly expensive hardware, and costs a great deal to produce. Consequently their general day-to-day usability in schools is very questionable.

The argument that I wish to develop is that schools, their teachers, pupils and current practices have to be the starting point for the educational development of interactive video, and that there is a strong argument for a 'Ford Model T' version rather than a 'Rolls-Royce'.

13.2 A PRIMARY SCHOOL CASE STUDY

In 1984, when interactive video was fast becoming a buzz word in the UK video and microcomputer worlds (they were largely quite separate worlds at that time), an opportunity arose to conduct a small evaluation study with videodisc players in primary schools. The study involved placing a player and three interactive videodiscs containing four programmes in each of four selected primary schools for a three-month term-time period in the Spring term 1984. The participating teachers, two headteachers and two class teachers, and the four schools, reflected a variety of school situations commonly found in the London area.

The project used prototype videodiscs that Thorn EMI had already developed, which, although not designed for school use but for home education, presented enough scope for an evaluation of this kind since we were concerned not simply with the discs themselves, but how teachers and children would react to and use the complete interactive video system in the schools. The discs comprised three programmes from the 'Adventures into Science — Start Here' series, designed to introduce aspects of physics to primary age children, and a programme entitled 'Mysteries of the Great Whales'. These programmes offered a linear sequence arranged in chapters followed by an indexed reference section.

The (VHD) system contained all the normal level 1 interactive video facilities including: remote control; rapid random access; still picture/page; page scan; repeat memory; autostop; fast scan/slow motion in forward and reverse (each with a variety of speeds available); stereo, mono and dual audio.

The programmes were designed to be used rather like a reference book but offered visual sequences and still pictures with stereo sound, or alternatively, dual audio-tracks that could be played separately allowing two soundtracks for the same visual sequence.

The teachers were introduced to the equipment and shown how to operate it, asked to make themselves familiar with the system and consider how they would introduce and monitor its use in their school. The introduction of the system into schools was to follow as natural a path as possible since the evaluation was to focus upon the ways in which teachers chose to use the system as well as its relative success within their normal work with children.

The teachers were left to their own devices for one month, then asked to attend a discussion meeting to compare their experiences and feelings about the system so far. The discussion was recorded and later analysed to form the first major piece of evaluation data. Teachers were given a list of items on which to make written comments and also invited to collect and send in any further views they were able to gather from colleagues and children as they arose, thus providing a second source of data. Other data was collected by observations during visits to the schools, conversations with the participating teachers and children, teacher colleagues' verbal and written comments. This information, essentially impressionistic and subjective, gave a broad notion of teacher and child experience and educational feeling about the system and provided mid-term evaluation which, through progressive focusing, enabled the construction of a more formal, 'key question' evaluation tool to be applied through individual interviews at the end of the field study phase.

The responses of the participating teachers showed that the videodisc system was positively received in almost every respect. Their comments concerned both pedagogic and implementation issues.

Pedogogic aspects
    Children reacted positively to the system and were able to use it in all appropriate situations, were motivated by it and maintained interest in it;
    The system was entirely compatible with current curriculum arrangements and teaching and learning methods;
    The rapid access and control functions were highly valued;

They advised a more 'open-ended' approach to programme design;
Teachers viewed the system as having exceptional potential for school use applications.

Implementation aspects

The system proved robust and reliable and no failure was reported;
Teachers would like to have several systems in their schools;
They felt that the cost of the system was reasonable and would be prepared to purchase them given good quality and quantity of software;
They felt strongly that educationalists and teachers should contribute to programme design;
They felt that a sponsored scheme for initial machine purchase was very desirable;
They tended to support multipurpose use of the system in schools and were less intersted in 'programmed learning' approaches;
They recognised the potential of interfacing the system with microcomputers and other devices;
They saw enormous potential for the system once it had established itself;
They would prefer the system to be more portable.

The evaluation showed that, as far as the four participating teachers were concerned, the interactive videodisc system was enthusiastically received by both teachers, pupils and teachers' colleagues. The system was used in a variety of ways including whole class work, small groups, individual learners, and for staff development. Its flexibility, user friendliness, reliability, and above all its ability to provide rapid access to quality information in sound and vision were much valued. The teachers were quick to see the future application potential of the system, not only for a variety of educational situations, subjects and pupils, but also the potential applications of level 2 and 3 systems (Mably, 1984).

The study demonstrated considerable enthusiasm for videodiscs in schools, and, coupled with the fact that most schools had by that time acquired microcomputers, indicated a need for further research and development. The report concluded that active development of good school-focused software and a sponsored scheme enabling schools to acquire videodisc players should begin without delay, and acknowledged that both potential publishers and relevant government initiatives were needed to support this.

As far as I know, this modest school-based project still remains the only UK research involving the general use of videodisc technology. By current standards the interactive aspect of it can only be described as crude. However, the central point to emerge — namely that the stand-alone videodisc player, given adequate quality and quantity of videodisc material, had a huge potential for wide use as a primary school resource — still remains good today despite all the higher technological educational development that has been the major focus since then. In reviewing the evaluation study, Jacquetta Megarry (1984) concluded:

> By revealing all these possibilities in an accessible, affordable package, the experiment has made its contribution to this field in a way which transcends any limitations of pilot discs made for a different purpose. Given imaginative use of computer-controlled interaction and video that has been carefully assembled and edited by teachers and educationalists, the potential impact of this medium is without precedent.

On reflection, perhaps the most crucial aspect of this study was that teachers were left in control, and made all the decisions using their own particular criteria within their own particular professional situations. The only element they had no control over was the videodisc content, and since this was largely arranged in indexed information modules (even the longer linear sequences were assembled as chapters, with absolutely no 'branching' or 'programming' built into their design) they had, and indeed made use of, a multitude of options in the way it could be used.

13.3 INTERACTIVE VIDEO AND SCHOOL EDUCATION

Perhaps the greatest problem with interactive video, at least in the context of broad education, is its name. The high-tech image it inspires does more for the technocratic mentality than it does for meaningful and purposeful education, leading to ideas about foisting a complex application on education, more for the sake of technical brilliance than an honest attempt to solve an educational problem. Prescribed programs are appropriate where objectives can be made very explicit and where the learning need is clearly defined, but the acquisition of understanding and learning often has more to do with experience and experiment than with working through a pre-specified program.

For educational purposes it might well be best to drop the term interactive altogether, or to define it in very wide terms. Teachers are unlikely to care whether they are dealing with level 1, 2 or 3 interactivity, focusing much more on how the new medium is genuinely useful in teaching and learning situations. The teachers and children in the evaluation study mentioned above simply saw the stand-alone player as an up-market cassette player. They recognised the power that fast random access and video material manipulation gave them and had no difficulty whatever in using it immediately. The fact they were operating at the bottom end of level 1 was quite irrelevant to them. Indeed, as time passed they themselves began to see the potential of up-grading to interfacing with a microcomputer, using it to drive the disc, or using the disc player as another computer peripheral. I suspect that had they been supplied with purpose-built level 2 hardware and software their reaction might have been very different. At level 1 the teacher and the pupil are fully in control; beyond that they become progressively controlled by the technology itself or, to be more accurate, the authors of the interactivity.

In schools today there is an evident need for good quality audio-visual material that can be accessed quickly and used in a variety of ways and levels that are largely determined by teachers and pupils themselves. The televisual medium is now a far more familiar informing experience than books and if it can be made available in a form which makes immediate sense to the practising teacher and adds significantly to their teaching and learning repertoire then a positive response is assured. It is clear that most teachers, on seeing interactive videodisc for the first time, are usually captivated by it and quick to see obvious applications within their own professional situations. Given the profession's well-known lack of enthusiasm for innovations, let alone technological innovations, the response is remarkable. The indications for the adoption of this technology in education are therefore very promising. However, moving from initial exposure of prototypes to the actual delivery of such systems to schools, in terms of appropriate software creation, awareness and especially cost, is far from simple. The basic questions 'do they want it? and 'do they need it?' have yet to be asked, not only in the UK, but also in the USA and Japan where development has been more rapid.

Interactive video probably will, and certainly should, only work in education where it is the best solution to educational problems and needs: the learning of mainstream school students should be qualitatively enhanced by its use. To put it more precisely, the important issue is not 'what system?' or 'which format?' but rather 'what kinds of educational problems can be solved by this technology in an effective and affordable way?'. Questions such as 'What is the likely impact of interactive video on schools?' or 'How should schools respond to this new technology?' are the wrong questions, but symptomatic of the kind of software development that is emerging.

Projects exploring the interactive technical capabilities of laser and microcomputer systems in an educational context seem to be the first major design initiatives. Most have in mind 'work station' i.e. an individualised teaching program a concept derived largely from behaviorist psychology and sanctified by corporate training, and one which has consistently been rejected by UK educationalists and teachers. In schools the 'work station' approach also fails in simple structural logistics wherever the 'station' is more than a modest cost. One unit (if that is all that is affordable), to be shared by several hundred pupils, is a nonsense no matter how elegant it may be. While such developments are valuable in extending the technical and programming possibilities, exploring the limits of what is possible, and especially breeding general awareness of the medium, their adoption in large numbers will depend on how well they fit with what is happening in the schools and whether they are perceived as cost-effective on educational criteria.

This recent developmental characteristic has also tended to mask the fact that the videodisc player, on its own, offers very wide scope for school use. In one recent study (Trowbridge, 1985) a stand-alone player and one disc has been shown to be all that is required. The player's ability to deliver dynamic visual and sound information not normally available to teachers and learners, is almost instantly a dramatic option for teaching and learning, albeit a very modest one in interactive terms. In this simple form it has the potential to be used in any educational context be it a formal lesson, group study, individual work, or as a teacher's and pupil's reference resource, and becomes a very desirable tool that does not prescribe the learning situation. Moreover, it does not need to assume a particular method of teaching and learning, it keeps the operation simple, offering very flexible and wide use, and it still allows the possibility of higher levels of interactivity to those who wish to develop it (in the school itself by teachers, or even pupils for example). The stand-alone player is also likely to be the only affordable option for most schools in the short term, though they may well become interested in up-grading as time goes by, by acquiring one of the cheap interface units already available that will link it to existing school microcomputers and associated hardware.

13.4 POTENTIAL SCHOOL USES

There are several ways in which interactive videodisc could be used in schools, including:

- as a teacher's lesson aid;
- as a resource for teacher planned group work;
- as an individual study (teacher-planned) resource;
- as an individual study (pupil-planned) resource;
- as a teacher in-service aid;
- as a televisual data-bank resource;
- as a programmed teaching/learning tool.

(There are also very specific uses such as customised systems for Special Educational Needs, English as a Second Language, systems that simulate particular scientific instruments such as an oscilascope, etc.).

None of these uses necessarily require interactivity past level 1 (i.e. computer linkage) and can be very successfully provided for by stand-alone videodisc players. Equally though, none are precluded from computer management or control. Provided the videodisc material is arranged suitably, the same discs could be used for both levels. However, if the initial design is dedicated to computer control, or if the disc design is heavily programmed (with a high degree of branching paths for example) the dual possibility is considerably reduced.

What is important is to consider the ways in which schools themselves are arranged and managed, because the introduction of systems of any type can never assume that the environment, structures, organisation and community attitudes are neutral. The less disruption or change required by the introduction of a new system the more likely it is to be found acceptable.

Conversely, a radical alteration necessary for a new system to be properly used will limit its easy adoption.

Primary schools, with their more integrated way of working, are likely to place different requirements on the medium than secondary schools where study is often more subject specific, and where the educational objectives are more closely defined. In primary schools resources are often shared throughout the school, whereas their secondary counterparts are mainly structured in subject departments, each with its own specific resources. This is not to imply that there is no overlap (many secondary schools operate close to primary school practice in the first two or three years) but simply to suggest that in broad terms the priorities, methods, structures, staff attitudes and budgetry arrangements are often different. The idea of a Craft Design and Technology Department of a large comprehensive secondary school sharing an interactive video system with the Modern Languages Department does not seem likely given the way in which secondary schools are currently arranged.

If interactive video is to be of any use at all it needs to be physically accessible at the moment when it is needed. While careful planning can overcome relatively minor accessibility problems, no teacher will be prepared to set out on a long journey to obtain the equipment any more than they do now with computers. In the same way that a secretary needs a desk-top system to use word processing profitably (the days of the 'word processing room' buried away in the basement are long since gone), so teachers and pupils in schools need the kit in close proximity for use.

Primary schools are used to making AVA and microcomputer equipment portable (often on trolleys), until such time as they have acquired enough hardware to provide every class with individual kit. The player is normally located in the school library/resources centre on a trolley, and simply moved to a classroom and other parts of the school when it is required. Primary schools have used a similar arrangement for videocassette for years.

Secondary schools tend to base equipment round subject departmental centres, and it is likely that initial software for secondary schools will be subject-specific. Whether it is the year's crop of Shakespeare and other A level set texts residing with the English Department, a skills videodisc and player located in the Craft Workshop, or a Physics Experiment videodisc, it is very unlikely that systems will be acquired for general school use in the first instance. Schools will not buy hardware for hardware's sake; rather they will buy software that answers a need they have, or that enhances practice. The fact that its delivery system is interactive video, provided it is affordable, will be comparatively incidental. Secondary schools especially will only buy software whose value speaks for itself.

It is worth noting here that one of the unique features for schools is the dual audio capability of videodisc systems. Two sound-tracks for the same piece of visual material opens up a huge educational dimension. In Japan, early science VHD videodiscs, made by JVC in collaboration with the central curriculum authorities, have used one sound-track for pupils, and the other for teachers. It is not difficult to see the inservice implications of this approach. Different comprehension levels, different languages, different information, are other obvious ways of using this special facility. To return to Shakespeare for a moment, one could use one sound-track for the actual play, the other for on-going literary criticism, and any remaining space on the discs for a reference section about the play (Shakespeare's portrayal of women, historical notes, linguistics of the time, etc.). It is this facility coupled with fast random access to quality audio-visual software material of the type mentioned above, that will sell the concept of interactive video to both secondary and primary schools. It will not sell on the basis of technical brilliance alone.

13.5 HARDWARE ISSUES

Not surprisingly perhaps, hardware has been a dominant concern in interactive video. It is important to realise that the hardware has been available for some time and is currently far from new. Early systems interfaced tape and microcomputers with reasonable technical success, but the linear emphasis in design, mainly to cut down wind-on/wind-back time, coupled with very slow access time made them very limited by today's standards. The emergence of videodisc, with its rapid access, addressable chapters, time-codes and frame/page numbers, and the dual audio-track capability presented a whole new possibility of design that is still far from its developmental limits.

Videodisc technology itself has been available for several years now, and while there continue to be many technical enhancements, the basic systems of LaserVision and VHD remain the same. The relatively slow utilisation and application of the systems outside Japan, and to a lesser degree the USA and Canada, relate to the large initial investment costs of creating the software for videodiscs, and also to the somewhat futile debates about which system to standardise upon. If innovation needs 'vision, courage and money' as some suggest, it is largely the lack of each of these that represent the major problem. Videodiscs are analogous to gramophone records. One begins to make profits when one has a mass market for them, or to put it more precisely, disc cost is a function of market size. Since very few discs exist, very few players are sold, producing a classic 'Catch 22' situation. In the UK especially, unlike Japan, videodisc player sales fell foul of the sudden, and unexpected impact of videocassette player sales, which through skilful marketing caught the imagination and spending power of the high street market. Thorn EMI cancelled its proposed high street launch of VHD at the last minute, avoiding a near certain commercial disaster in addition to the investment costs it had already incurred. Today some 70% of schools in the UK have VHS videocassette recorder/players.

By contrast the Japanese were not such enthusiastic buyers of videocassette players, with the result that videodisc player sales have been more dramatic there than in any other part of the world. The most recent statistics show that 4% of Japanese households have a videodisc player already (approximately a quarter of a million players), and the market is accelerating. The total videodisc player population is about 750 000 with half a million in industry and education added to the home market. The competing LaserVision and VHD systems share this market at approximately 55% to 45% respectively and some 5000 videodisc titles are available and growing.

To stimulate the school market JVC, who manufacture VHD players, have produced a collection of eight double-sided videodiscs for junior high school science (physics, chemistry, biology and earth science) complete with teachers' guidebooks. The discs are modular, nothing more than a vast televisual store of classical scientific experiments or phenomena, beautifully shot and stored on the discs as a long list of references. The series provides 16 hours worth of visual material, with two sound tracks (one for the pupils and one for the teacher) designed to be used with a stand-alone player and remote key-pad. Clearly it would be quite easy to write a computer management program if necessary. Schools have been using these discs for several years now with considerable success. JVC have further series in production and are looking to others, notably publishers, to produce more once the school player population makes this a viable prospect.

The videodisc player population in the USA and Canada is also growing steadily, largely on NTSC LaserVision, though VHD is becoming more available there, and there are approximately 100 educational titles listed covering all levels of education.

In the UK progress has been slow. Hardware has been caught up in the raging, but educationally irrelevant, debate about which system (LaserVision or VHD) to standardise upon. In general LaserVision appears to be winning this dubious battle, partly on the grounds that it is an optical system and therefore seen as 'tomorrow's technology' with the expected growth of optical memory systems. In addition, LaserVision has a very clean freeze frame facility of 54 000 frames, and tends to be marginally faster in access terms. In most other respects it behaves in the same way as VHD, at least as far as the user is concerned.

VHD is a high density capacitance system where the signal is read by a sensor which rests on the surface of the disc. Pundits suspect disc or sensor wear may prove a problem (though there is no evidence of this to date) and point to its poor random freeze frame facility (there are two frames on every revolution of the disc, and since freeze frame keeps the sensor on one revolution it reads the two frames, producing a 'wobble' effect). VHD offers fewer individual frames at 45 000 (though a picture store facility is being developed which will double the capacity and produce a rock hard freeze), but each disc can accommodate 60 minutes of video and dual audio-tracks on each disc side compared with 37 minutes on LaserVision.

There is no doubt that LaserVision is the more elegant system, but a debate about which system should or could be used in education and schools depends much more on the kind of school use envisaged than the relative merits of the technological specifications of a particular system. The 'optical' technology argument is a digression. Current LaserVision may be optical, but anything made for it now will not in future interface with optical memory systems. Both systems will be ultimately eclipsed by Direct Read After

Write (DRAW) systems which enable users to record onto discs and which will require a completely new player at the very least. And these will be made obsolete by further technological marvels that we do not even know about yet. Standardisation of systems has always proved a very mixed blessing except in the very short term.

The main consideration is probably cost. While one can appreciate the technical beauty of LaserVision and its good freeze frame, it is at least twice as expensive as VHD, and I suspect that its limit of 37 minutes per side compared with 60 minutes per side is a great disadvantage in general educational use. Hardware in this context is mainly a question of what will do the educational job adequately in the most cost-effective way, emphasising again that the real issue is software not hardware.

Other hardware issues revolve around how the televisual images are accessed and delivered. With more sophisticated TV monitors, and some extra components, notably a GENLOCK board, it is possible to overlay computer generated text and graphics on top of the video picture. This can be very useful where the user needs indicators that point out various parts of the picture on the screen (arrows showing precisely an engine component, of the roots of a plant for example). Text windows can be created on the micro which allow sub-titles to be overlaid on the video picture. In fact there are many applications for overlay which could be effected. For 'work station' use overlay is often very useful indeed, as the user only has to look at one screen to work with the system. On the other hand, the cost is high because schools do not possess such TV monitors, nor the appropriate interfacing in their existing equipment, and it is doubtful if the 'work station' approach is the most useful one for schools anyway.

Using two screens, one a conventional TV, the other the existing microcomputer monitor, is a good alternative which in some instances may even be preferable. Since video material is often made for viewing from a distance (unlike computer text and graphics), it makes sense to have the TV screen further away than the micro monitor. There is a limit to how much text can be overlaid anyway, and sometimes text gets in the way of video. With separate screens computer text can be held, like a reference notebook, while the video sequence is rolling. Again, cost may well be a strong determining factor here. Since schools already have all the hardware they need, other than the videodisc player and microcomputer interface, they will be tempted to do without the finer refinements, at least at first.

Other hardware peripherals relate mainly to accessing. It is possible to use a variety of devices such as light pens, touch sensitive screens, barcode readers, tracker balls, the mouse, and 'concept' keyboards. The same basic argument applies here too. While applications of these devices can be imagined (especially for children with special education needs for example), they will not be of immediate concern except in very specific instances. Schools are likely to want to keep it simple at first and develop into the use of these devices when and where there is an obvious educational reason for doing so. A further hardware issue is whether to link the video to microcomputers. There are perhaps two predominant ways of using this facility. The first is simply to use the computer as a management tool for video. The second is to see the video player as a computer peripheral. There is a difference here, but the choice is largely determined by the availability of video material.

It is worth remembering that hardware is a delivery system which makes possible the manipulation of software, in this case visual and audio software, and the finest delivery system is only as good as the software available or creatable for it. For this reason it is crucial that software should not be locked into particular hardware systems. This may seem a trivial point, but the consequences of machine specific software are very far-reaching indeed. Moreover the costs of software production are so huge, that it makes economical nonsense to develop program(me)s that can only possibly be accessed on one form of the technology. Recent examples have shown the folly of a 'system dominated' approach to software generation, where technological developments (e.g. CD-ROM) overtake the developmental process in midstream. Who knows what is just round the corner? Looking back over just the last five years of development in the information technology field tells us that the only certain thing is that today's hardware delivery systems will shortly be eclipsed by new, better, faster, cheaper, and extended versions.

From an educational point of view it is therefore essential to view software separately from hardware, at least in part, and more important still to generate the kind of software that can be easily adapted converted or complemented to be available on new hardware as it arrives. This is the lesson that both microcomputers and early interactive video systems should have taught us. I can think of no examples in either where any software developed for a specific hardware system has survived in its original form. In general the rule seems to be that the closer the software/hardware relationship, the shorter the life.

Hardware has become a never-ending issue for debate in the Interactive Video industry itself, and in some ways educational thinking has been seduced by this tendency. This is mainly because those who initially respond to interactive video within education tend to be those who are particularly enamoured of technology and systems, especially those closely involved with microcomputers. This is inevitable perhaps, but we should not lose sight of the point that if interactive video is to be a good useful tool in schools then it is the non-specialist teacher who must respond with enthusiasm, and they will do that not on hardware issues, but on educational use issues. In this domain it is software that is the key and hardware is simply perceived as the 'box' that it works on. All that is required of hardware is that it does the job effectively, and is affordable.

13.6 SOFTWARE — A MODULAR APPROACH?

So far I have used the term 'software' to distinguish it from 'hardware' but it is necessary to think of software in interactive video in two separate ways (though in some instances they can be so closely interrelated that they are one). Software, in the way I have used it refers to both the material contained on a videodisc (visual sequences, sound-tracks, still pictures and text, together with any built in control features such as autostops, chapters, time code and frame/page addresses), and also associated computer software normally contained on floppy disc, mini-disc, ROM chips, etc.

The linking of these two types of software, and more importantly the hardware they run on, has been the basis of interactive video, bringing video under computer control and allowing the user to 'interact' with it. Inevitably perhaps these two types of programming have been getting closer, and one of the special features of the BBC's Domesday Disc is that the computer programming is contained on one sound-track of the videodisc itself. This is called Laser-Vision Rom (LV Rom), but it requires a high-level videodisc player with an added sensor to read the digital microcomputer information. Compact Disc Rom (CD-Rom) is thought to have special possibilities for interactive video, and the Philips Sony Compact Disc (CDI) which can define a system for an infinitely flexible mix of music, still pictures, text graphics and computer programs on a compact disc may well extend this technology further. In fact software and hardware in this sense are getting closer.

Videodisc 'software' at level 1 concerns the images and sound material as no computer is involved. It is this medium which I have argued is of most general use to schools, and most understood by teachers and pupils. Moreover, video has the power to bring into a classroom, laboratory or school library/resource centre very real vicarious experiences which cannot be had first hand (whales spouting in the South Atlantic, explosions, complex industrial processes, distant locations, etc.). Videotape can of course deliver these sequences too, but cannot be accessed quickly, and usually only offers one sound-track (most school VCRs are mono, as is most broadcast televison material). Videotapes are usually constructed as films, linear programmes with a beginning, middle and end, where the user is expected to be largely a passive watcher.

For school use, it may be sensible to think of putting video material onto disc in the form of modules of information, rather like a reference book, where each module can be indexed. Thus a child, or a teacher who wishes to find out something to do with their study would use the videodisc collection alongside all the other resources (reference books, videotapes, slides, audiotapes, etc.). One can imagine the school library having shelves of videodiscs together with its more normal contents and a videodisc player available. This is using the technology at its simplest, but in a way which it performs very well. For a primary school one can envisage a range of titles on Science, others on Mathematics, Nature, History, and so on. Given the integrated curriculum approach of many primary schools, discs on themes and topics, such as People, Travel, Homes, could be treated in this way.

Secondary schools could also make very good use of this simple format. A disc that contains craft skills, well filmed (dovetail jointing, how to use a wood plane, soldering and welding, etc.) could be an invaluable resource in the Craft and Design Technology workshop, where a pupil needing a particular skill or craft element could simply access it from the disc, watch the expert way to do it and listen to two sound-tracks, freeze it, play it in slow motion, put it on repeat mode, without taking individual time from a busy teacher, and without wastefully using up craft materials in demonstration. I am not, of course, advocating that this should be at the expense of the pupil actually using the skill, merely suggesting that a modular disc of craft skills and elements could help them to choose the best method of achieving the design requirement and inform themselves about the particular skill to be employed in the task before doing it for real. A similar disc for PE sports and games would be invaluable. Imagine the best exponents in the land at trampolining, gymnastics or swimming captured on film and modularised into accessible elements, where pupils and teachers can look closely at a particular technique they are trying to develop, and can manipulate it in any way they choose. Such applications are so simple and yet so valuable in school use terms that it can only be a queston of time, and cost-effectiveness before they are developed.

Making a videodisc is a very expensive business, but the costs are substantially reduced if archive or existing visual material can be used — possibly one-third less (though it is worth noting that copyright is a huge and largely unresolved issue in the field of interactive video, see section 14.3). Extensive archives exist from a whole variety of sources, but the most important for schools has to be television broadcasting.

Schools' television broadcasting began in the UK almost exactly thirty years ago with Associated Rediffusion. Since that time the BBC and a number of the independent television companies have refined schools broadcasting to a fine art. The archive material they hold is in itself a very rich resource indeed. The main problem is that each programme has been constructed in a rigid linear form. Broadcasters are essentially slot-fillers in that they have to fill a fixed time slot. The programme has to be designed to capture uninterrupted attention of a viewing audience which is, by definition, passive. This is a long way from interacting with the material in the ways described above. However, a great deal of this material could be adapted into a usable form, could be modularised, could be given new sound-tracks (which is not expensive), and 'live' in another extended form. The broadcasters are the most professional and prolific producers of television material, and great expense is involved in producing any broadcast television programme. And yet it is comparatively rare for any television programme to be broadcast more than once. Videodisc offers a continuing use for existing material, and indeed a further income for it. School broadcasting should be considering not only how it could make its archive store available for videodisc and other uses, but should also begin to make new broadcast material in such a way that it has this extended use in mind from the start. Broadcast television companies are the most obvious providers of material for general educational videodiscs.

The modular approach also has some other aspects to recommend it. The dual audio facility which allows the possibility of two sound-tracks for the same sequence could be used in a number of ways. For example visual sequences are not necessarily age-specific and could probably serve several age ranges, provided the sound-tracks reflected them. In some cases, using the second track to simply double the sound information (playing the sequence twice but using track B the second time) may be a good use, depending on the nature of the visual sequence. But perhaps the most exciting possibility is to think of sound track A for the pupil and B for the teacher. With careful design it should be possible to provide teachers with an on-the-spot inservice tool at one and the same time as material for pupil use. Science, is an obvious subject for this kind of treatment, being an acknowledged problem area in primary schools, and it is not surprising that the Japanese have already produced a successful series in just this format.

Modules do not have to be simply chunks of information for it is quite possible to design them in such a way that they cannot be passively viewed and forgotten. Using the autostop facility a module could be stopped during a sequence and frozen on a text card which asks questions, promotes consideration, suggests activities that the user might engage in, or directs the user to other references. Branching would be required if answers were to be given by the user, but sometimes it is enough to simply ask questions to focus attention and consideration. This makes sequences 'open ended', and at the very least forces the user to do something before continuing, if only to press the play button.

One of the beauties of the modular approach is that it provides a videodisc that is in a very good format for up-grading into level 2 interactivity. The disc is a store of information that can be drawn upon for a microcomputer program. A teacher, with modest programming skill, could assemble a series of sequences, with added computer text, without too much difficulty and there are enough teachers with computer skills to be able to experiment with a whole variety of interactive programs. Teachers are in the very best position to develop this since they will write for known needs and situations. However, if videodiscs of this type do become available it would not be long before professional writers of school computer programs began to produce and market associated software. This 'bottom-up' process has much to recommend it.

The microcomputer can provide a very useful function on its own in terms of indexing. A relatively simple filing system with a search facility could be utilised to help pupils and teachers locate what modules exist on the disc collection through a key-word indexing system. Type in 'air pressure' and up would come a list of modules that include a reference to the topic together with the title of the disc they are on and their access number. Something like this facility may be the best way in which to ease the ordinary teacher into level 2 interactive video since it is friendly, useful and not intimidating to the uninitiated.

Most important of all, the modular format makes possible the very widest use of the medium. All the seven uses mentioned earlier are possible, from teachers' classroom teaching aid (teachers could even use a third sound-track, their own voice, by muting the sound), through project work, to programmed learning (for those that support it). Finally, the modular format is transferable to any system including VHD, LaserVision, or anything else that emerges. Arranging today's discs in this way does not lock them into a specific hardware system.

13.7 AFFORDABILITY

I started my argument by saying that what is needed is a system that answers an educational need effectively and that is affordable. I believe that discs designed in the way I have described would attract wide use in schools. For the first time large production runs from the same disc master would be possible. Schools may be small in comparison with the consumer market, but they do represent the second largest likely market for videodiscs other than the home. Disc cost is a function of numbers of discs pressed, and if several thousand copies can be made and sold the costs should be quite easily affordable (about the equivalent of a set of textbooks or even one high quality reference book, a pre-recorded videotape, or a quality microcomputer program).

If the player requirement is simply that it can do the job effectively, can be up-graded by the addition of a microcomputer interface, and is compatible with normal school health and safety rules then the stand-alone videodisc player could be our initial 'Model T Ford'. It should be possible for a school to acquire a player and six or seven discs for a few hundred pounds. But the way to make this technology available is through rental arrangements, perhaps utilising existing rental agencies. This way the costs for the user are spread and clearly budgetable on an annual basis, and the equipment can be returned if found to be no longer required, can be fully maintained, and can be replaced by new systems as they become available without vast extra expense.

I am very conscious that my thoughts are the product of the present with an eye to a future that is characterised by 'change', but 'changes' which are not necessarily clear. Schools themselves may ultimately become relics of the past (fantasies about home based education using new technology have been spoken about for some time now), and certainly technology will march relentlessly onward. But of one thing I am certain. For the foreseeable future learning will still involve teachers and, in the business of 'learning to learn', videodisc offers a unique resource that is too valuable to miss. If the right educational needs are addressed, in the right way and at the right price, educational videodisc should sell like hot cakes.

REFERENCES

Mably, C. (1984) Interactive videodiscs in primary schools — An evaluation study, North East London Polytechnic (unpublished).

Megarry, J. (1984) *Times Educational Supplement*, 29 June.

Trowbridge, N. (1985) *Video Database Evaluation*, published by Hampshire Education Authority.

14

Producing resource discs — the Domesday Project experience

Peter Armstrong

14.1 INTRODUCTION

It is probably true to say that if we had known at the beginning all that we know now about the difficulties of producing a full-scale resource disc we would never have undertaken the Domesday Project. As I write we are ten weeks away from the official completion date and we are still up to our necks in computer code, test discs that sometimes mysteriously fail and reports from university mainframes running checks round the clock. The role of pioneer is rarely a comfortable one, however strongly you continue to believe in the importance of the product you see in your dreams.

We began the project two years ago in an atmosphere of enthusiasm and optimism. The idea was to commemorate the 900th anniversary of the production of the Domesday Book under William the Conqueror in 1086. He had wanted to take stock of what his newly acquired kingdom contained, and we wanted to do the same. To take a snapshot in pictures, text and data of the state of the United Kingdom in the late twentieth century, at a time of crucial social change. I felt sure that if computers had been available to William this was just what he would have wanted to do for his own time.

Interactive videodisc was the ideal medium, since we knew we wanted to include both high quality still images in very large numbers as well as film. We were not interested in incorporating any teaching strategy into the discs, nor indeed of adding any significant layer of interpretation to the raw data. These were to be resource discs in the sense that users, particularly in the educational community, could draw on them as a resource for research or teaching about Britain in the 1980s in disciplines like social science, environmental studies or economics.

I had not been impressed, however, by the clumsy way in which microcomputers had been interfaced with such discs. Authoring languages were quite well developed, but not the kind of retrieval software packages which would allow a user to move smoothly and intelligently around tens of thousands of images. Such software would depend in turn on large indexes, tens of megabytes in volume. Our discs had therefore to carry a large digital content in some form or other.

In the event we developed two strategies. First, to develop with Philips, Eindhoven a new form of LaserVision—LV ROM—in which the sound part of the recorded waveband for any one frame can be used instead for 6 kilobytes of error-checked data. This gives a total capacity (where no sound is required) of 324 megabytes per disc side. Unlike some other digital recording systems, this does not impinge on the picture content of the disc—the full 54 000 frames are still available. The format for the data is exactly based on that for CD–ROM, which allowed us to work in that format as well. It remains to be seen whether the convenience of LV–ROM where everything is held on a single disc will be preferred in the market-place to the greater flexibility of the LaserVision/CD-ROM disc combination where two optical heads work in parallel and where digital-only updating is easier. Our experience in demonstrating the system is that it is easy to underestimate the depth of techno-fear among managers and educators. This makes very attractive any system which combines sophisticated but hidden computer power with a very simple human interface. This may prove to be the decisive advantage of LV–ROM over systems which depend on manipulating three different types of disc (floppy, CD and LaserVision) in three different drives.

By contrast, imagine a user of the Domesday Discs coming into a library equipped with the BBC LV–ROM videodisc player attached to a microcomputer and screen. They select one of the discs and put it in the player. The micro now takes all the software it needs from the videodisc and offers the user a map of Great Britain. The user is now in total control. They simply move the screen pointer with the mouse and zoom into a closer map. Next photographs or text about the map area on the screen can be summoned up from the options menu. Alternatively, users can enter a topic of interest —'fish and chips' or 'contemporary sculpture'—and be taken to picture sets, film sequences, data maps, graphs and charts, surrogate walks or text articles as they choose. The index searching, cross-referencing and loading of specialised software all happens without the user being aware of it. Users should be able to navigate smoothly through this massive database without thinking about anything except the path that is opening up in front of them.

We had particular problems on the Domesday Project because we were inventing a new medium as well as publishing a large data-base in it. We also had the task which we expected of editorial selection and physical manipulation of very large volumes of material: around 24 000 maps, 51 000 still images, 250 000 screen pages of text, 200 million cell values of statistical data, and so on. We knew too that it would be difficult to co-ordinate the work of more than one million volunteers in local data collection, text input and picture taking. Those were all the problems we knew we had. What I intend to describe here are the problems we did not anticipate and the issues that arise from them. This is perhaps where our experience could be of some

Ch. 14] PRODUCING RESOURCE DISCS — THE DOMESDAY PROJECT 207

help to other teams planning resource discs. Almost all the issues are consequences of the sheer volume of material involved.

14.2 BUILDING THE DATA-BASE

The first surprise was in the area of pre-mastering. The digital content of our discs has been collected and manipulated on a VAX 11/750 minicomputer with 2 gigabytes of on-line disc storage. This does not mean, however, that the data can be held in the same format on these discs as it will be on the final videodiscs. The format that is appropriate to a data-base that is being assembled, edited, aggregated and indexed is not the same as that required for optimum performance from a videodisc. The process of creating the second from the first took 34 days of virtually continuous machine time, working on a 24-hour basis. This resulted in five computer tapes for each of the disc sides which were then mastered by Philips together with the videotape. Only when each disc was pressed could the validity of the digital content be checked by running it with the retrieval software in the target microcomputer. If faults came to light then, the enormous build time had to be undertaken again before they could be corrected. This meant the discs were created by lurches forward (and sometimes backwards) at bimonthly intervals, rather than by a continuous process of small improvements.

Clearly the answer to this problem is to emulate the final digital content of the videodisc on the mainframe and use this for test purposes. This was not possible for us because of a prior decision on optimisation at the replay end. We were publishing a system that would run with a comparatively small, 8-bit micro with only 128K of core memory. Data had therefore to be available to it from the videodisc in the optimum form: for example, picture captions had to be held in physical proximity to their analogue picture frames. Secondly, we wanted to use the full capacity of the videodisc in order to have comprehensive coverage of the country. This meant that statistical data files were compressed in such a way that they could be read and displayed as fast as possible.

Now with the data in this form, it could not be edited. To add a new section to a compressed data file meant uncompressing it, making the change, recompressing it and then adjusting a number of pointers in the resulting files and indexes. This in turn led to the long build times as the original files were edited and then re-built into the videodisc format. It is ironic that in creating an interactive system we have used such an un-interactive pre-mastering process.

The alternative is to trade such optimisation against the advantages of emulation: i.e. accept less performance from small micros or less data on each disc, in return for a much greater ease of data-base construction by the creation of a virtual videodisc on the mainframe. The issue can be put like this: should the digital data on the published videodiscs be in a true data-base format? If they are, they can be edited on the mainframe throughout the pre-mastering and the effect on the retrieval software checked interactively, but the final videodiscs will work more slowly and contain less data. This is the approach we will take on future discs.

14.3 THE COPYRIGHT NIGHTMARE

The second issue that has come to dominate our thinking in the management of the project during the last two years is the issue of copyright. On the Domesday Project we were, for the most part, publishing other people's material, whether it was newspaper articles, satellite images or Ordnance Survey maps. Whereas in conventional publishing or television production one may need clearance of a small amount of material for limited markets, the resource videodisc producer tends to need all types of non-theatric rights for a very great deal of material. The standard rate for a colour transparency for television use in the UK in 1986 is around £50. So anyone cheerfully planning to fill a disc with 100 000 commercial stills is looking at a bill of £5 million for picture copyright alone.

Our approach has been threefold. Wherever possible we have used our own BBC material, particularly our film and video archives. This is one of the main reasons why I believe broadcasting organisations are bound to become significant players in the interactive video game—we already have such large pictorial libraries. Secondly we used the idea of a national photographic competition (with good prizes) to generate 5000 photographs with copyright assignment. Even apart from the chance of winning a prize, amateur photographers in the United Kingdom seem to have liked the idea of their pictures appearing in a prestigious, national archive like Domesday. For more commercial discs, however, this approach could rightly be seen as a form of exploitation and could only be embarked on with great care. Thirdly, we negotiated royalty agreements with picture agencies for large numbers of pictures at special rates, allowing for the advantage to them of linking their name with a product that we hope will be very widely used.

In other cases the problem was not the cost of copyright charges but the difficulty of clearance itself. For example, the Domesday Discs contain a number of surrogate travel sequences. These involve comprehensive photographic coverage of a particular area—for example a town centre. A particular wall cannot be avoided because it contains a copyright poster and a shot of a shop window full of album covers cannot be missed out, even though it could tie up a researcher for weeks. Moreover, a particular poster may contain copyright material belonging to a number of different people—some of whom may have died, leaving us to deal with their estates! Given that coverage of a town centre might easily contain 2000 individual shots, the organisational problem is obvious; and shots cannot be dropped without destroying the geographical logic of the walk.

We have responded to this problem in a number of ways. At first we hoped that the full rigour of the 1956 Copyright Act might not apply to us if we could be classified as a 'cinematograph film'—albeit a very slow moving one. Unfortunately the legal advice we were given was that an interactive videodisc is not a film in the terms of the legislation. Nor could our use of the copyright material be considered 'incidental' since we gave the user the facility to dwell on it. We were therefore forced back to a pragmatic approach. We did not shoot material that might have a copyright element in it (e.g. a product logo on a package) in sufficient close up for it to be clearly identified. Where this could not be avoided, we put the image through a paintbox to blur the outlines. Where neither was possible we set our copyright researchers the very difficult task of tracing and attempting to clear whatever copyright might exist. But in spite of this careful approach, we are fully aware that there may be copyright material on the disc that we have failed to spot and which could lead to litigation.

14.4 CHECKING AND DOUBLE CHECKING

When the Oxford University Press was completing the latest supplement to its celebrated English dictionary in machine-readable form it employed 55 proof readers for more than two years to read through the entries three times. That is an indication of the level of effort required to check the accuracy of the huge volumes of material that can be produced by electronic publishing techniques.

In the case of the Domesday Discs, we estimate that it would take an individual seven years of full time effort to examine every item on the two discs in reasonable detail. Teams of people in six universities have therefore had to be involved in the checking process. But what are they to check the output of the test discs against? In the case of spelling the answer is easy, but how do you check a table of 10 000 numbers that has arrived from a Government Department purporting to be unemployment figures in certain industries in particular years. Only a specialist can say whether the numbers look approximately right. Only the Department that created them can say if they have been reproduced accurately. And no one can say whether they are in reality 'right' in an absolute sense.

Becoming a knowledge broker is a tricky business, because the customer's first expectation is that you have checked the accuracy of what you are selling. In the case of Domesday, we have tried to communicate an opposite emphasis: saying in effect—'this is life in Grimsby as people there saw it; this was what happened in the Falklands as Fleet Street wrote it up, and these were the unemployment figures as the Government published them. Please make up your own mind about how much credibility to assign to each.' But avoidable errors will occur and in the final analysis, like some book publishers and most software publishers, we have to rely on the general public spotting errors that have slipped through our checking procedures, so that we can put them right in subsequent editions of the Domesday Discs. We are also inviting the general public to make sugges-

we could be classified as a 'cinematograph film'—albeit a very slow moving one. Unfortunately the legal advice we were given was that an interactive videodisc is not a film in the terms of the legislation. Nor could our use of the copyright material be considered 'incidental' since we gave the user the facility to dwell on it. We were therefore forced back to a pragmatic approach. We did not shoot material that might have a copyright element in it (e.g. a product logo on a package) in sufficient close up for it to be clearly identified. Where this could not be avoided, we put the image through a paintbox to blur the outlines. Where neither was possible we set our copyright researchers the very difficult task of tracing and attempting to clear whatever copyright might exist. But in spite of this careful approach, we are fully aware that there may be copyright material on the disc that we have failed to spot and which could lead to litigation.

14.4 CHECKING AND DOUBLE CHECKING

When the Oxford University Press was completing the latest supplement to its celebrated English dictionary in machine-readable form it employed 55 proof readers for more than two years to read through the entries three times. That is an indication of the level of effort required to check the accuracy of the huge volumes of material that can be produced by electronic publishing techniques.

In the case of the Domesday Discs, we estimate that it would take an individual seven years of full time effort to examine every item on the two discs in reasonable detail. Teams of people in six universities have therefore had to be involved in the checking process. But what are they to check the output of the test discs against? In the case of spelling the answer is easy, but how do you check a table of 10 000 numbers that has arrived from a Government Department purporting to be unemployment figures in certain industries in particular years. Only a specialist can say whether the numbers look approximately right. Only the Department that created them can say if they have been reproduced accurately. And no one can say whether they are in reality 'right' in an absolute sense.

Becoming a knowledge broker is a tricky business, because the customer's first expectation is that you have checked the accuracy of what you are selling. In the case of Domesday, we have tried to communicate an opposite emphasis: saying in effect—'this is life in Grimsby as people there saw it; this was what happened in the Falklands as Fleet Street wrote it up, and these were the unemployment figures as the Government published them. Please make up your own mind about how much credibility to assign to each.' But avoidable errors will occur and in the final analysis, like some book publishers and most software publishers, we have to rely on the general public spotting errors that have slipped through our checking procedures, so that we can put them right in subsequent editions of the Domesday Discs. We are also inviting the general public to make suggestions on additional material they would like to see included. In this way too the creation of the discs will be an interactive process.

14.5 CONCLUSIONS

In fact we probably would—if we had our time again—still want to undertake the Domesday Project. Discs which can offer a socially significant resource by bringing together pictures, text and data in a creative way are going to be crucial, in my view, to the success of the interactive videodisc revolution. But next time we will give ourselves more time and aim to produce 80% of the original dream with capacity in hand, rather than 120% with a very high risk of failure. Resource discs on this scale should—like marriage—be entered into 'not lightly or wantonly, but soberly and in the fear of God'.

15

Videodisc and Videotex: Love-match or passing acquaintance?

Colin Jackson

15.1 INTRODUCTION

In the early days of information technology we heard a great deal about the 'convergence of technologies'. When videodisc became readily available a natural question to pose was — with which already existing technology would videodisc happily converge? The ability to store a very large visual database coupled with the videodisc player's ability to allow for random access of that database pointed to an answer — a very large randomly accessed textual database. Brighton Polytechnic's Computing Department became involved in interactive videodisc applications as soon as PAL equipment became available. Rather than concentrate on learning packages of one sort or another the philosophy adopted was to consider applications involving these two types of databases. Both databases would be about the same topic and each would complement the other. Pictures are splendid ways to communicate essentially qualitative information but they are generally not precise enough to communicate quantitative information. A picture of the beaches and hotels in Corfu may convince us that that is the place we would like to go — but can we afford it; how much does it cost and what are the flight times? Such quantitative information is so much better conveyed by textual methods and in addition tends to be more volatile and thus better suited to the ease of updating offered by editing systems.

15.2 THE PROJECT

Examples of large textual databases are those hosted on Viewdata systems and in particular on Prestel. These databases were considered to be in need of enhancement as their picture producing capabilities are virtually non-existent; the best that can be done is by using block graphics — imagination on the viewer's part is essential.

212 EXPLOITING THE TECHNOLOGY

The Department of Industry agreed to privide matched funding for a videodisc/videotex application project and the hunt was on for the application. The English Tourist Board provided an ideal solution. ETB use Prestel to host several hundred pages detailing hotels and accommodation in England and so the project became one of marrying their well-developed textual database with a newly developed, and equivalent visual database. The pilot scheme was to run in an ETB Information Centre and possibly in an ABTA travel agent's premises as well.

15.3 INTERFACE DESIGN

Much of the planning time was spent in discussion of the 'user concepts'. ETB naturally wished to keep to their well tried page format which basically consisted of information concerning three hotels or three attractions near to the town under consideration. Routeing through these pages was accomplished in the normal Viewdata manner, namely of pressing the keys of a numeric keypad. As the project was viewed as a public information system from the outset, the operation of a keypad by members of the public was viewed with some alarm. First, there are those who would not know what to do with it and secondly yet others who would know only too well! Of course it would be possible for software to intercept characters from the keyboard and filter out all those except bona fide ones; however, this seemed likely to produce a hacker's dream. As the amount of equipment to support videodisc work increased in variety the use of a touch screen became rather more than an interesting proposition. Menu driven applications are those where the user is presented with a series of options. The user inputs the option of their choice and the program proceeds accordingly. Touch screens were becoming more popular as an input device for menu-driven programs and most people feel more at home pressing a designated area of the screen rather than hunting around a 'qwerty' keyboard. For these reasons the following user concepts were agreed to maximise the efficiency of the system.

(1) The videodisc player and the Prestel database would be 'driven' by a touch screen.
(2) Users would be enticed to use the system by a 'teaser' sequence from the videodisc. On pressing the screen another picture from the disc invites the user to press 'PRESS' in English French or German and a response from that invitation starts a video sequence that keeps the user occupied while the system automatically logs on to Prestel.
(3) The sequence stops with an appropriate message in the selected language on termination of the log-on sequence.
(4) The root page of the ETB database is displayed and progression through the database is by touching the screen on symbols placed near to the required items.

(5) When a 'three line page' is displayed a touch on the appropriate symbol places the system into videodisc mode and pictures of the items described are shown. In this mode various options are available. Briefly these are

— to browse around pictures of the hotel or attraction
— to browse around the 'head' picture of each hotel or attraction in the same town
— to have the position of the town indicated on a map of the area
— to obtain further textual information about the hotel or attraction currently being viewed.

This last option means a return to Prestel mode with the appropriate page being displayed.

The new dimension provided by the visual database gave us the problem of how to control it. The method adopted was the obvious one of placing the control information relevant to a particular Prestel page on that page. Consider a 'three line page' giving details of three hotels in a town. For reasons of readability there are blank lines in the text. Each blank line represents 40 characters worth of information and using the 'conceal' facility of Prestel we can have 39 further characters of control information which to the viewer appears as a blank line. ETB, like most other information providers, use double height characters to produce banner headlines. The second line of a double height line is in effect invisible and this gave us the use of such lines for further control information. The information required was:

(1) The type of page; this is needed to determine the videodisc picture of the background.
(2) An 'end page flag' denoting the last page of the sequence.
(3) The number of the first Prestel three line page for hotels.
(4) The number of the first Prestel three line page for attractions.
(4) The videodisc number of the relevant region map together with a map reference.
(6) The frame number on the videodisc of the first or 'head' picture of the hotel.
(7) The number of further pictures in a contiguous sequence.
(8) The type of picture — landscape or portrait (described below).

To cater for the browsing of head pictures of other hotels in the same town we devised a method of automatically switching between videodisc and videotex modes. Thus if the system had detected that pictures of the third hotel on the page were being displayed and that the user was interested in seeing further hotels, then the next page would be requested and obtained, the control information extracted and used to present the next picture.

Much thought was given as to how the control information was to be held. Transmission of Prestel pages often introduces erroneous characters and whereas the user can live with a spelling error, the control system could not tolerate incorrect data. We decided to use the standards devised by the Council for Educational Technology for the transmission of telesoftware. Briefly this entails bracketing the control data between standard character pairs and ending each such bracketed set by three check digits. On receipt of a page by the system, the code sequence is found, check digits calculated and compared with the transmitted check digits. If the two sets do not match then a repeat transmission of the page is requested. Figure 15.1 shows

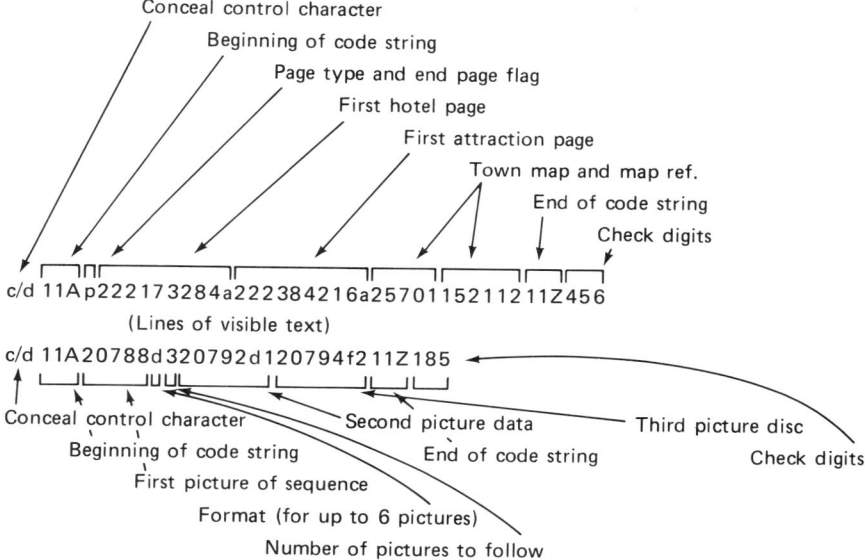

Fig. 15.1 — Control character sequences embedded into a Prestel page.

typical character sequences embedded into a Prestel page.

15.4 HARDWARE

The original equipment used for the project development was a Philips VP705 Professional videodisc player and a Rediffusion Teleputer 3 microcomputer. The Teleputer 3 was provided by Rediffusion Computers Ltd (now ROCC Computers Ltd) as part of their contribution to the project. The other company participating in the matched funding was Aragon International. The Prestel 'look-alike' system IVS3 (and later IVS 100) was installed on the Polytechnic's VAX computer system. This combination of hardware and software was invaluable in the early months of the project when innovative ideas were devised and tested. However the Teleputer, although endowed with Viewdata software had no touch screen and this was considered essential to the project. Sony Ltd then became involved in the project and generously loaned us an SMC70 microcomputer, a videodisc player and a monitor with touch screen. The software provided for the SMC70 did not include a Viewdata package and once again the project was kept going by Sony offering to write such a package for us. Their extensive support provided without any commitment and at no cost was very much appreciated by the project team.

There were many difficulties that became apparent during development.

(1) The complexity of the system ruled out writing the software in Basic; there was insufficient storage on the SMC70. The programmer employed on the project had to write in assembler to overcome this problem with consequent delays to the project timetable.
(2) The touch screen (to be fair an experimental model) had a grid that in no way matched the lines and columns of computer produced text. This meant that symbols designed as touch areas had to be well separated to ensure that no cases of ambiguity arose.
(3) There is no way of knowing when the transmission of a page of Prestel is complete although the system should be sure of receipt of a complete page before it starts searching for control strings. One approach would be to edit in to each page an 'end of page' character which on receipt would signify that no further characters were to be transmitted. However, this did not meet with favour because

— It would have to be validated, and this would mean eight characters of additional information on a line that was already well used by ETB.
— it is possible for a Prestel frame to be transmitted in an order different from the conventional top down left to right approach, by using cursor control characters. Thus a character while logically being the last one on a page may in fact not be the last character transmitted.

The solution adopted was to assume transmission was complete when no characters were received in a small period of time. This did seem a little risky but appeared to work in practice!

15.5 CONTENT AND ORGANISATION OF THE DISC

The SMC70 generates its display within a border area which is considerably larger than many other microcomputer systems and this fact was instrumental in the design of the content of the videodisc. Each page on the ETB Prestel database was classified into one of several types, for example a town index, a three-line page of hotels, a three-line page of attractions with only two attractions listed and so on. Each computer generated page of text was displayed on a background from the videodisc which gives a more pleasing effect than the bald video text. Figure 15.2 illustrates this effect; the 'What to see' heading and the three touch screen symbols to the right are from the videodisc, and the Prestel text is overlaid onto the remaining black area.

Apart from these backgrounds the disc contained:

(1) Several thousand stills. These were overall views of the hotel or attraction or of a typical bedroom or of the conference suite or the swimming pool etc. These stills were mainly taken from 35 mm stock held in the ETB archives and were transferred to the master tape in two distinct formats.

— Portrait. The picture occupied approximately the left two-thirds of the screen area. The purpose of the remaining unused black area was so that the name of the hotel or attraction could be superimposed without obscuring picture detail and to ensure contrast.
— Landscape. The picture occupied approximately the top three-quarters of the screen, the remaining area being used as before.

(2) The moving sequences on the disc were of nine 'selected places' in England and were generally each of about a minute in duration. The sequences were created in two different ways: On some locations 35 mm film had been used which was then telecined to videotape, while on others the sequence had been shot by video-camera. The differences between these two approaches has to be considered carefully when the use of the disc is being planned. Each picture from the disc is displayed as a standard TV frame composed of two interlaced fields, each field being scanned in one-fiftieth of a second. If the original material is from a TV source then that too will have fifty potentially different pictures per second and when replayed there is a difficulty arising when 'still framing'. When the player is in still frame mode two contiguous fields are repeatedly scanned to produce one complete picture and if the two fields are substantially different (for example if the sequence includes fast movement) then the effect is rather unfortunate with the picture having a distinct 'jitter'. If on the other hand, the original material is shot from 35 mm film then during mastering of the disc it can be arranged so that the two fields scanned are in fact identical. This is straightforward as film-shot material is at a rate of 25 pictures a second rather than 50. (Film shot at the standard 24 frames per second is suitably 'moulded' to 25 frames per second during the telecine process — often simply by speeding it up!). In the part of the project being described care was taken so that the last few frames of each sequence were of a stationary view so that on stopping at the end of a sequence no jitter was apparent.

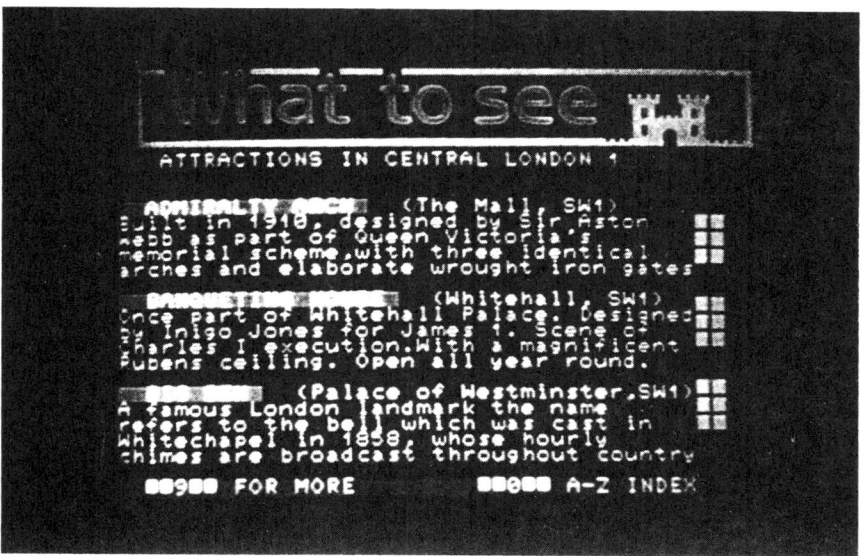

Fig. 15.2 — Computer-generated text displayed on a background from the videodisc.

15.6 SYSTEM PROBLEMS

The whole concept of the project was that the viewdata database contained the control information for the disc player. It was unreasonable to expect ETB to manually insert the information into their pages; as the format of the control strings adhered to a rigid syntax they would have to be computer–generated with much scope for error during the input stage. The method adopted was that the ETB database as generated by them was downloaded onto tape and loaded onto one of the Polytechnic's VAX computers. Apart from the programmer employed on the project full-time we also had the shared services of one of the Department's sandwich course students and most of her work was in writing a suite of programs for the editing of the Prestel database and for the input of raw information for these programs to process. The amount of work was not inconsiderable. The database consisted of some 1500 pages and every page had to be edited to include a control string (see Fig. 15.1). In some cases this was minimal, for example a single character to indicate the type of page involved — although such a short string still had to be bracketed and provided with check digits as described earlier. In other cases the control strings were not far short of the maximum length provided by the number of blank lines on a page. Two databases were created, one detailing every Prestel page to be used, the page number, the names of the hotels, and so on. The other database described the disc, e.g. the frame number, the name of the hotel it represented, whether it was the head picture, its format, etc. This data entry phase took several weeks to complete because of the sheer volume of data.

The first software package created a third database out of the original two. That highlighted errors — for example spelling inconsistencies prohibited cross-matching, with the third database consequently deficient. Another program produced the code strings for insertion into every page and a final program was written to edit the Prestel page file for tape preparation and ultimate upload to Prestel.

The listing of the code strings to be inserted was invaluable in the final phase of the project because it was possible to check that the system worked before a complete live Prestel file was available. The IVS 100 system was used to manually edit a sufficient number of pages to enable checking of all the concepts to take place. The double height facility of Prestel was not provided for the SMC70, the principal reason for this being that its architecture did not cater for Viewdata compatibility. This obviously detracted from the appearance of the Prestel pages and the final test involving the uploaded database was never completed.

15.7 THE LESSONS LEARNED

The pilot scheme, when tested, did prove that interation between Viewdata and Videotex was possible and worked very well. The combination of computer-generated symbols (for the touch areas used for menu options) superimposed on a picture from the disc offered a pleasant screen to look at and a system which was easy to use. So what were the lessons learned?

(1) The touch screen used for the test, while adequate for testing purposes would not have been suitable for public use. The main problem was the difference between touch grid and line layout referred to previously. Present day equipment has overcome this registration problem as touch screens are now designed as an integral part of the monitor rather than being an 'add on' item.
(2) As noted earlier the SMC70 was not designed for Viewdata applications and a fully operational Viewdata software package was not used. In this sense it was not an appropriate machine to use. Many of today's microcomputers do have Viewdata capability as well as having the necessary input and output ports to support the control of a videodisc player.
(3) While the previous two lessons learnt could be acted upon, the major difficulty lay in communications costs. Once logged on to Prestel the system remained connected until a period of inactivity was detected, and at this stage the connection was terminated. However, the system was designed for the user to spend long periods of time looking at pictures from the videodisc, and during these periods the link with Prestel is still in effect — and has to be paid for! It is obviously impractical to disconnect from Prestel when a page is neither being viewed by a user nor scanned by the system. More accurately, disconnection is no problem but the re-establishment of a link with the consequent time delay is and could not be tolerated.

15.8 PROJECT PHASE TWO — A DIFFERENT APPROACH

It is the last observation that prompted ETB to consider another way of holding the textual database, namely of holding it locally rather than remotely. After all, the cost of disc storage on microcomputers had been dropping all the time.

Thus phase two of the project was conceived, but this time as a commercial venture. The Department of Industry was not involved and neither was the Polytechnic. The production house responsible for the disc in phase one — Focus Invision — contracted with ETB to build phase two and the author acted as computing consultant with Focus Invision.

The requirements of phase two were:

(1) The textual database is to be hosted on a microcomputer and in such a form that modifications to the database could be effected simply.
(2) Operation of the system is to be by touch screen.
(3) The user concepts are similar to phase one:
   — A 'Teaser sequence', that is a short video sequence repeatedly displayed should attract the attention of a user and invite them to press the screen.
   — Once hooked the user is shown a map of the United Kingdom and invited to touch one of four triangles positioned at the centres of England, Wales, Scotland and Northern Ireland. If they select England a map of England is displayed with triangles positioned on each of the twelve regions designated by the English Tourist Board.
   — Having routed through the map(s) — from the videodisc — the system shows a video sequence of the region selected (the smaller countries count as regions for this purpose). Superimposed on the video is a computer-generated symbol inviting the user to touch for display of an index of towns for the selected region.
   — Each town index is generated from datafiles associated with the region. There are up to ten towns listed per page and the screen display is augmented by computer-generated triangles for the user to select the town of their choice.
   — Selection of a town results in a picture of that town being displayed together with the text associated with it. Two symbols also appear, one inviting the user to return to the main index (the UK map) the other providing more 'options'. While the user reads the text, further pictures of the two are displayed. The options, each associated with a symbol replacing the full text:

   Main index
   Town index — for back routing
   Places to stay — for information and pictures of hotels in the town.
   Places to visit — for information and pictures of attractions in the town.
   More detail — a return to the original display with full text.

— The browsing concepts are retained from phase one. Several pictures for each hotel or attraction are automatically cycled at intervals of one second, while browsing through hotels or attractions in the same town is performed by the user by touching the appropriate symbol.
— London region is dealt with slightly differently. A town index is not appropriate and is replaced by a sub-index (e.g. inner London attractions, outer London attractions, places to stay etc.). A further option is a 'day trips' index and in this way the user is able to examine towns, hotels and attractions in other regions within reasonable travelling distance from London.

The production of the disc required little new footage (the exception being the regional video sequences). However, all the stills were reformatted. The stills that were used in phase one were reduced in size so as to fit into a border. The space above this bordered area was for the name of the region and the space below the bordered area was for the computer-generated text.

Data input programs were written for ETB to use, allowing separate files for (a) towns and (b) hotels and attractions for each of the fifteen regions, each file containing disc information as well as the text associated with each town hotel or attraction. There is one other file for the index pages. In this way the data is split into manageable sizes for editing and for reading into main store from fixed disc.

The equipment used was an NCR PC6 (an IBM PC compatible machine) with display fitted with touch screen and a Philips VP835 videodisc player. The system was commissioned for installation mounted in a cabinet for the new Travel Centre in London's Lower Regent Street — formally opened by the Prime Minister in June 1986. Since then the data available has and still is being expanded.

Updating of the data files can be done on site or at ETB's main offices and transferred by diskette. Should the system be adopted for use in Tourist Information Centres throughout the country then network transmission of data files would seem appropriate.

The system records which regions have been requested by users. Such information should be useful for ETB for forthcoming promotions.

15.9 SUMMARY

The concept of remotely held Viewdata pages containing textual information visible to the user together with invisible information to control a videodisc player proved to be successful. The advantage of such a system is the ease with which both sorts of information can be altered at the information provider's office. Once the host computer's files have been updated then the users at sites spread around the country can immediately have access to the new information. For volatile information such as price this is obviously a great advantage.

The disadvantage of using a remote Viewdata database is the communcation problem, that is, the time spent in establishing a connection and the cost of that communication link being maintained while the user is viewing pictures from the local database. The problem of frequent transmission errors also has to be taken into account.

When using local databases the communications problems are not present, although a hard disc system is necessary for any sizeable database. The disadvantage of local databases is that modification of the data held is more difficult. Copies of modified files created at the information provider's office may be sent on diskettes to the remote sites providing that the consequent delay can be tolerated. As mentioned before a data transmission network could be utilised to automatically send files to the remote sites if those sites were supplied with auto-answering equipment.

The choice is — as always — dependent on the application but both methods have been proved to work.

Postscript: Future Directions

If interactive media are to become part of the mainstream of instructional technology there must be a greater willingness on the part of practitioners to record, analyse and articulate their experiences, their successes and their failures. The authors contributing to this book have all attempted to provide some building blocks for future practitioners to work with, but this is only a beginning and there is a lot more work to be done. In many projects to date, the emphasis has been on exploring what the technology can do, finding out how to use it, and demonstrating its features, all of which make it a solution in search of some educational problems. Now that it has established itself as both pedagogically and economically feasible in the right applications, it should be possible for research and development to be taken seriously in this field, in a way that will contribute to our understanding of how students learn from teaching methods of this type. Designers of interactive media material will pay more attention to research findings on how students learn through the individual media of text, computer-based learning, video, and audio, and will develop their own research findings for the particular combinations of computer, video and audio discussed in this book.

Similarly, along with developments in stand-alone computer-based teaching there will have to be some investigation of how Artificial Intelligence techniques can further enhance the value of interactive media. AI researchers have made considerable advances in structuring and accessing data in ways that conceivably complement human thought processes. This is precisely what practitioners of interactive media need to help them understand how best to exploit the vast storage capacity and immediate access facilities at their disposal. And yet there has been very little commerce between the two fields so far.

The education and training worlds have tried hard to embrace the new technology, but once our appetite was whetted for new and exciting forms of pedagogy, we discovered how many constraints and limitations the technology imposed, many of them documented in this book. In the coming years practitioners will look for developments in the technology that will serve our ambitions rather than frustrate them. And the key areas are not those imminent developments such as writeable discs—not a single author in this volume has found their absence a stumbling-block—it will be developments such as easier and cheaper mastering, and more inter-system compatibility that will be welcomed most.

Interactive media will undoubtedly survive in the education and training worlds in some form, but what will that be? The debates encountered here will continue: on whether resource discs are a better way to use videodisc than those that embody some particular teaching objectives; on whether interactive video is computer-enhanced video or video-enhanced computer-based learning; on whether CD–ROM will replace videodiscs; on whether analogue video will play an important role in a future that offers digitised video as well; on whether interactive audio will be more efficient than interactive video; on who should take overall control of an interactive media development project? The survival of this technology as a mainstream instructional method depends crucially on the quality of material being produced, on the compatibility of the hardware and software with the practitioners' requirements, and on the flexibility of existing education and training systems to adapt to the kinds of resourcing demands such a technology makes. The authors in this book have furnished the experience and the arguments to elaborate these points. We hope they provide a sound basis for other practitioners to work on and ensure the future of interactive media as a valuable educational resource.

Bibliography

Alty, J. L. & Coombs, M. J. (1978) Proceedings of the Workshop on Computing Skills and Adaptive Systems, University of Liverpool, Liverpool, 21–22 March.

Aspen Disc (1983).

Ayscough, P. B. (1977) Calchem: Final Review Report, Department of Physical Chemistry, The University of Leeds.

Bandura, A. (1982) Self-efficacy mechanism in human agency, *Amer. Psychologist*, **37**, 122–148.

Barker, P. G. (1983–85) A practical introduction to authoring for computer-assisted instruction: Parts 1–5, *British Journal of Educational Technology,* **14**, 16, 174; **15**, 82; **16**, 115, 218.

Barker, P. (1985) Information technology, education and training, *British Journal of Educational Technology,* 16/2, May, 103–115.

Barker, P. (1986) The many faces of human–machine interaction, *British Journal of Educational Technology,* 17/1, 74–81.

Barnes, D. (1973) *Language in the Classroom*, Open University.

Bates, A. W. (1983) Selecting media and possible roles for interactive video in the Open University, in R. G. Fuller (ed.), *Using Interactive Videodiscs in Open University Courses, I.E.T. Papers on Broadcasting,* No. 218, June 1983.

Bayard-White, C. (1985) *Interactive Video Case Studies and Directory*, Council for Educational Technology.

Bayard-White, C. (1985) *An Introduction to Interactive Video*, UK National Interactive Video Centre and the Council for Educational Technology.

Bayard-White, C. (1986) *Interactive Video Case Studies and Directory*, UK National Interactive Video Centre and the Council for Educational Technology, pp. 27–42.

Beckwith, D. (1983) The nature of learners as total systems, *Journal Visual and Verbal Languaging*.

Bernstein, B. (1971) *Class Codes and Control*, Routledge & Kegan Paul, London.

Bork, A. (1980) Development of the intelligent disc, *Videodisc News*, **1**, 5, June.

Bork, A. (1980) *Computer Assisted Learning in Physics Education*, Pergamon Press, Oxford.

Bork, A. (1981) *Learning with Computers,* Digital Press, Bedford, Massachusetts.

Bork, A. (1981) Aspects of marketing intelligent videodisc learning material, *Proceedings of Conference on Interactive Video Learning Systems,* Society for Applied Learning Technology, August 1981.

Bork, A. (1984) Producing computer based learning material at the Educational Technology Centre, *Journal of Computer-based Instruction,* **11,** 3, Summer.

Bork, A. (1984) Production systems for computer-based learning. Decker F. Walker & Robert D. Hess (eds.), in *International Software: Principles, and Perspectives for Design and Use,* Wadsworth Publishing Company, Belmont, California.

Bork, A. (1985) Why has the interactive video had so little impact in education?, *The Videodisc Monitor,* **111,** 8, September.

Bork, A. (1985) *Personal Computers for Education,* Harper & Row, New York.

Bork, A. (1987) *Learning with Personal Computers,* Harper & Row, New York.

Bork, A. & Weinstock, H. (eds.) (1987) *Designing Computer–based Learning Material,* Springer, in press.

Bosco, J. (1986) An analysis of evaluations of interactive video, *Educational Technology,* May, 7–17.

Boud, D. & Pearson, M. (1978) *Bringing Reality into the Classroom: The Use of Trigger Films in Introducing Socio-emotional Aspects of Learning in the Health Sciences,* Tertiary Education Research Centre, University of New South Wales, Australia.

Boud, D. & Pearson, M. (1979) The trigger film: a stimulus for effective learning, *PLET,* **16** (1).

Boyd, G. M. & Jaworski, W. M. (1985) PALS, PATHS, PLACES and PRODUCERS: four more appropriate forms of computer aided education, *Proceedings of COMPINT85,* pp. 614–616, IEEE Computer Society Press, Washington DC.

Braten, S. (1982) Simulation and self-organisation of mind, University of Oslo, *Contemporary Philosophy. A New Survey,* Vol. 2, pp. 189–218.

Brooks, Jr., F. P. (1975) *The Mythical Man-Month,* Addison-Wesley.

British Garden Birds (1983) BBC Enterprises Ltd.

Butcher, P. G. & Harding, C. J. (1978) *Electronic Configurations,* Academic Computing Service, The Open University, Milton Keynes.

Butcher, P. G. (1986) Computing aspects of interactive video, *Computers and Education,* **10,** 1.

Card, S. K., English, W. K. & Burr, B. (1977) Evaluation of mouse, rate-controlled isometric joystick, step keys and text keys for text selection on a CRT, Xerox Palo Alto Research Centre, SSL–77–1, April.

Chorover, S. L. (1984) Cautions on computers in education, *Byte,* **9,** 6, 223–227.

Clark, D. R. (ed.) (1980) *Computers for Imagemaking,* Pergamon Press, Oxford.

Clark, D. R. (1983) Interactive video discs, *Professional Video*, 24–25, February.
Clark, D. R. (1984) Interactive videodisc in education and training, *Media in Education and Development*, 190–194, December.
Clark, D. R. (1984) The role of videodisc in education and training, *Media in Education and Development*, 17/4, December, 190–192.
Clark, D. R. & Sandford, N. (1986) Semantic descriptions and maps of meaning for videodisc images, *Programmed Learning and Educational Technology (PLET)*, **23,** 84–90, February.
Clark, J. (1984) How do interactive videodiscs rate against other media?, *Instructional Innovator*, 29/6, 12–16.
Committee of Vice-Chancellors and Principals (1980a) *University Statistics*, No. 5, Code of Practice for Academic Staff Training, Spring.
Compact Disc Digital Audio (1982) *Philips Technical Review*, **40,** 6.
Coombs, M. J. & Alty, J. L. *General Proposals for the Design of a Knowledge-Based Consultant: Rationale and a Cartoon*, Dept. of Computer Science, University of Strathclyde, Glasgow, Scotland, UK.
Copeland P. (1983) Cavis — from concept to system, *Media in Education and Development*, 16/2, June, 74–79.
Dalton, D. W. (1986) How effective is interactive video in improving performance and attitude?, *Educational Technology*, January, 27–29.
Daniel, J. S. (1974) *Knowables, Conversations and Learning: A Summary of Recent Work at Systems Research Inc.*, Tele-University, Quebec, Canada.
Daniel, J. S. (1975) Learning styles and strategies, in N. Entwhistle & D. Hounsall (eds.), *How Students Learn*, University of Lancaster, Lancaster, UK.
Daynes, R. & Butler, B. (eds.) (1984) *The Videodisc Book, A Guide and Directory*, John Wiley, New York.
Dean, C. & Whitlock, Q. (1983) *A Handbook of Computer Based Training*, Kogan-Page.
Doulton, A. (1984) Interactive video in training, *Media in Education and Development,* 17/4, December, 205–206.
Duke, J. L. (1983) Interactive Video: Implications for Education and Training, CET Working Paper, Council for Educational Technology, 5, 7.
Eco, U. (1979) Can television teach?, *Screen Education,* **31,** 15–24.
EETPU (1985) *An Introduction to Solid State Electronics*, EPIC.
Elliott, I. (1986) A Specification for an Interactive Video Tutor, Paper presented at GIREP Conference, 18–23 August 1986, on 'COSMOS — An Educational Challenge' in Elsinore, Denmark. European Space Agency, November 1986, ESASP–253.
Elton, L. R. B. (1977) Innovation and the role of educational media, in J. K. Beug (ed.), *Innovation and Improvement in Teaching and Learning in Higher Education*, Higher Education Authority and Irish Federation of University Teachers.
Entwhistle, N. (1978) Knowledge structures and styles of learning: a

summary of Pask's recent research, *British Journal of Educational Psychology,* **48,** 255–265.

Fiske, J. (1982) *Introduction to Communication Studies,* Methuen.

Fleetwood-Walker, P., Mathias, H. & Rutherford, D. (1985) Continuing Education in Universities, paper delivered at the SRHE Conference.

Floyd, S. (1982) Thinking interactively, in *Handbook of Interactive Video,* S. Floyd & B. Floyd (eds.), Knowledge Industry Publications, p. 22.

Floyd, S. & Floyd, B. (eds.), (1982) *Handbook of Interactive Video,* Knowledge Industry Publications.

Fox, B. (1985) Light at the end of the video tunnel vision, *Electronic Times,* 10 October 1985.

Frye, N. (1957) *The Anatomy of Criticism,* Princeton University Press.

Fuller, R. G. & Zollman, D. (1984) *Energy Transformations Featuring the Bicyle,* Great Plains Media Centre, University of Nebraska — Lincoln, Lincoln, NE.

Fuller, R. G., Zollman, D. & Campbell, T. C. (1982) *The Puzzle of the Tacoma Narrows Bridge Collapse,* John Wiley, New York.

Gaines, B. R. & Shaw, M. L. G. *Is There a Knowledge Environment?,* Dept. of Industrial Engineering, University of Toronto and Dept. of Computer Science, York University, Canada, 1983.

Gayeski, D. M. & Williams, D. K. (1984) Interactive video in higher education, in O. Zuber-Skerritt (ed.), *Video in Higher Education,* pp. 64–74.

Gerrit, C., van der Veer, Jos J. Beishuizen, Learning Styles in Conversation — A Practical Application to Pask's Learning Theory to Human–Computer Interaction. Vrije Universiteit, Amsterdam, Netherlands.

Glanville, R. (1975) A cybernetic development of epistemology and observation, applied to objects in space and time (as seen in architecture), Ph.D. thesis, Dept. of Cybernetics, Brunel University.

Griffiths, M. (1984) Planning for interactive videodisc, *Media in Education and Development,* 17/4, December, 196–200.

Hannapin, M. J. (1985) Empirical issues in the study of computer assisted interactive video, *Educational Communications Technology Journal,* **33,** 4, Winter, 235–248.

Harris, T. A. (1973) *I'm OK — You're OK,* Pan Books, London (previously published as *The Book of Choice,* Jonathan Cape, London, 1970).

Hart, A. P. (1984) Not just a bit of an extra, *Media in Education and Development,* 17/3, September, 162–167.

Hart, A. P. (1985) Making connections: higher education and cable television in Britain, *Media in Education and Development,* 18/3, September, 116–120.

Hawkes, Jacquetta (1953) *A Land,* The Cresset Press, London.

Hawkridge, D. (1981) The telesis of educational technology, *British Journal of Educational Technology,* 12/1.

Hills, P. (1979) *Teaching and Learning as a Communication Process,* Croom Helm.

Hoffos, S. & Parsloe, E. (1984) *Interactive Video,* Sigma Technical Press.

Holland, G. (1984) Business and open learning, Conference report, Open University.
Horlock, T. H. (1986) Continuing education for industry, Lecture at the Open University, 17 February, 1986.
Hounsell, D. & Entwhistle, N. (1975) *How students learn. Readings in higher education*, 1. Lancaster, Institute for Research and Development in Post-Compulsory Education.
Hutt, G. (1986) Using interactive videodisc, *Interactive Learning International*, **2,** 4, April, 26–28.
Johnson, C. G. (1984) TenCORE and PC PILOT — a comparison of two authoring languages, *Interactive Learning International*, **1,** 2, Oct.- –Dec., 27–30.
Johnson, D. W. & Johnson, R. T. (1975) *Learning Together and Alone: Cooperation, Competition and Individualization*, Prentice-Hall, Englewood Cliffs, NJ.
Jaworski, W. M. & Hinterberger, H. (1981) Controlled program design by use of the programming concept ABL, *Angewandte Informatik*, July, pp. 302–310.
Kagan, N. (1975) Influencing human interaction — eleven years with IPR, *The Canadian Counsellor*, 9.
Kemmis, S. (1976) *The Education Potential of Computer Assisted Learning: Qualitative Evidence about Student Learning*, University of East Anglia, Centre for Applied Research in Education.
Kozma, R. B. (1978) Faculty development and the adoption and diffusion of classroom innovations, *Journal of Higher Education*, 49/1, January, 316–328.
L'Allier, J. J. (1983) Interactive Video — an Elephant in Search of a Definition, *Performance and Instruction Journal*, November, 4.
Laurillard, D. M. (1981) Interactive computer simulations in undergraduate teaching, *Proceedings, Second International Microcomputers in Education Congress*, London, 1980, Harvester, London.
Laurillard, D. M. (1982) The potential of interactive video, *Journal of Educational Television*, 8/3, 173–180.
Laurillard, D. M. (1983) Interactive video and the control of learning, *IET Papers on Broadcasting*, No. 231, 1983.
Laurillard, D. M. (1984) *Videodisc Evaluation Report: 'The Teddy Bear's Disc'*, November, 1984.
Laurillard, D. M. (1985) The teddy bear's disc, *Media in Education and Development*, March.
Laurillard, D. M. & Marante, G. J. L. (1981) *A view of computer assisted learning in the light of conversation theory*, Open University, Institute of Educational Technology, Milton Keynes, United Kingdom.
Lee, H. M. (1984) *The Practice of Conversation Theory: Understanding and Encouraging Innovation*, US Army Research Institute for the Behavioural and Social Sciences, Great Britain.
Lepore, E. (1986) *Truth and Interpretation: Perspectives on the Philosophy of Donald Davidson*, New York.

Lewis, B. N. & Pask, G. L. (1965) The theory and practice of adaptive teaching systems, in R. Glasser (ed.), *Teaching Machines and Programmed Learning*, Vol. II, National Education Association, Washington DC.

Life and Energy (1987) An Environmental science disc for 9–13-year-olds. One of the Interactive Video in Schools (IVIS) project, 1987 (DTI). Prodeuced by BBC Open University Production Centre in conjunction with Bulmershe College of Higher Education.

Lindsey, J. (1984) The challenge of designing for interactive video, *Instructional Innovator,* September, 17.

Lindstrom, B. (1983) *Learning styles and teaching strategies: Conversation theory. The Work of Gordon Pask*, University of Gothenburg, Department of Education, Gothenburg, Sweden.

Lippman, A. & Backer, D. S. (1982) Personalized aids for training: an assault on publishing, *Proceedings of the Fourth Annual Conference on Video Learning Systems*, Society for Applied Learning Technology, Warrenton, VA.

Lloyd, P. (1986) Exploring the thinkies, *AudioVisual*, 46–7, September.

Luria, G. R. (1961) *The Role of Speech in the Regulation of Normal and Abnormal Behaviour*, Pergamon Press, London.

Luria, G. R. (1968) *The Mind of a Mnemonist*, Basic Books, New York.

Mabley, C. (1984) Interactive videodiscs in finishing schools — an evaluation study, North East London Polytechnic (unpublished).

McAleese, R. (1986) The representation of knowledge in authoring environments, in N. Rushby and A. Howe (eds.), *Aspects of Educational Technology XIX*, Kogan-Page, pp. 104–113.

McAleese, R. (1986) Computer-based authoring and intelligent interactive video, in *International Yearbook of Educational and Instructional Technology 1986/87,* Kogan-Page, pp. 63–81.

MacDonald, B., Atkin, R., Jenkins, D. & Kemmis, S. (1977) Computer assisted learning: its educational potential, *National Development Programme in Computer Assisted Learning*, Final Report of the Director.

Macintosh, P. (1984) Educational technology past and present, *Interactive Learning International*, 1/1, Jul.–Sep., 12–14.

McKenzie, J. Interactive computer graphics for undergraduate science teaching, *Computers and Education*, **2**, 25–48.

McLuhan, M. (1964) *Understanding Media*, Abacus.

McQuail, D. & Windahl, S. (1981) *Communication Models*, Longman.

Master Driver (1984) Seoul Metropolitan Subway Corporation. Designed by Marconi Simulation, Dunfermline.

Mathews, W. (1986) Report of the Courseware Committee, Irish Dept. of Industry and Commerce, February 1986, Published by Her Majesty's Stationery Office.

Megarry, J. (1984) *Times Educational Supplement*, 29 June.

Meurrens, M. W. F. (1986) An intelligent approach to computer aided learning: in F. Percival (ed.), *Aspects of Educational Technology*, XX,

Kogan-Page, London.

Miller, F. (1970) *Amer. J. Phys.*, 39 (1), 5–8.

Milton Keynes Information Technology Disc (1982) First PAL interactive laserdisc produced in the UK. Produced by BBC Open University Production Centre on behalf of the Milton Keynes Development Corporation for part of an Information Technology Exhibition in 1982.

Minutes of the Second Optical Disc Forum (1986) Commission of the European Communities, Luxembourg, May 1986.

Mitchell, P. D. & Dalkir, K. (1986) C/CASTE and artificial intelligence based computer aided learning system, in J. Brahan (ed.), *Proceedings of the Fifth Canadian Symposium on Instructional Technology*, NCR, Ottawa.

Mole, J. & Langham, J. (1982) *Pilot Study of the Application of Video Disc Technology at the Public Archives of Canada*, Ottawa (DSS catalogue number SA2–139/1982).

Moore, D. M. & Hunt, T. L. (1980) The nature of resistance to the use of instructional media, *British Journal of Educational Technology*, 11/2, May 141–147.

Morris, H. & Archer, D. (1977) *The Interpretation of NMR Spectra*, CALCHEM, Department of Physical Chemistry, The University, Leeds.

Nicol, D. (1985) New information technologies in higher education, *Media in Education and Development*, 18/4, December, 184–186.

Ogborn, J. (1987) *Conversation: Theory; epistemology; heuristic?*

Open University (1984) *An Eye for an Eye (The Teddy Bear Disc)*, Open University Educational Enterprises, Milton Keynes.

Palmarozza, P. H. (1984) Trends in training: an historical perspective, *Interactive Learning International*, 1/1, Jul.–Sep., 9–11.

Parsloe, E. (ed.) (1983) *Interactive Video*, Sigma Technical Press.

Papert, S. (1980) *Mindstorms: Children, Computers and Powerful Ideas*, Basic Books, NY.

Pask, G. (1961) *An Approach to Cybernetics*, London, Hutchinson, reprinted 1968, 1972.

Pask, G. (1971) A comment, a case history, and a plan, in J. Reichardt (ed.), *Cybernetics: Thought and Ideas*, Studio Vista, London. Also 1963, 1966, 'Fun Palace' and 'Proposals for a Cybernetic Master', reprints with Lewis, B. N., Littlewood, J. & Price, C.

Pask, G. (1972) A fresh look at cognition and the individual, *Int. J. Man–Machine Studies*, **4**, 211–216.

Pask, G. (1975) *The Cybernetics of Human Learning and Performance*, Hutchinson, London.

Pask, G. (1975) *Conversation, cognition and learning, A Cybernetic Theory and Methodology*, Elsevier, Amsterdam.

Pask, G. (1976) Conversational techniques in the study and practice of education, *British Journal of Educational Psychology*, **46**, 12–25.

Pask, G. (1976) *Conversation Theory: Applications in Education and Epistemology,* Elsevier, Amsterdam.

Pask, G. (1977) Knowledge, innovation and 'learning to learn'. *Proceedings, NATO — ASI Structural/Process Theories of Complex Human Behaviour*, Banff Springs, Canada, Noordhoff, Alphan aan den Rijn.

Pask, G. & Scott, B. C. E. (1972) Learning strategies and individual competence, *Int. J. Man–Machine Studies*, **4,** 217–253.

Pask, G. & B. C. E. (1973) A theory of conversations and individuals (exemplified by the learning process in CASTE), *Int. J. Man–Machine Studies*, **5,** 443–566.

Pask, G., Kallikourdis, D. & Scott, B. C. E. (1975) The Representation of Knowables, *Inter. J. Man–Machine Studies*, **17,** 15–134.

Pask, G., Ensor, D., Scott, B. C. E. & Pask, E. (1977) Cartoons. Tests for learning 'style'. Forms III, V, VI (Computer adminstrated versions are also issued), Systems Research Ltd, Richmond, Surrey.

Petri, C. E. (1978) *Concepts of Net Theory and Concurrency*, GMD, Bonn.

Rees, M. J. & Robson, D. J. (1985) Video-slide: a presentation aid for the BBC computer, *Software Practice and Experience*, 15/9, September.

Rescher, N. (1973) *The Coherence Theory of Truth*, Oxford University Press.

Roach, D. K. (1983) Who, What, Where?, *Videodisc Newsletter*, 2, October.

Roach, D. K. (1984) Interactive video: the Cardiff experience, *Media in Education and Development*, 17/4, December, 187–189.

Rosenblatt, L. M. (1978) *The Reader, the Text, the Poem: the Transactional Theory of the Literary Work*, Carbondale, Southern Illinois University Press.

Schofield, A. (1982) Call Yourself a Manager? — a new approach to using simulation in management training, in L. Gray & I. Waitt (eds.), *Perspectives on Academic Gaming and Simulation 7: Simulation of Management and Business Education*, Kogan-Page, London.

Shannon, C. & Weaver, W. (1949) *The Mathematical Theory of Communication*, University of Illinois Press.

Smith, R. C. (1983) Development of computer assisted learning/videodisc based training for newly-hired workers in Florida's umbrella social work agency, *Proceedings of the Conference in Interactive Instruction Delivery*, Society for Applied Learning Technology, Warrenton, VA, 9–11 February 1983.

Smith, R. C. (1984) Full scale pilot testing of Florida's videodisc training project, *Proceedings of the Second Conference on Interactive Instruction Delivery*, Society for Applied Learning Technology, Warrenton, VA, 15–17 February 1984.

Smith, R. C. (1984) First results from Florida's interactive training program, *News*, **6,** 1. Videodisc Design Production Group, University of Nebraska, Lincoln.

Smith, R. C. (1984) University of West Florida training project, *Videodisc Monitor*, **2,** 12–14.

Smith, R. C. (1984) Management of a microcomputer-assisted learning project, *Comput. Educ.*, **8,** 197–201.

Sperry, R. (1982) Nobel Prize Speech, 8 December 1981, *Science*, September, 1223.
Stress at Work (1987) An MSC funded project. Produced by BBC Milton Keynes. A level 3 stress awareness package.
The Body Disc (1984) Level 1 disc produced by New Media.
The First National Kiddisc (1982) Level 1 disc NTSC. Published by Optical Program Associates.
The Teddy Bear Disc (1983) A materials science disc produced for Open University Summer School Use. Published by Open University Educational Enterprises.
Trowbridge, N. (1985) Video database evaluation. Published by Hampshire Education Authority.
Van der Veer, J. P. (1957) *A Psychological View of Problem Solving*, Leiden.
Van der Veer, G. & Van der Wolde, J. (1980) *Psychological Aspects of Problem Solving with the Help of a Computer Language*, Vrije Universiteit, Amsterdam.
Weightworld (1987) A weight training videodisc. The first of a series of discs produced by the BBC Open University Production Centre in conjunction with the National Coaching Foundation.
Weil, S. & Schofield, A. (1984) *Integrating Theory and Practice: the Use of Triggers in Professional Education and Training*, Centre for Staff Development in Higher Education, London.
Weisgerber, R. A. (1968) Higher education and media innovation, in R. A. Weisgerber (ed.), *Instructional Process and Media Innovations*, Rand McNally.
Wells, G. & Nicholls, J. (1985) *Language and Learning: A Transactional Perspective*, Falmer.
Williams, K., Wright, M. et al. (1984) *Introduction to Materials Science*, Open University/BBC, Milton Keynes, UK.
Williams, R. (1974) *Television: Technology and Cultural Form*, Fontana.
Wilson, L. (1983) Interactive video — a step toward natural learning, *Performance & Instruction Journal*, November, 32–33.
Worcester, C. (1983) Interactive video — a new video, *Performance and Instruction Journal*, November, 14–16.
Wright, E. (1986) The Jello Plan and other pitfalls, (unpublished).
Zollman, D. & Fuller, R. G. (1983) *Studies in Motion*, Great Plains Media Centre, University of Nebraska — Lincoln, Lincoln, NE.

About the contributors

Dr D. M. Laurillard
Diana Laurillard is Head of the Centre for Information Technology in Education, which is part of the Institute of Educational Technology at the Open University. Formerly lecturer in Computer Assisted Learning at the University of Surrey, while completing a Ph.D. thesis on student learning, she has spent some twelve years on research and development of the design and use of instructional media and computer-based materials (including tutorials, simulations, interactive video) for education and training, covering a wide range of subject areas. This work has been disseminated through journal articles, invited contributions to books, international conferences, lecture tours and consultancies. Contributions to conferences include keynote lectures at conferences on cognitive psychology and student learning, and computer-based learning. Most recently, she has developed (with Dr P. Lefrere) the MSC-funded pack 'Introduction to Computer-Based Training'. Current work includes research on a prototype for an expert system in training needs analysis.

Mr Peter Armstrong
After eight years at Oxford where he completed degrees in Philosophy, Psychology and Theology, Peter Armstrong joined the BBC in 1969 where he has since worked as a Producer and Head of Department in both television and radio.

In 1984 he devised the Domesday Project and edited the two Domesday discs which were published in 1986. He is at present Head of Television for the BBC South and East region.

Professor Alfred Bork
Alfred Bork is Professor of Information and Computer Science, and Professor of Physics at the University of California, Irvine. He directs the Educational Technology Center, a research and development group in computer-based learning.

Recent research projects include a study of screen design, a study of small group usage of computer learning material, and a study of computer use in California classrooms. Recent developments of computer-based learning material address problems of learning about the methods of science, improving reasoning capability, teacher training, the problems of weak students in beginning science courses, and learning Japanese. The Scientific Reasoning Series is now commercially available. Professor Bork has published many papers on the design of computer-band learning materials, in addition to the following books: *Learning with Computers* (Digital Press, 1981), *Personal Computers for Education* (Harper & Row, 1985), *Learning With Personal Computers* (Harper & Row, 1986), and *Designing Computer Based Learning Material* (co-edited with Harold Weinstock, Springer-Verlag, 1986).

Professor Gary Boyd
Gary McIntyre Boyd was born in Toronto of Scottish and English ancestry. He received a B.Sc. in Physics from Carleton University, Ottawa, an M.SC. in Radiophysics from the University of Saskatchewan and the Ph.D. in Geophysics from the University of British Columbia. He ran the Alert 1GY–1GC Station in the Northwest Territories.

He taught physics at Royal Roads Military College in Victoria, B.C., and then became one of the founders of the Educational Technology graduate programme at Concordia (SGWU) in Montreal in 1968. There he developed and has given courses in Educational Cybernetics since that time. He was a visitor with the UK National Development Program in Computer Assisted Learning in 1975, and has been an active member of the UK Association for Educational and training technology.

As Assistant Director for Research and Development for the Concordia Audiovisual Department he helped foster the development and production of the award winning PIVOT-1 level 4 interactive videodisc telephone trainer system by Paul Vinet in conjunction with Northern Telecom, Sony and Bell Canada. He is currently collaborating with Dr Mariela Tovar on three interactive video projects.

Mr Philip Butcher
Philip Butcher has an MA in chemistry from the University of Oxford and an M.Phil in computer-based education from the University of Leeds. He has been involved in computer-based education since 1974 when he joined the CALCHEM project for the UK National Development Programme in Computer Assisted Learning. For the past 10 years he has worked for the Open University Academic Computing Service where he is currently the Senior Software Designer with responsibility for CAL applications in OU courses. In this position he designed and implemented the software accompanying the OU's first interactive videodisc for undergraduate use, *The Teddy Bear Disc*, which received the gold award for best disc in the UK Philips' Interactive Videodisc Awards of 1984.

Dr Bert Camstra
Bert Camstra finished his studies in educational psychology in 1972 at the University of Amsterdam. After being employed by the same university as an educational researcher, he started his own company Courseware Europe

b.v., in 1982. The company carries out development of computer-assisted learning programs, and authoring systems for computer-based training, as well as knowledge engineering applications. Courseware Europe has now been expanded into a Europe-wide network of courseware development companies called the Courseware Group. The Group employed about 50 people in its companies in Holland, Ireland, Denmark, Germany and Belgium in early 1987, while companies in Spain, Portugal, Italy, Austria and Greece will be added during 1987. Camstra is President of the Courseware Group and director of most of the companies.

Dr David R. Clark
David Clark was awarded a Ph.D. in physical chemistry at the University of Manchester. He became Assistant Professor in the Department of Chemistry at the University of Toronto in 1966. In 1971 he joined the Audio-Visual Centre of the University of London as Producer, becoming its Director in 1984. He has made a wide range of films and video programmes for higher education. In 1979 he was awarded a grant by the Film Production Board for his version of *Film*, by Samuel Beckett, three of whose plays for radio he has also produced. He is editor of *Computers for Imagemaking* (1981) and has published many articles on computer graphics, three-dimensional imagery, and videodisc development. He is currently in charge of the University's major videodisc project, which is supported by Thorn EMI Ltd and the Department of Trade and Industry, and is closely involved in the implementation of the new interactive video network linking seven major sites of the University.

Dr Rupert Dowling
Rupert Dowling graduated in mathematics from University College Dublin. He then trained as a courseware designer/programmer with AnCO (Ireland's industrial training authority), where he helped to design a 15-hour IV course on welding, developed for the IVIS system. He later worked as a consultant on the shooting and production of the video disc for the course — the first interactive videodisc to be produced in Ireland. Since 1984 he has worked for Courseware Ireland Ltd in Dublin, part of the European Courseware Group.

Professor Robert G. Fuller
Robert Fuller (Ph.D. in condensed matter physics, University of Illinois) of the University of Nebraska–Lincoln has been developing physics videodisc lessons since 1979. He is the co-author of one of the first commercially available interactive educational videodiscs, *The Puzzle of the Tacoma Narrows Bridge Collapse* (John Wiley, 1982). He served as an interactive videodisc consultant to the British Open University 1982–83. He is currently (1987–88) serving as a Distinguished Visiting Professor of Physics at the United States Air Force Academy where he is working on two new videodiscs, *Skylab Physics,* and *The Science of Powered Flight*.

Dr Andrew Hart

Andrew Hart is a lecturer in the Faculty of Educational Studies at the University of Southampton where he runs postgraduate courses on media studies. During the last decade he has been involved in the design, production and evaluation of a wide range of educational media packages for staff and students in higher education. He has written several articles on the media and on educational technology and is author of *Teaching Television: The Real World,* Cambridge University Press (1987). He is editor of *Media-in-Education Research* and a consultant to the BBC's *Media Studies* series.

Mr. Colin Jackson

Colin Jackson's career started in the aircraft control industry where he was employed as an Electronic Engineer working on military projects. He then moved into Education as a lecturer at Brighton Polytechnic and has remained with the Polytechnic, currently as Deputy Head of the Department of Computing and Cybernetics.

He became interested in computer-controlled videodisc applications at the time that videodisc players working to PAL specifications first became readily available in the UK. In particular the integration of videodisc and videotex technologies became a research interest.

Colin Jackson is married with three children and lives close to the South Downs just outside Lewes in East Sussex.

Dr Colin Mably

Colin Mably is principal lecturer in Teacher Education at the School for Independent Study, North East London Polytechnic, and has been working with both pre-service and in-service schoolteachers for approximately ten years, following a similar time period as a primary school teacher himself.

As head of the Polytechnic's Short Course Unit, he organized the first UK national conference on Interactive Video in July 1983, and from this was Director of the first evaluation study of the use of interactive videodiscs in UK primary achools in 1984. He is Educational Consultant to Thorn EMI Videodisc Ltd and is actively involved in researching and promoting the development of interactive videodisc use in schools and colleges.

Among other things Colin Mably is a member of both the UK 'Parliamentary Information Technology Committee', and the Association for Teacher Education in Europe's 'Information Technology Working Group'.

His work and writing on information technology and education has led to speaker and consultant invitations from many parts of the world including Eastern and Western Europe, North and South America, and the Middle and Far East.

Mr David Nelson

David Nelson is Executive Producer in charge of videodisc production and, in addition, all programmes on technology and design at the BBC Open University Production Centre at Milton Keynes. He produced the first videodisc to be made at the Production Centre: The Milton Keynes Information Technology disc.

He has been with the BBC since 1969, producing numerous programmes about all aspects of technology and industry. Before that he spent five years in industry after graduation from Nottingham University.

Professor Gordon Pask
Gordon Pask studied at Downing College, Cambridge, University College London (Ph.D. — Psychology) and the Open University (D.Sc. — Cybernetics). His first academic post at the University of Illinois, Urbana, was followed by appointment as a Professor in Cybernetics when the department was founded at Brunel University.

Since 1981 Gordon Pask has served as Research Professor in Educational Technology and co-director of the CSRKE at Concordia University, Montreal. He currently holds posts at the Architectural Association School of Architecture, in London, and as Professor at the University of Amsterdam.

Dr N. J. Rushby
Nick Rushby has been involved with the use of computers in education and training for over sixteen years. Following a first degree in electronic engineering at the University College of North Wales, and postgraduate work at Imperial College London, he worked in industry before moving to Brighton Polytechnic as senior programmer in their computer centre. Between 1975 and 1977 he was a project coordinator with the UK National Development Programme in Computer Assisted Learning, responsible for a group of institutions developing a large-scale computer-managed learning and training system. At the end of the National Programme he returned to Imperial College to set up and direct computer-based learning activities rhere, running CEDAR, the national information service on the use of computers in education and training, and CITAR, a unit providing workshops and consultancy on the use of new technologies in training. In 1984 he moved to the London Centre for Staff Development in Higher Education where he is responsible for new technologies in training. He is author and editor of a number of books and papers on CBL and CBT, and is an active member of the Association for Educational and Training Technology.

Dr Ricard Smith
Richard C. Smith is Technical Director for The University of West Florida's Office for Interactive Technology and Training. He serves also as Chairman of the Department of Physics. His interest in learning technologies dates from the mid-1970s, when he began applying mastery techniques to computer-assisted instruction. His current interests include distance learning delivery with computer conference techniques.

Mr Martin Wright
Martin Wright is Senior Producer at BBC Videodisc Development Group at

the Open University Production Centre, Milton Keynes. Has been involved in IV production since 1982, from a background of educational TV production.

Index

access to knowledge, 13
Acorn BBC microcomputer, 123, 126
active learning, 16, 26
activities, 11
Ada, 40
ADAPT authoring system, 156
analogue
   pictures, 66, 67
   video, 63, 64, 223
answer matching, 53, 54, 78, 84
Apple, 137
Apple II, 155
Apple Super Pilot, 151, 154
Artificial Intelligence, 52, 222
audio track(s), 55, 56, 153, 162, 191, 197, 198
author languages, 45, 51, 53, 55
authoring, 109, 110
   languages, 39, 126, 154, 157
   languages and systems, 42
   systems, 13, 39, 40, 94, 135, 137, 145, 154, 155

BBC B+, 126
BBC's 'Domesday' projects, *see* 'Domesday'
budget, 24, 26, 41, 127
'Building Block' systems, 154–156

CAL (Computer-assisted learning), 44, 45, 47, 52–54, 56, 58, 81, 94, 133
   tutorials, 90
CALCHEM program, 47, 48
   project, 47
capacity of a videodisc, 61, 68
CAVIS, 151, 154, 155
CBL (Computer-based learning), 34, 37, 116, 128, 129, 222
CBT (Computer-based training), 124, 127, 128, 132, 145, 146, 147, 153, 154, 157, 167, 169
CD (Compact disc), 63–65, 69, 72
CD-I (Compact-disc interactive), 41, 158, 201
CD-ROM, 108–110, 112, 147, 156, 200, 201, 206, 223

chemistry, 53
commands, 55
computer, 119, 164
   control, 121, 128, 195, 201
   controlled, 122
   dialogue, 31, 35
   overlay(s), 22, 24, 26, 56, 161
Concept disc(s), 72, 73
conjectural paradigm, 47, 49, 50
control, 14, 57, 83, 88, 89, 121, 123, 155, 206, 213, 214, 217
controlling, 45
conversation theory (CT), 14, 91–93, 94, 95–98, 103, 107, 108
copyright, 208, 209
cost(s), 19, 25, 26, 156, 174, 194, 204
   matching, 24
costing, 127
Critical Path, 142
Critical Path Method (CPM), 141

data base, 162, 207
dedicated systems, 154, 155
design, 22, 42, 82, 88, 92, 119, 124, 132, 169, 212
   team, 44, 58
designers, 133, 136, 140, 222
   training, 38
designing interactive material, 37
development team, 142
Development Testing, 124, 127
dialogue, 82
digital data, 60, 63–67, 69
Digital Equipment Corporation's (DEC) IVIS system, 45, 155, 156
Domesday, 208
   disc, 49, 55, 96, 143, 201, 206, 208, 209
   project, 66, 162, 167, 190, 205

engineering, 49
entailment meshes, 95, 97, 98, 100, 103, 109
evaluation, 21, 23, 35, 40, 42, 75–78, 81, 84, 85, 88, 91, 125, 190–193

existing film, 19, 41
existing material, 117

features of IV, 12
FELIX, 155
   interaction, 16, 28, 29, 32, 34–36, 38, 41, 42, 47, 50, 52, 54, 55, 57, 70, 71, 76, 81, 85–89, 166, 167, 172, 173
   forms of, 13, 14, 80, 84

games, 147
GENLOCK, 199

hardware, 24–26, 46, 128, 143, 145, 146, 148–150, 156, 157, 171, 174, 193, 197, 199, 200, 204
human-computer
   interaction, 30
   interface, 121
hypothesis-testing, 49

IBM PC, 31, 32, 137, 145, 147, 156
image compression, 162, 163
images, 44, 56, 72, 146, 160, 164–166, 169, 172
information storage, 147
instructional, 13, 14, 21, 22
   design, 75, 85, 97, 127, 135
   designer(s), 12, 76, 85, 86, 88, 91, 130
   T.V., 93
   paradigm, 47, 58
intelligent tutoring systems, 30
interactive media, 11
interactivity levels, 15
interpersonal skills, 116, 117, 119, 128, 129
interviews, 77, 79, 81, 84
IVIS system, 45, 155, 156

languages, 39
Laservision, 64, 66, 78, 152, 162, 197–199
Laser-Vision Rom (LV Rom), 63, 65, 73, 122, 126, 201, 204, 206
'learner control', 92, 94
learning dialogue, 29
   gains, 81
   objectives, 75
level of interactivity, 146, 148, 156
level two, 21

mastering, 19, 67, 222
mastery learning, 33, 37
mathemagenic, 11
   activities, 11
MCQs, 88, 89
Mentor II, 154
methods, 142
MIC, 157
microplato, 154
Microtext, 72, 127, 154, 157

MicroTICCIT, 156
MIT Movie Manual, 140
Modula II, 40
motivation, 34, 41
multiple choice, 35, 36, 42, 47, 153, 167
   question(s) (MCQs), 13, 35, 72, 88, 89
mutual control, 92

Nebraska Videodisc Design/Production group, 20
needs analysis, 75
NTSC, 65, 151–153, 156, 160, 198

objective(s), 76, 88, 168
observation, 76, 79, 84
open learning, 153
Open University, 20, 23, 51, 54, 55, 77, 78, 116
overlaid, 216
overlays, 55, 164, 165, 199

PAL, 61, 65, 151–153, 156, 165, 211
Pascal, 24, 25, 39, 40
pedagogical design, 38
Performance Evaluation and Review Technique (PERT), 141
Philips, 45, 66, 152, 153, 165, 201, 206, 207
   ILVAS, 155
   Laservision, 78
physics, 15–17, 22
picture(s), 61, 71, 72, 86, 89, 95
Pioneer, 152, 153, 155
Pioneer's P-Basic, 155
planning, 12, 133, 163
point of sale, 147
pre-existing film, 19
pressing the master disc, 128
producer, 165
Production Database, 141
production schedules, 169
   team, 84
Professional-350, 155
program control, 84
programmer(s), 12, 25, 84, 150, 156
   conmtrol, 92
programming, 132
project scheduling, 141

questionnaires, 77, 79, 81, 84

Resource, 72, 73, 208
resource discs, 205, 208, 210
revelatory paradigm, 49
revolutionary paradigm, 47

script, 38, 39, 137, 138
scripting, 127, 132
scriptpage, 136, 137, 142

SECAM, 151
selection of the topic, 12
simulation(s), 49, 51, 55, 71, 81, 86, 87, 92, 95, 98, 110, 116, 129
'slotable' systems, 151, 154, 156
Socrates, 29
software engineering, 39, 40, 42
Sony, 152, 153, 155, 215
STAF2 authoring language, 78
student-CAL interaction, 47
   -computer interaction, 35
   -controlled, 84
   -constructed input, 84, 88
   -constructed replies, 32
subject expert, 12
system, 39
systems analyst, 12

team, 21, 23
Teletape's MIC, 156
teletext, 45, 78, 166
   overlay, 78
TenCORE, 154, 157
'The Instructor', 154
Thorn EMI, 190, 197
training need, 119
Transaction Analysis, 123
trigger(s), 118, 162
trigger episodes, 129
   video, 116, 117, 119, 120
tutorial(s), 82, 83
tutorial system, 29

two screen system, 24

UK National Development Programme in Computer Assisted learning, 45
user control, 160

VAX Computer, 45
VHD, 122, 123, 125, 126, 152, 191, 196–199, 204
videodisc
   design and production, 18
   'generic', 41
video equipment, 150
   formats, 151
   image(s), 22, 45, 56, 160
   mixing, 45
   picture, 55
   producer(s), 12, 44, 58, 141, 142, 160
   production, 128, 133, 143, 169
videotape formats, 151
Videotex, 211, 218
videotext, 144
Viewdata, 211, 215, 217, 218, 222
VISAGE, 156, 157
visual images, 22, 71

WISE, 154

Xerox PARC, 70

OHIO UNIVERSITY LIBRARY

Please return this book as soon as you have finished with it. In order to avoid a fine it must be returned by the latest date stamped below.

QUARTER LOAN
SEP 11 1989

RETURN BY
MAR 16 1994

MAR 11 1994

AUG 9 1989

RETURNED BY:
NOV 15 1994

RETURN BY
NOV 02 1994

NOV 16 1990

NOV 15 1990

JUN 15 1997

NON.

APR 26 1997

DEC 20 1990

DEC 21 1990

RETURN BY

NOV 02 1993

RETURN BY
NOV 27 1993

CF NOV 19 1993